Casseroles:

365 Days of Fast, Easy & Delicious Casserole Recipes

By

Julianna Sweeney

As a "Thank You" for purchasing this book, I want to give you a gift absolutely 100% Free

**** Follow the instructions at the end of this book to receive Holiday Casserole Recipes FREE ****

Table of Contents

Introduction

Congratulations and Thank You!

I want to start by thanking you for downloading the book, "*Casserole Recipes: 365 Days of Fast, Easy & Delicious Casserole Recipes*" I am honored to be helping you on this journey to create quick & easy Casserole Recipes!

One of the staples of a warm home-cooked meal for years has been the classic casserole. Each family has their own variation of what a casserole should look like, taste like, and which ingredients to keep in this truly timeless recipe. Casseroles are extremely popular when serving a large amount of people for dinner; they are hearty, usually require very little cleanup, and can make for some great leftovers the next day. What many people do not know is that the casserole itself is one of the most versatile dishes you can create for your family. There are limitless combinations to the ingredients you can put in your casserole, as you will see when you go through this e-book.

Luckily, you will not have to wrack your brain to come up with these seemingly endless possibilities; there are 365 recipes right in this e-book that you can refer to in order to ease the process of choosing what to make for dinner. With so many options, you are bound to find casserole recipes that will appease even the pickiest eater. You might even find a few new options to try out on your family and friends, instead of serving them the same old recipe time after time. And rest assured that there will indeed be some delicious leftovers for the next day, which you can also get creative in how you serve. Whether you are using leafy vegetables, tender meats, or some starches to balance out the meal, you will find a casserole to fit each person and every event that you find yourself cooking for.

Thanks again for downloading this book, I Hope You Enjoy It

Secrets To Making A Perfect Casserole

Here are a few of our favorite tricks and tips to help you create the best casserole possible

1.Improve the flavor of your favorite casserole by sprinkling it with a yummy topping before baking. Some of our favorite toppings are buttered breadcrumbs, French fried onions, crushed potato chips, shredded cheese or cooked, crumbled bacon.

2.Remove Extra Moisture from Wet Vegetables Before Cooking. Frozen vegetables can be add extra moisture to a recipe which can ruin it. Thaw frozen vegetables in a strainer so they lose their extra liquid.

3.Don't meat all the way before using in a Casserole. If you cook meat all the way, it may overcook. Cook your meat up to 2-4 minutes less than the suggested cooking time.

4.Make Sure Your Casserole Is the Right Temperature Before Baking It. Be sure to defrost your casserole completely in the refrigerator before you bake it. This can take up to 2 days. Also, let it come up to room temperature as your oven preheats. If you put a cold casserole in the oven, the outer edge could cook too fast while the middle cooks too slowly

5.When making a casserole to freeze, line the dish with foil, allowing 3 inches of foil to hang over each side. Arrange the casserole as directed; cover and freeze. When frozen, use the foil to lift the casserole out of the dish. Peel off the foil, wrap the casserole in freezer paper and return it to the freezer. When ready to bake, unwrap and place the casserole back in the pan.

TOP SECRET

365 Casserole Recipes

Here you will find fun and easy Casserole Recipes Have Fun!!

Three Topping Sweet Potato Casserole

INGREDIENTS:

2 1/2 lbs. sweet potatoes (about 5 medium)
2 tbsp. butter, softened
1/2 cup firmly packed brown sugar
1/2 cup 2% reduced-fat milk
1 large egg
1/2 tsp. salt
1/2 tsp. vanilla extract
Vegetable cooking spray
1 1/4 cups cornflakes cereal, crushed
1/4 cup chopped pecans
1 tbsp. brown sugar
1 tbsp. melted butter
1 1/4 cups miniature marshmallows

INSTRUCTIONS:

•Prepare filling by preheating the oven to 400°F.
•Then bake the sweet potatoes on a baking sheet for about 1 hour or until tender.
•Reduce oven temperature to 350°.
•Let the potatoes to cool down until it could be touch.
•Peel the potatoes
•Mash it with a potato masher.
•Then beat the mashed sweet potatoes, butter, brown sugar, milk, egg, salt, and vanilla at medium speed with an electric mixer until smooth.
•Spoon the mixture into an 11- x 7-inch baking dish coated with cooking spray.
•Prepare toppings by Stirring together crushed cornflakes cereal, pecans, brown sugar, melted butter and marshmallows.
•Sprinkle over sweet potato mixture in diagonal rows by 2 inches apart.
•Bake at 350° F for about 30 minutes.
•Remove from oven; let stand for another 10 minutes.
•Sprinkle miniature marshmallows in alternate rows between cornflake mixture, and bake for about 10 more minutes.

Macaroni and Cheese Casserole

INGREDIENTS:

1 lb. uncooked cellentani (corkscrew) pasta
2 tbsp. butter
1/4 cup all-purpose flour
3 cups fat-free milk
1 (12-oz.) can fat-free evaporated milk
1 cup (4 oz.) shredded smoked Gouda cheese
1/2 cup (2 oz.) shredded 1.5% reduced-fat sharp Cheddar cheese
3 oz. fat-free cream cheese, softened
1/2 tsp. salt
1/4 tsp. ground red pepper, divided
1 (8-oz.) package chopped smoked ham
Vegetable cooking spray
1 1/4 cups cornflakes cereal, crushed
1 tbsp. butter, melted

INSTRUCTIONS:

•Preheat oven to 350°F.
•Cook cellentani pasta according to package directions.
•In the meantime, melt 2 tablespoon of butter in a Dutch oven over medium heat.
•Whisk the flour gradually for about 1 minute until it becomes cook.
•Add the milks while whisking slowly until it becomes smooth.
•In about 8 to 10 minutes constant beating must be done or until it slightly thickened.
•Add the Gouda cheese, cheddar cheese, cream cheese, salt, ground red pepper while whisking constantly or until it becomes smooth.
•Remove from the heat and mix the ham and pasta.
•Spoon out the pasta mixture into a 13- x 9-inch baking dish coated with cooking spray.
•Mix together the crushed cereal, melted butter, and remaining ground red pepper, then sprinkle it over the pasta mixture.
•Bake at 350° F for about 30 minutes or until golden and bubbly.
•Let stand for about 5 minutes before serving.

Chicken Coated With Panko Crumbs Casserole

INGREDIENTS:

4 chicken breasts
1/4 cup bread crumbs
1/4 cup Parmesan cheese
1 tsp. seasoned salt or garlic salt
1 tsp. Mrs. Dash seasoning
Freshly cracked black pepper
1 can Cream of Chicken
1/2 pint sour cream
3 cans broth or milk or water
salt

INTRUCTIONS:

•Clean and rinse chicken and pat dry with paper towel.
•Slice them into pieces and put them in a bowl.
•Pour small amount of cooking oil on the chicken.
•Combine seasoned salt, Mrs. Dash and black pepper and sprinkle it on the chicken pieces.
•Cover the bowl and refrigerate for few hours or overnight.
•Mix bread crumbs and the Parmesan cheese to coat the chicken pieces.
•Arrange chicken in a deep dish or deep pan.
•Bake in a preheated 375°F oven for about 25 minutes.
•While chicken is baking make the Cream Sauce by mixing the Cream of Chicken, sour cream, broth, and salt if needed.
•Take the chicken out of the oven and pour the sauce over it.
•Reduce oven temperature to 350°F then put back the chicken to bake for about 1 hour or until the chicken are fork tender.
•Serve hot over rice or mashed potatoes.

Crab Meat Noodle Casserole

INGREDIENTS:

1 (15 oz.) can peas, drained
1 (8 oz.) package extra wide egg noodles
1 tbsp. butter
1/2 bunch celery, chopped
1/2 sweet onion (such as Vidalia), chopped
2 zucchini, quartered and sliced
1 (10.75 oz.) can condensed cream of potato soup
1 (10.75 oz.) can condensed cream of celery soup
1 3/4 cups milk
4 cups shredded Cheddar cheese, divided
1 lb. imitation crabmeat, flaked
Salt and ground black pepper to taste

INSTRUCTIONS:

•Preheat the oven to 350 degrees F
•Put grease in a 9x13-inch baking dish.
•Open the can of peas and drain well.
•Set aside the peas in the freezer.
•Fill water with a sprinkle of salt in a large pot, then bring it to boil.
•When water reaches to its boiling point, put the egg noodles and stir constantly until the pasta is cooked (pasta is firm when bite).
•Get the cooked pasta, put it in the colander and drain well in the sink with water.
•Heat a large saucepan with a medium heat, melt the butter, cook the celery and onion, and see to it that the onion become translucent in about 3 minutes.
•Add zucchini in the saucepan and cook it until the color become bright green and tender, this takes for about 5 to 8 minutes.
•Put the potato, celery, milk and half of the Cheddar cheese in the saucepan.
•Allow all the mixture to stand for about 5 minutes, and then gently put the cooked noodles, imitation crab, and the peas while stirring infrequently.
•Seasoned it with salt and pepper to add taste, and then take out the saucepan, spread the mixture into the greased baking dish with cheddar cheese as toppings of the casserole.
•Bake the casserole in the oven for about 30 minutes.

•Remove the baked casserole, cover it with foil, and allow it to stand for about 10 to 15 minutes

Cobbler Mushroom Chicken Casserole

INGREDIENTS:

6 tablespoons melted butter, divided
4 cups cubed sourdough rolls
1/3 cup grated Parmesan cheese
2 tablespoons chopped fresh parsley
2 medium-size sweet onions, sliced
1 (8-ounce) package sliced fresh mushrooms
1 cup white wine
1 (10 3/4-ounce) can cream of mushroom soup
1/2 cup drained and chopped jarred roasted red bell peppers
2 1/2 cups shredded cooked chicken

INSTRUCTIONS:

•Mix 4 tablespoons melted butter with cube sourdough rolls, grated Parmesan cheese and chopped fresh parsley, and then set aside.
•In a large skillet, sauté the onion with the remaining 2 tablespoons of butter over medium to high heat for about 15 minutes or until it become golden brown.
•Add mushroom and cook in 5 minutes.
•Put wine, mushroom soup, roasted bell peppers and shredded chicken while stirring constantly until it become bubbly and cooked.
•Spoon the mixture into the 9 inch square baking dish, slightly greased and top it with bread mixture, evenly.
•Bake the casserole at around 400°F for about 15 minutes or until golden brown.

Ham-and-Vegetable Casserole

INGREDIENTS

1/4 cup butter
1/4 cup all-purpose flour
3 1/2 cups milk
1/2 tsp. dried thyme
1 tsp. chicken bouillon granules
2 cups diced cooked ham
1 (10-oz.) package frozen sweet peas and mushrooms
1 cup frozen crinkle-cut carrots
1 (14.1-oz.) package refrigerated piecrusts

INSTRUCTIONS

•Preheat oven to 450°F.
•Melt butter in a large saucepan over medium heat.
•Gradually whisk in flour, and cook, whisking constantly for about 1 minute.
•Add milk, dried thyme, and chicken bouillon granules, stir constantly until cook or in about 6 to 8 minutes when become thick and bubbly.
•Add ham, frozen crinkle –cut carrots, and refrigerated pie crust, let it cook for about 4 to 5 •minutes or until the mixture is thoroughly heated.
•Spoon it into a lightly greased 11 x 7 – inch baking dish.
•Unroll each piecrust on a lightly floured surface.
•Cut the piecrust into 1 ¼ - inch – wide strips and arrange it in a lattice design over the ham mixture.
•Then bake the casserole in a 450° F for about 40 minutes or until crust is brown and the filling is bubbly.

Beefy Lasagna a la Vanessa's Make-Ahead Casserole

INGREDIENTS

12 uncooked lasagna noodles
1 container 4% small-curd smooth-and-creamy cottage cheese
1 (16-oz.) container ricotta cheese
2 large eggs, lightly beaten
1/2 cup refrigerated pesto
1 tsp. salt
2 1/2 cups (10 oz.) shredded mozzarella cheese, divided
1 lb. lean ground beef
1/2 cup finely chopped onion
2 (24-oz.) jars tomato-and-basil pasta sauce

INSTRUCTIONS

•Preheat oven to 375°F.
•Prepare noodles according to package directions.
•Meanwhile, stir together cottage cheese, large eggs, refrigerated pesto and salt with mozzarella cheese.
•In a large skillet, cook ground beef and onion over medium-high heat.
•Stir often, 6 to 7 minutes or until meat become crumbles.
•Drain the meat and put pasta sauce while stirring it constantly.
•Put at least 3 layers of beef mixtures, noodles and cottage cheese in a lightly greased 13x9 inch baking dish.
•Over the top of the layered mixtures, sprinkle it with the remaining 1 1/2 cups mozzarella cheese.
•Then, cover the casserole and bake it at 375° F for about 40 to 45 minutes.
•Add another 20 minutes to cook while the dish is uncovering and or until the cheese is browned.
•Let it stand for about 10 to 15 minutes before serving.

Spring Onion Pie with Gruyere Cheese

INGREDIENTS:

10 thin spring onions
4 large eggs, lightly beaten
1 cup milk
3/4 cup all-purpose flour
1 tsp. kosher salt
1/2 tsp. baking powder
1/4 tsp. freshly ground pepper
2 tbsp. butter
5 oz. Gruyere cheese, cubed

INSTRUCTIONS:

•Preheat oven to 400°F.
•Heat a 10-inch cast-iron skillet in oven.
•Clean the onions, then take out the roots and chop it into half.
•Whisk together the eggs and milk.
•Sift together flour, kosher salt, baking powder and ground paper.
•Gradually add flour mixture to egg mixture.
•Beat the mixture rapidly for about 20 to 30 seconds or just until it blended and become smooth without lumps.
•Stir in the chopped onions.
•Let it sit for about 5 minutes.
•Carefully remove hot skillet from oven.
•Add the butter, and let it melt.
•Place skillet over medium-high heat, and pour butter into skillet.
•Arrange the cheese and the remaining whole onions over top of butter.
•Cook it for about 30 seconds to 1 minute or until edges begin to set.
•Transfer skillet to top oven rack, and bake at 400° for about 22 to 25 minutes or until golden brown and becomes puffy.
•Serve immediately.

Scalloped Potato with Parmesan Cheese

INGREDIENTS:

2 lbs. Yukon gold potatoes, peeled and thinly sliced
3 cups whipping cream
1/4 cup chopped fresh flat-leaf parsley
2 garlic cloves, chopped
1 1/2 tsp. salt
1/4 teaspoon freshly ground pepper
1/2 cup grated Parmesan cheese

INSTRUCTIONS:

•Preheat oven to 400°F.
•Layer the potatoes in a 13- x 9-inch or 3-qt. baking dish.
•Stir together cream, parsley, garlic cloves and salt in a large bowl.
•Pour cream mixture over potatoes.
•Bake at 400°F for about 30 minutes.
•Stir gently every 10 minutes.
•Sprinkle the top with cheese.
•Bake again for about 15 to 20 minutes or until bubbly and golden brown.
•Let it stand on a wire rack in about 10 minutes before serving.

Chicken Mozzarella Cheese Risotto Casserole

INGREDIENTS

2 tbsp. butter
2 1/2 cups chicken broth
1 cup uncooked Arborio rice (short-grain)
1/2 small onion, diced
1/2 tsp. salt
2 cups chopped deli-roasted chicken
1 (8-oz.) package fresh mozzarella cheese, cut into 1/2-inch cubes
1 cup cherry or grape tomatoes, halved
1/4 cup shredded fresh basil

INSTRUCTIONS

•Preheat the oven to 400°F.
•Spread butter in a 13- x 9-inch baking dish;
•Bake for about 5 minutes or until melted.

•Stir in broth, Arborio rice, onion and salt.
•Cover the baking dish and bake at 400° F for about 35 minutes.
•Remove the dish from oven.
•Fluff rice with a fork.
•Add the chicken, mozzarella, and tomatoes.
•Sprinkle it with shredded basil.
•Serve it directly.

Stovetop Chicken Pie Casserole

INGREDIENTS:

8 frozen buttermilk biscuits
1 small sweet onion, diced
1 tbsp. canola oil
1 (8-oz.) package sliced fresh mushrooms
4 cups chopped cooked chicken
1 (10 3/4-oz.) can reduced-fat cream of mushroom soup
1 cup low-sodium chicken broth
1/2 cup dry white wine
1/2 (8-oz.) package 1/3-less-fat cream cheese, cubed
1/2 (0.7-oz.) envelope Italian dressing mix (about 2 tsp.)
1 cup frozen baby peas, thawed

INSTRUCTIONS:

•Bake biscuits according to package directions.
•In a large skillet, sauté the onion in the hot oil over medium-high heat until it become golden.
•Add mushrooms and cook for about 5 minutes or until become tender.
•Mix the cooked chicken, cream mushroom soup, chicken broth, white wine, cubed cream cheese, and Italian dressing mix.
•Frequently stir the mixture for about 5 minutes or until the cheese is melted.
•Add the thawed peas and cook more for about 2 minutes.
•Spoon chicken mixture on top of the hot split biscuits.

Chicken Veggie Enchilada Casserole

INGREDIENTS:

3 cups chopped cooked chicken
2 cups (8 ounces) shredded Monterey Jack cheese with peppers
1/2 cup sour cream
1 (4.5-ounce) can chopped green chilies, drained
1/3 cup chopped fresh cilantro
8 (8-inch) flour tortillas
Vegetable cooking spray
1 (8-ounce) container sour cream
1 (8-ounce) bottle green taco sauce
Toppings: diced tomato, chopped avocado, chopped green onions, sliced ripe olives, chopped cilantro

INSTRUCTIONS:

•Mix together the chopped cooked chicken, shredded Monterey Jack cheese with pepper, sour cream, green chilies, and fresh cilantro.
•Spoon the mixture evenly over each tortilla, and roll it up.
•Arrange in a lightly greased 13- x 9-inch baking dish.
•Coat tortillas with vegetable cooking spray.
•Bake at 350° F for about 35 to 40 minutes or until golden brown.
•Stir together sour cream and taco sauce.
•Spoon over hot enchiladas, and sprinkle with the toppings.

Skillet Chicken Mushroom Pot Pie

INGREDIENTS:

1/3 cup butter
1/3 cup all-purpose flour
1 1/2 cups chicken broth
1 1/2 cups milk
1 1/2 teaspoons Creole seasoning
2 tablespoons butter
1 large sweet onion, diced
1 (8-oz.) package sliced fresh mushrooms
4 cups shredded cooked chicken
2 cups frozen cubed hash browns
1 cup matchstick carrots
1 cup frozen small sweet peas
1/3 cup chopped fresh parsley
1 (14.1-oz.) package refrigerated piecrusts
1 egg white

INSTRUCTIONS:

•Preheat the oven to 350°F.
•Melt 1/3 cup butter in a large saucepan over medium heat.
•Add all-purpose flour and whisk it constantly for about 1 minute.
•Then add chicken broth and milk gradually while whisking it constantly for about 6 to 7 minutes to cook or until it become thick and bubbly.
•Remove it from the heat, and stir in Creole seasoning.
•Melt 2 tablespoon of butter in a large Dutch oven over medium-high heat.
•Add the onion and mushrooms, and sauté it in about 10 minutes or until tender.
•Stir in the chicken, hash browns, matchstick carrots, sweet peas, parsley, and the sauce.
•Prepare the crust by putting 1 piecrust in a lightly greased 10-inch cast-iron skillet.
•Spoon the chicken mixture over piecrust, and top with remaining piecrust.
•Whisk egg white until foamy.
•Brush the top of piecrust with egg white.
•Cut 4 to 5 slits in top of pie for steam to escape.

•Bake at 350°F for about 1 hour to 1 hour and 5 minutes or until golden brown and bubbly.

Chicken Biscuit Pot Pie Casserole

INGREDIENTS

1/3 cup butter
1/3 cup all-purpose flour
1 1/2 cups chicken broth
1 1/2 cups milk
1 1/2 teaspoons Creole seasoning
2 tablespoons butter
1 large sweet onion, diced
1 (8-oz.) package sliced fresh mushrooms
4 cups shredded cooked chicken
2 cups frozen cubed hash browns
1 cup matchstick carrots
1 cup frozen small sweet peas
1/3 cup chopped fresh parsley
1/2 cup cold butter, cut into 1/2-inch cubes
2 cups self-rising flour
3/4 cup (3 oz.) shredded sharp Cheddar cheese
1/4 cup finely chopped cooked bacon
2 tablespoons chopped fresh chives
1 cup whipping cream
2 tablespoons butter, melted

INSTRUCTIONS

•Preheat oven to 425°F, then in a large saucepan melt the 1/3 cup butter over medium heat, and then add all-purpose flour while whisking constantly, 1 minute to cook.
•Add the chicken broth and milk gradually.
•Whisk the mixture in the saucepan constantly for about 6 to 7 minutes or until thickened and bubbly and then remove it from the heat, and stir with Creole seasoning.
•Melt 2 tbsp. butter in a large Dutch oven over a medium-high heat.
•Add onion and mushrooms, and then sauté for 10 minutes or until tender.
•Mix in the chicken, hash browns, matchstick carrots, sweet peas, parsley and the sauce.

•Spoon the mixture and fill it into a lightly greased 13- x 9-inch baking dish.
•Using the pastry blender or fork, cut the butter cubes into self-rising flour until becomes crumbly and the mixture will resemble into small peas.
•Stir the cheese, bacon, chives, and whipping cream and add it to the dry ingredients to become moistened.
•Get the dough out and put it into a lightly floured surface, and then massage it lightly 3 or 4 times.
•Roll and pat the dough to 3/4-inch thickness and cut it with a 2 1/2-inch round cutter to form 15 biscuits.
•Bake Chicken Pie Filling at 425°F for about 15 minutes.
•Remove the chicken pie filling from oven, and arrange biscuits on top of hot chicken mixture.
•Bake 25 to 30 more minutes or until biscuits become golden brown and the chicken mixture is bubbly.
•Remove it from oven, and then brush the biscuits with the melted butter.

Tetrazzini Marsala Chicken

INGREDIENTS

1 (8-oz.) package vermicelli
2 tbsp. butter
1 (8-oz.) package sliced fresh mushrooms
3 oz. finely chopped prosciutto
3 cups chopped cooked chicken
1 cup frozen baby English peas, thawed
1 (10 3/4-oz.) can reduced-fat cream of mushroom soup
1 (10-oz.) container refrigerated light Alfredo sauce
1/2 cup chicken broth
1/4 cup Marsala
1 cup (4-oz.) shredded Parmesan cheese

INSTRUCTIONS

•Preheat oven to 350°.
•Prepare pasta according to package directions.
•Meanwhile, melt butter in a large skillet over medium-high heat;
•Add mushrooms and prosciutto, and sauté for 5 minutes.

•Stir together mushroom mixture, chicken, English peas, mushroom soup, Alfredo sauce, •Marsala and 1/2 cup cheese.
•Add pasta constantly.
•Spoon mixture into a lightly greased 11- x 7-inch baking dish.
•Sprinkle with the remaining 1/2 cup cheese.
•Bake at 350°F for about 35 minutes or until bubbly.

Onion-Topped Sausage 'n' Mashed Potato Casserole

INGREDIENTS

1 (19.5-oz.) package sweet ground turkey sausage, casings removed
2 (14.5-oz.) cans diced tomatoes in sauce
1/4 cup loosely packed fresh basil leaves, chopped
1 shallot, chopped
1 teaspoon salt-free garlic-and-herb seasoning
1 (24-oz.) package refrigerated garlic-flavored mashed potatoes
1 (8-oz.) package shredded Italian five-cheese blend
1/4 teaspoon dried Italian seasoning
1 cup French fried onions

INSTRUCTIONS

•Preheat oven to 350°F.
•Put the turkey sausage in a large skillet over medium-high heat.
•Stirring often, 6 to 8 minutes or until meat crumbles and is no longer pink; drain.
•Stir in tomatoes, basil leaves, shallot, and salt-free garlic and herb seasoning, mixing stirring occasionally, 5 minutes. Transfer sausage mixture to a lightly greased 11- x 7-inch baking dish.
•Stir together mashed potatoes, cheese, and Italian seasoning in a large bowl. (Mixture will be dry.)
•Spread potato mixture over sausage mixture in baking dish.
•Bake at 350° F for about 35 to 40 minutes or until bubbly.
•Top with fried onions, and bake 5 more minutes.
•Let stand 5 minutes before serving.

Cranberry-Pecan Turkey Pot Pie

INGREDIENTS:

3 tbsp. butter, divided
2 large sweet onions, diced
1/2 cup all-purpose flour
1 tsp. salt
1 tsp. pepper
4 (12-ounce) turkey tenderloins cut into 1 1/2-inch cubes
2 tbsp. vegetable oil
1 1/2 cups chicken broth
1 cup milk
1 (10-ounce) package fresh spinach, torn

INSTRUCTIONS:

•Melt 1 tablespoon butter in a large skillet over medium-high heat.
•Add onions, and sauté for 15 minutes or until caramel colored.
•Place onions in a bowl, and set aside.
•Combine all-purpose flour, salt, and pepper, and then dredge turkey tenderloins in flour mixture.
•Melt remaining 2 tablespoons butter with oil in skillet over medium-high heat.
•Add the turkey tenderloins, and brown on all sides.
•Gradually stir in chicken broth and milk.
•Bring to a boil, and cook, stirring constantly, 1 minute or until thickened.
•Stir in onions and add spinach, stirring just until wilted.
•Pour turkey mixture into a lightly greased 13- x 9-inch baking dish.
•Bake, covered, at 350°F for 30 minutes.
•Remove from oven, and arrange desired amount of Cranberry-Pecan Crusts over pie before serving.
•Serve with any remaining Cranberry-Pecan Crusts on the side.

Chicken Tetrazzini Classic Style

INGREDIENTS:

1 1/2 (8-oz.) packages vermicelli
1/2 cup butter
1/2 cup all-purpose flour
4 cups milk
1/2 cup dry white wine
2 tbsps. Chicken bouillon granules
1 tsp. seasoned pepper
2 cups freshly grated Parmesan cheese, divided
4 cups diced cooked chicken
1 (6-oz.) jar sliced mushrooms, drained
3/4 cup slivered almonds

INSTRUCTIONS:

•Preheat oven to 350°.
•Prepare pasta according to package directions.
•In the meantime, melt butter in a Dutch oven over low heat and then whisk in flour until smooth.
•Cook for 1 minute while whisking constantly.
•Gradually whisk in milk and wine; cook over medium heat, whisking constantly for about 8 to 10 minutes or until mixture is thickened and bubbly.
•Whisk in bouillon granules, seasoned pepper, and 1 cup Parmesan cheese.
•Remove from heat; stir in diced cooked chicken, sliced mushrooms, and hot cooked pasta.
•Spoon mixture into a lightly greased 13- x 9-inch baking dish; sprinkle with slivered almonds and remaining 1 cup Parmesan cheese.
•Bake at 350° for 35 minutes or until bubbly.

Tomato and Egg in Indian-Spiced Casserole

INGREDIENTS:

1 ½ pounds fingerling potatoes
Kosher salt
¼ cup vegetable oil
1 yellow onion, diced
1 poblano pepper, seeded if desired, finely chopped
2 jalapeño peppers, seeded if desired, finely chopped
2 tablespoons finely chopped peeled ginger
3 garlic cloves, finely chopped
1 teaspoon ground cumin
1 teaspoon ground garam masala
½ teaspoon ground coriander
1 28-ounce cans whole peeled tomatoes
¼ cup chopped fresh mint, more for garnish
2 tablespoons chopped cilantro or basil, more for garnish
6 eggs
Black pepper, as needed

INSTRUCTIONS:

•Prepare a large pot with salted water.
•Place potatoes in the large pot and bring it to a boil until potatoes are cooked and become tender.
•Remove and drain the potatoes.
•Slice it into 1/2-inch-thick rounds.
•Heat oil in a large skillet over medium-high heat and then add the onion followed by peppers, ginger, garlic, cumin, garam masala and coriander.
•Cook it for about 10 minutes.
•Stir in tomatoes and 1/2 teaspoon salt and simmer it over medium-low heat for around 15 minutes.
•Break tomatoes with a fork and mix in mint, cilantro or basil.
•Taste and adjust seasonings.
•Heat oven to 375°F.
•Place potatoes in a 9-inch-square baking dish and file it in a single layer.
•Pour the hot tomato sauce over potatoes.
•Set the pan to oven and bake for about 20 minutes.
•Make six wells in the tomato mixture.
•Crack the eggs and put it into the wells.

•Season with salt and pepper.
•Bake until egg whites are set but yolks are still runny, this take for about 8 to 13 minutes, depending on how much the potatoes and sauce cooled before baking.
•Serve garnished with herbs.

Vegetable Delight Casserole

INGREDIENTS:

1 large eggplant or 2 medium (1 pound), peeled if desired, cut in half lengthwise, then sliced about 1/2 inch thick
Salt to taste
3 tablespoons extra virgin olive oil
1 large onion, sliced thin across the grain
2 to 4 garlic cloves (to taste), minced
1 (28-ounce) can chopped tomatoes
2 tablespoons tomato paste
Pinch of sugar
⅛teaspoon cinnamon
1 sprig basil
1 (15-ounce) can chickpeas, drained
3 tablespoons chopped flat-leaf parsley (optional)

INSTRUCTIONS:

•Preheat the oven to 450°F.
•Pile a baking sheet with aluminum foil, and brush the foil with olive oil.
•Place the eggplant slices on the foil, sprinkle with salt and brush each slice lightly with oil.
•Put in the oven for about 15 minutes or until lightly browned.
•Remove from the heat, and carefully fold the foil in half over the eggplant.
•Tuck the edges together, so that the eggplant is sealed inside the foil and will continue to steam and soften.
•Leave it for at least 15 minutes.
•Meanwhile, prepare the tomato sauce.
•Heat 2 tablespoons olive oil in a large, heavy skillet over medium heat.
•Add the onion.
•Cook, stirring often, until tender, for about five minutes, and add the garlic and a pinch of salt.
•Cook, stirring, until the garlic is fragrant, in about a minute.

•Add the tomatoes, tomato paste, sugar, cinnamon, basil and salt to taste.
•Bring to a simmer, and stirring it often, for 20 to 25 minutes or until the sauce is thick and fragrant.
•Add freshly ground pepper, then taste and adjust seasoning.
•Remove the basil sprig, and mix the drained chickpeas.
•Preheat the oven to 350 degrees.
•Greased a 2-quart baking dish or gratin.
•Cover the bottom with thin layer of tomato sauce, and make a layer of half the eggplant.
•Spoon half the remaining sauce over the eggplant, and repeat the layers.
•Bake for about 30 minutes, until bubbling.
•Remove it from the heat, and allow cooling for at least 10 to 15 minutes.
•Sprinkle the parsley on the top of the dish before serving.

Noodle Casserole with Chicken and Spinach

INGREDIENTS:

6 tablespoons unsalted butter
1/4 cup all-purpose flour
4 cups whole milk
1 cup sour cream kosher salt and black pepper
12 ounces egg noodles
4 slices sandwich bread
2 cups shredded cooked chicken or rotisserie chicken
5 ounces baby spinach, chopped
2 teaspoons dried thyme

INSTRUCTIONS:

•Heat oven to 400° F.
•Thaw 4 tablespoons of butter in a large saucepan over medium heat.
•Add the flour and stir gradually until cook for about 1 to 2 minutes or until foamy.
•Put the milk and whisk slowly until simmered and thickened for about 3 to 5 minutes.
•Remove from heat.
•Mix the sour cream, 1 teaspoon salt, and ¼ teaspoon pepper and then whisk constantly until it blended.

•Meanwhile, cook the noodles according to the package directions.
•Drain and return them to the pot.
•Thump the bread in a food processor until coarse crumbs form.
•Melt the remaining 2 tablespoons of butter in a microwave-safe bowl.
•Add the milk mixture, chicken, spinach, and thyme to the noodles and toss to combine. •Transfer to a 9-by-13-inch or some other 3-quart baking dish, sprinkle with the bread crumbs, and drizzle with the melted butter.
•Bake until the bread crumbs are golden and the filling is bubbling for about 8 to 10 minutes.
•Let the food sit before serving.

Chicken Enchilada Casserole

INGREDIENTS:

Cooking spray
4 bone-in chicken thighs, skinned
1/3 cup chopped fresh cilantro, divided
1 cup frozen corn kernels, thawed
1/3 cup (3 ounces) 1/3-less-fat cream cheese, softened
1/2 tsp. ground red pepper
1/2 tsp. ground cumin
1/4 tsp. kosher salt
1/4 tsp. black pepper
2 cups chopped onion, divided
6 garlic cloves, minced and divided
1 cup fat-free, lower-sodium chicken broth
2/3 cup salsa verde
1/4 cup water
2 tbsp. chopped pickled jalapeno pepper
9 (6-inch) corn tortillas
1/4 cup (1 ounce) shredded sharp cheddar cheese

INSTRUCTIONS:

•Preheat oven to 425°F and in a medium-high heat put a large ovenproof skillet.
•Coat the pan with cooking spray and then sauté chicken for about 4 minutes.
•Place skillet in oven; bake at 425°F for 10 minutes or until done.
•Remove chicken from pan; let stand for around 15 minutes, then shred the meat and discard the bones.

•Put the chicken in a medium bowl and add 1 1/2 tablespoons cilantro, corn, cream cheese, red paper, cumin, salt, and then toss to combine.

• Again place the chicken mixture in a pan and then add the 1/2 cup onion; sauté in for about 5 minutes in medium-high heat, stirring occasionally.

•Continue to sauté and then add 3 garlic cloves, stirring constantly in about 30 seconds.

•Add onion mixture to chicken mixture; stir to combine.

•Combine remaining ingredients; 1 1/2 cups onion, 3 garlic cloves, broth, salsa, 1/4 cup water, jalapeño in a saucepan, and then bring it to boil over medium-high heat.

•Reduce heat, and let it simmer for about 15 minutes while stirring occasionally.

•Remove from heat; let stand in about 10 minutes.

•Carefully pour mixture into the blender, and then add 2 tablespoons of cilantro blend it until become smooth and next is heat a large skillet and then add 2 tortillas cook it for 1 1/2 minutes on each side.

• Remove tortillas from pan; repeat procedure with remaining tortillas and then cut tortillas into quarters, then next is spread 1/2 cup salsa mixture in the bottom of an 8-inch square glass or ceramic baking dish coated with cooking spray.

•Arrange 12 tortilla quarters over salsa mixture and spoon half of chicken mixture over tortillas. Repeat layers, ending with tortillas. Pour remaining salsa mixture over tortillas; sprinkle evenly with cheddar cheese. Bake at 425° for 15 minutes or until bubbly and lightly browned. Top with remaining cilantro.

Broccoli and Rice with Cheese Casseroles

INGREDIENTS:

2 cups 1% low-fat milk
1 cup water
1 (3 1/2-ounce) bag boil-in-bag long-grain rice
3 cups small broccoli florets
Cooking spray
1/3 cup chopped onion
1/3 cup chopped celery
1/3 cup chopped green bell pepper
1/4 cup (2 ounces) 1/3-less-fat cream cheese
2 ounces light processed cheese, cubed
2 cups shredded skinless, boneless rotisserie chicken breast
1/4 teaspoon salt
1/4 teaspoon freshly ground black pepper
1/4 cup (1 ounce) grated Parmesan cheese

INSTRUCTIONS:

•Preheat oven to 375°F.
•Boil the milk and water in a medium saucepan, and then add the rice.
•Cook it for about 10 minutes.
•When the rice is cooked removes it and keeps it warm.
•Continue to simmer the milk and then add the broccoli; cook it for about 5 minutes.
•Drain the broccoli and discard the milk mixture.
•In a medium-high heat Dutch oven place the pan coated with cooking spray and then add the following onion, celery, and bell pepper.
•Sauté the mixture for 5 minutes, and adds cream cheese and processed cheese.
•Stir it constantly until cheese melts.
•Remove from heat and then mix the rice, broccoli, chicken, salt, and black pepper.
•Spoon 1 cup rice mixture into each of 4 (10-ounce) ramekins coated with cooking spray.
•Sprinkle each serving with 1 tablespoon Parmesan.
•Bake at 375°F for 10 minutes or until cheese melts.

Eggplant Parmesan Casserole

INGREDIENTS:

Eggplant
2 large eggs, lightly beaten
1 tablespoon water
2 cups whole-wheat panko (Japanese breadcrumbs)
1/4 cup (1 ounce) grated fresh Parmigiano-Reggiano cheese
2 (1-pound) eggplants, peeled and cut crosswise into 1/2-inch-thick slices
Cooking spray
1/2 cup torn fresh basil
1/4 cup (1 ounce) grated fresh Parmigiano-Reggiano cheese
1/2 teaspoon crushed red pepper
1 1/2 teaspoons minced garlic
1/4 teaspoon salt
1 (16-ounce) container part-skim ricotta cheese
1 large egg, lightly beaten
1 (24-ounce) jar premium pasta sauce
1/4 teaspoon salt
8 ounces thinly sliced mozzarella cheese
3/4 cup (3 ounces) finely grated fontina cheese

PREPARATION:

•Preheat oven to 375°F.
•Prepare two shallow dishes, in one dish combine the 2 eggs and 1 tablespoon water, and on the second dish combine panko and ¼ cup Parmigiano-Reggiano.
•Dip eggplant in egg mixture and then dredge in the panko mixture by pressing it gently to adhere and shaking off the excess mixture.
•In a cooking spray coated baking sheets, place eggplant 1 inch apart.
•Bake at 375°F for 30 minutes or until it become golden.
•Turn and rotate the baking sheets every after 15 minutes.
•Prepare the filling, combine basil and next 6 ingredients (through egg).
•To assemble, spoon 1/2 cup pasta sauce in bottom of a 13 x 9-inch glass baking dish coated with cooking spray. Layer half of eggplant slices over pasta sauce. Sprinkle eggplant with 1/8 teaspoon salt. Top with about 3/4 cup pasta sauce; spread half of ricotta mixture over sauce, and top with a third of mozzarella and 1/4 cup fontina. Repeat layers once, ending with about 1 cup pasta sauce. Cover tightly with

aluminum foil coated with cooking spray. Bake at 375° for 35 minutes. Remove foil; top with remaining third of mozzarella and 1/4 cup fontina.

•Bake at 375° for 10 minutes or until sauce is bubbly and cheese melts; cool 10 minutes.

Vegetable with Alfredo Sauce Lasagna

INGREDIENTS:

1 (6-oz.) package fresh baby spinach, thoroughly washed
1/3 cup refrigerated pesto sauce
1 (15-oz.) jar Alfredo sauce
1/4 cup vegetable broth
1 (25-oz.) package frozen cheese-filled ravioli (do not thaw)
1 cup (4 oz.) shredded Italian six-cheese blend
Garnishes: chopped fresh basil, paprika

INSTRUCTIONS:

•Heat oven to 375°F.
•Chop spinach, and toss with pesto in a medium bowl.
•Combine Alfredo sauce and vegetable broth.
•Spoon one-third of Alfredo sauce mixture (about 1/2 cup) into a lightly greased 2.2-qt. or 11- x 7-inch baking dish.
•Top with half of spinach mixture.
•Arrange half of ravioli in a single layer over spinach mixture.
•Repeat layers once. Top with remaining Alfredo sauce.
•Bake at 375° for 30 minutes.
•Remove from oven, and sprinkle with shredded cheese.
•Bake 5 minutes or until hot and bubbly.
•Garnish, if desired.
•Chicken broth may be substituted.

Bread Pudding Casserole

INGREDIENTS:

1 bunch Swiss chard (about 1 lb.)
6 large eggs
1 cup milk
2 tsps. Dijon mustard
1 1/4 tsp. salt
3/4 tsp. pepper
3 cups cubed ciabatta bread (about 1-inch cubes)
1 1/2 cups freshly grated Parmesan cheese, divided
1 (8-oz.) package sliced fresh mushrooms
1 red bell pepper, chopped
1 small onion, chopped
1 tsp. minced garlic
2 tbsps. Olive oil

INSTRUCTIONS:

•Preheat oven to 350°.
•Remove and discard ribs from Swiss chard.
•Rinse with cold water; drain and coarsely chop.
•Whisk together eggs, milk, mustard, salt and pepper in a large bowl;
•Add in bread and half of cheese.
•Sauté mushrooms, bell pepper, onion and minced garlic in hot oil in a large skillet over medium-high heat for 8 minutes.
•Stir in Swiss chard and sauté for 2 minutes.
•Fold vegetable mixture into egg mixture. Pour into a lightly greased 11- x 7-inch baking dish. Sprinkle with remaining cheese.
•Bake at 350° for 35 to 40 minutes or until center is set. Let stand 5 minutes.

Bread Pudding with Okra and Tomato

INGREDIENTS:

6 large eggs
1 cup milk
1 1/4 tsp. Cajun seasoning
1/2 tsp. pepper
3 cups cubed ciabatta bread (about 1-inch cubes)
1 1/2 cups Monterey Jack Cheese
1 (8-oz.) package sliced fresh mushrooms
1 green bell pepper, chopped
1 small onion, chopped
1 tsp. minced garlic
2 tbsps. Olive oil
2 medium tomatoes

INSTRUCTIONS:

•Preheat oven to 350°.
•Remove and discard ribs from Swiss chard.
•Rinse with cold water; drain and coarsely chop.
•Whisk together eggs, milk, tomato, salt and pepper in a large bowl;
•Add in bread and half of cheese.
•Sauté okra, bell pepper, onion and minced garlic in hot oil in a large skillet over medium-high heat for 8 minutes.
•Stir in mushrooms and sauté for 2 minutes.
•Fold vegetable mixture into egg mixture. Pour into a lightly greased 11- x 7-inch baking dish. Sprinkle with remaining cheese.
•Bake at 350° for 35 to 40 minutes or until center is set.
•Let stand 5 minutes.

Veggie Lover Lasagna

INGREDIENTS:

4 medium zucchini halved lengthwise and thinly sliced (about 1 1/2 lb.)
1 (8-oz.) package sliced fresh mushrooms
2 garlic cloves, minced
Vegetable cooking spray
1 medium-size red bell pepper, chopped
1 medium-size yellow bell pepper, chopped
1 yellow onion, chopped
1/2 teaspoon salt
1 1/2 cups fat-free ricotta cheese
1 large egg
2 cups (8 oz.) shredded part-skim mozzarella cheese, divided
1/2 cup freshly grated Parmesan cheese, divided
5 cups Basic Marinara Sauce
1 (8-oz.) package no-boil lasagna noodles

INSTRUCTIONS:

•Preheat the oven to 450°F.
•In a jelly roll-pan coated with cooking spray, put the zucchini, mushrooms, and garlic and then bake for about 12 to 14 minutes or until vegetables are crisp-tender.
•With the same procedure, bake the peppers and onion and be sure to reduce the oven temperature to 350°F.
•Mix together the vegetables and salt in a bowl.
•Make the ricotta mixture by stirring together the ricotta, egg, 1 1/2 cups shredded mozzarella cheese, and 1/4 cup grated Parmesan cheese.
•Spread 1 cup Basic Marinara Sauce in a 13- x 9-inch baking dish coated with cooking spray. •Top with 3 noodles, 1 cup sauce, one-third of ricotta mixture, and one-third of vegetable mixture, and repeat procedure twice to make it layered.
•Then sprinkle with remaining 1/2 cup shredded mozzarella and 1/4 cup grated Parmesan.
•Bake, covered, at 350°F for about 45 minutes.
•Uncover and bake again to about 10 to 15 more minutes or until cheese is melted and golden.
•Let stand for 10 minutes.

Easy Green Bean Lasagna

INGREDIENTS:

12 uncooked lasagna noodles
1/4 cup butter, divided
2 (14.4-oz.) packages frozen French-cut green beans, thawed
2 large sweet onions, halved and sliced
8 ounces assorted fresh mushrooms, trimmed and sliced
1/4 cup white wine
1 (15-oz.) container ricotta cheese
Parmesan cream sauce
5 cups (20 oz.)Shredded Italian cheese blend, divided
1 1/2 cups crushed round buttery crackers
1 (6-oz.) container French fried onions
3 tablespoons butter, melted

INSTRUCTIONS:

•Preheat oven to 350°F.
•Drain the green beans and then pat dry with paper towels.
•Prepare the noodles according to its package directions.
•Meanwhile, melt 2 Tbsp. butter in a large skillet over medium-high heat.
•Add onions and sauté for 15 minutes or until golden brown.
•Transfer onions to a large bowl.
•Again melt the remaining 2 Tbsp. butter in skillet and add the mushrooms.
•Then sauté for about 4 to 5 minutes or until tender.
•Add wine, and sauté 3 minutes or until liquid is absorbed.
•Add mushrooms and green beans to caramelized onions in bowl and then toss.
•Stir together ricotta cheese and 1 cup Italian cheese blend.
•Layer 1 cup Parmesan Cream Sauce, 3 noodles, half of green bean mixture, and 1 cup cheese blend in a lightly greased 15- x 10-inch baking dish.
•Top with 1 cup Parmesan Cream Sauce, 3 noodles, and all of ricotta cheese mixture.
•Top with 3 noodles, remaining green bean mixture, 1 cup cheese blend, and 1 cup Parmesan Cream Sauce.
•Top sauce with remaining 3 noodles, 1 cup Parmesan Cream Sauce, and 2 cups cheese blend.

•Bake at 350°F for 50 minutes or until bubbly and golden brown.
•Toss together crackers, French fried onions and melted butter.
•Remove lasagna from oven and then sprinkle the cracker mixture over the top.
•Bake for about 10 more minutes.
•Let stand on a wire rack for 20 minutes before serving.

Flavorful Tomato Cobbler

INGREDIENTS:

1 medium-size sweet onion, chopped
1 tablespoon olive oil
1 large tomato, chopped
3 garlic cloves, minced
3 pounds assorted small tomatoes, divided
1 tablespoon Champagne vinegar or white wine vinegar
1 tablespoon cornstarch
1 teaspoon kosher salt
1 teaspoon freshly ground black pepper
1 teaspoon fresh thyme leaves
1 1/2 cups self-rising soft-wheat flour (such as White Lily)
1/2 cup stone-ground yellow cornmeal
1/2 teaspoon baking powder
1/2 cup cold butter, cut into 1/4-inch-thick pieces
3/4 cup (6 oz.) freshly shredded Jarlsberg cheese
1/4 cup chopped fresh basil
2 tablespoons chopped fresh chives
1 1/4 cups buttermilk

INSTRUCTIONS:

•Preheat oven to 375°F.
•In a large skillet, sauté onion in hot oil over medium-high heat for about 5 to 6 minutes or until tender.
•Add the chopped tomato, garlic, and 1 1/2 cups small tomatoes, and again sauté it for about 10 minutes or until tomatoes are softened.
•Remove from heat, and stir in vinegar, cornstarch, kosher salt, ground black pepper and fresh thyme leaves.
•Place the remaining small tomatoes in a 13 x 9-inch baking dish.
•Spoon the onion mixture over tomatoes, and gently toss to coat.
•Bake at 375°F for 10 minutes.

•In the meantime, stir together flour, stone-ground yellow cornmeal and baking powder in a large bowl.
•With a pastry blender mix the cut butter and flour until mixture resembles small peas; •Cover and chill for 10 minutes.
•Stir cheese, fresh basil and fresh chives into the cold flour mixture.
•Add buttermilk, stirring just until dry ingredients are moistened.
•Blob mixture by 1/2 cupful's onto tomato mixture. (Do not spread.)
•Bake at 375°F for 30 to 35 minutes or until golden brown.
•Let it cool on a wire rack for 30 minutes before serving.

Lasagna Rolls with Tomato and Basil

INGREDIENTS:

10 uncooked lasagna noodles
1 cup finely chopped sweet onion
2 teaspoons olive oil
3 garlic cloves, minced and divided
1 (24-oz.) jar tomato-and-basil pasta sauce
1 1/2 teaspoons sugar
1/4 teaspoon dried crushed red pepper
1 cup low-fat ricotta cheese
2 ounces 1/3-less-fat cream cheese, softened
1 (14-oz.) can baby artichoke hearts, drained and quartered
1 large egg white, lightly beaten
1/4 cup torn fresh basil
1/4 cup (1 oz.) freshly shredded Parmesan cheese
Toppings: fresh basil, Parmesan cheese

INSTRUCTIONS:

•Warm the oven to 350°F.
•Cook the pasta according to its package directions for al dente.
•Drain pasta and arrange in a single layer on a piece of lightly greased aluminum foil or wax paper.
•Sauté onion in hot oil in a 3-qt. saucepan over medium heat for about 7 to 8 minutes or until caramelized.
•Add two-thirds of minced garlic, and cook, stirring constantly for 1 minute.
•Stir in tomato sauce, sugar and red pepper.
•Bring mixture to a boil, stirring often.
•Reduce heat to low and let it simmer by stirring often for about 5 minutes.

•Set aside.
•Stir together ricotta and cream cheese until smooth.
•Stir in artichoke hearts, egg white, fresh basil and shredded Parmesan cheese with the remaining minced garlic.
•Spread 1/4 cup cheese mixture on 1 noodle and then roll up firmly.
•Place the roll with the seam side down into a lightly greased 11- x 7-inch baking dish. •Repeat procedure with the remaining noodles and cheese.
•Spoon tomato sauce over lasagna rolls.
•Bake, covered, at 350°F for 45 to 50 minutes or until thoroughly heated and bubbly.
•Let stand for 5 minutes and then sprinkle with desired toppings.

Pastatta with Spinach-and-Herb

INGREDIENTS:

1 (10-oz.) package frozen chopped spinach, thawed
1 (16-oz.) package mezze penne pasta
2 1/2 tablespoons butter
3 large shallots, sliced
2 tablespoons all-purpose flour
1 1/2 cups half-and-half
1/2 cup ricotta cheese
1 cup (4 oz.) freshly shredded Asiago cheese, divided
10 large eggs, lightly beaten
1/3 cup loosely packed fresh flat-leaf parsley leaves, coarsely chopped
1 tablespoon finely chopped chives
2 teaspoons kosher salt
1 teaspoon freshly ground pepper
Garnishes: fresh flat-leaf parsley leaves, shaved Parmesan cheese

INTRUCTIONS:

•Warm the oven to 325°F.
•Drain the spinach well by pressing between paper towels.
•Prepare pasta according to its package directions.
•For the time being, melt butter in a medium saucepan over medium heat.
•Add shallots, and for 5 minutes or until golden brown.
•Whisk in flour until smooth and then cook for 1 minute by whisking constantly.

•Gradually whip in half-and-half and cook over medium heat while whisking it constantly until thickened and bubbly.
•Whisk in ricotta and 1/2 cup Asiago cheese until smooth and then remove it from heat.
•Beat eggs in a bowl until frothy.
•Fold in shallot mixture, spinach, parsley, chives, kosher salt and ground pepper.
•Stir in the cooked pasta.
•Sprinkle 1/4 cup Asiago cheese on inside rim of a lightly greased 9-inch spring form pan. •Pour pasta mixture into pan.
•Bake at about 325°F for 55 minutes to 70 minutes or until set.
•Let stand for 10 minutes and remove the sides of the pan.
•Sprinkle with remaining 1/4 cup Asiago cheese and serve.

Sweet Potato, Cauliflower, and Greens Casserole

INGREDIENTS:

1 head cauliflower (1 1/2 to 2 lb.), cut into small florets
1 (8-oz.) package fresh cremini mushrooms, stemmed and halved
6 tablespoons olive oil, divided
1 teaspoon ground cumin, divided
1 teaspoon kosher salt, divided
1/4 teaspoon freshly ground black pepper, divided
3 large sweet potatoes (2 1/2 to 3 lb.), peeled and cut into 1/4-inch-thick slices
2 garlic cloves, minced
4 cups chopped fresh kale, collards, or mustard greens
2 teaspoons red wine vinegar
1 (14-oz.) can butter beans, drained and rinsed (optional)
Easy Cheese Sauce
1/2 cup panko (Japanese breadcrumbs)
1 tablespoon chopped cilantro
1 teaspoon extra virgin olive oil

INSTRUCTIONS:

•Warm oven to 475°F.
•Toss together the cauliflower, mushrooms, 2 1/2 Tbsp. oil, 1/2 tsp. cumin, 1/2 tsp. salt, and 1/8 tsp. pepper in a medium bowl.
•Spread cauliflower mixture in a single layer jelly-roll pan.

•Toss together sweet potatoes, 2 1/2 Tbsp. oil, remaining cumin, salt, and pepper.
•Spread in another single layer jelly-roll pan.
•Bake potatoes and cauliflower at 475°F for about 10 to 12 minutes or until browned and just tender, turning once.
•Let it cool on wire racks for 10 minutes.
•Reduce the oven temperature to 375°F.
•Heat the remaining 1 Tbsp. oil in a large skillet over medium-high heat.
•Add garlic and cook by stirring it often for 1 minute.
•Add kale and cook by stirring it occasionally for 10 minutes or until tender.
•Add salt and pepper to taste and add vinegar.
•Layer half each of sweet potatoes, cauliflower mixture, beans (if desired), kale, and 1 1/2 cups Easy Cheese Sauce in a lightly greased 13- x 9-inch baking dish.
•Repeat the layer once.
•Top with remaining 1/2 cup cheese sauce.
•Mix together panko, chopped cilantro, and olive oil, and then sprinkle crumb mixture over casserole.
•Bake at 375°F for 20 to 25 minutes or until thoroughly heated, bubbly, and golden brown. •Let stand for 5 minutes before serving.

Cheesy Chili Hash Brown Bake

INGREDIENTS:

1 1/2 pounds lean ground beef or turkey
1 (15.5-oz.) can original sloppy joe sauce
1 (15-oz.) can chili with beans
1/2 (30-oz.) package frozen country-style shredded hash browns (about 4 cups)
2 cups (8 oz.) shredded Cheddar cheese

INSTRUCTIONS:

•Preheat oven to 425°F.
•Cook ground beef in a large skillet over medium-high heat and stirring often for about 7 to 10 minutes or until meat crumbles and is no longer pink.
•Mix in sloppy joe sauce and chili.
•Spoon chili mixture into 8 lightly greased 10-oz. ramekins and then top it with frozen hash browns.
•Bake and covered at 425°F for 30 minutes.
•Uncover the casserole and bake for 10 more minutes or until browned and crisp.
•Sprinkle with cheese, and bake for 5 more minutes or until cheese is melted.

Enchilada Casserole con Texas-Style

INGREDIENTS:

1/2 medium-size red onion, chopped
1 (4-ounce) can diced green chilies
1 pound ground chuck
12 (6-inch) corn tortillas cut into 1-inch pieces
1 (10 3/4-ounce) can cream of mushroom soup
1 (2 1/4-ounce) can sliced ripe black olives
1 cup mild enchilada sauce
1/2 cup sour cream
1 (8-ounce) block sharp Cheddar cheese, shredded and divided $
Toppings: shredded lettuce, diced tomato, finely chopped red onion $

INSTRUCTIONS:

•Cook the red onion, green chilies and ground chuck in a large skillet over medium-high heat by stirring it until the beef crumbles and is no longer pink.
•Drain well.
•Place beef mixture in a large bowl and then stir in tortilla pieces, cream of mushroom soup, black olives, enchilada sauce, sour cream, and 1 cup cheese.
•Spoon mixture into a lightly greased 11- x 7-inch baking dish.
•Sprinkle the remaining 1 cup cheese evenly.
•Bake at 400°F for about 20 to 25 minutes or until bubbly.
•Serve casserole with desired toppings.

Tomato 'n' Beef Casserole with Polenta Crust

INGREDIENTS:

1 teaspoon salt
1 cup plain yellow cornmeal
1/2 teaspoon Montreal steak seasoning
1 cup (4 oz.) shredded sharp Cheddar cheese, divided
1 pound ground chuck
1 cup chopped onion
1 medium zucchini, cut in half lengthwise and sliced (about 2 cups)
1 tablespoon olive oil
2 (14 1/2-oz.) cans petite diced tomatoes, drained
1 (6-oz.) can tomato paste
2 tablespoons chopped fresh flat-leaf parsley

INSTRUCTIONS:

•Turn on oven to 350°F.
• In a 2-qt. saucepan, bring to boil the 3 cups water and 1 tsp. over medium-high heat. •Whisk in cornmeal and reduce heat to low and then let it simmer by whisking constantly for about 3 minutes or until thickened.
•Remove from heat, and mix the steak seasoning and 1/4 cup Cheddar cheese.
•Spread cornmeal mixture into a lightly greased 11- x 7-inch baking dish.
•Cook the ground chuck in a large nonstick skillet over medium-high heat by stirring it often for about 10 minutes or until meat crumbles and is no longer pink.
•Drain and transfer to a bowl.

•Sauté onion and zucchini in skillet over medium heat for 5 minutes or until crisp and tender.
•Combine the beef, tomatoes, tomato paste with onion and zucchini.
•Let it simmer by stirring often for about 10 minutes.
•Pour beef mixture over cornmeal crust.
•Sprinkle with remaining 3/4 cup cheese.
•Bake at 350°F for 30 minutes or until bubbly.
•Sprinkle casserole with parsley just before serving.

Mushroom and Tomato Pie

INGREDIENTS:

1 1/2 pounds ground round
1 cup chopped onion
1/2 (8-oz.) package fresh mushrooms, sliced
1 garlic clove, minced
1 cup frozen peas, thawed
4 teaspoons beef bouillon granules
1/2 teaspoon salt
1/2 teaspoon dried thyme
1/4 teaspoon freshly ground pepper
1 tablespoon all-purpose flour
1 (14 1/2-oz.) can stewed tomatoes
1 bay leaf
2 tablespoons red wine vinegar

INSTRUCTIONS:

•In a large skillet make the beef become brown by heating over medium-high heat and stirring it often for 10 minutes or until meat crumbles and is no longer pink.
•Remove the ground beef from skillet using a slotted spoon.
•Set aside 2 Tbsp. dripping in skillet.
•Reduce to medium heat.
•Use the reserve dripping to sauté onion, mushrooms, and garlic over medium heat for about 10 to 11 minutes or until tender.
•Stir in ground beef, peas, beef bouillon granules, salt and dried thyme.
•Sprinkle flour over meat mixture.
•Increase heat to medium-high and cook by stirring it constantly for 1 minute.

•Stir in whole tomatoes, bay leaf, and vinegar and then disintegrate large tomato pieces with a spoon.
•Reduce to medium heat and cook by stirring often for 3 minutes or until slightly thickened. •Remove bay leaf.
•Transfer mixture to a lightly greased 3-qt. baking dish or pan.
•Spoon Cheese-and-Carrot Mashed Potatoes evenly over meat mixture by smoothing it with the back of the spoon.
•Bake at 400°F for 15 minutes or until thoroughly heated.
•Let stand for 5 minutes before serving.

Meatball Pasta Casserole

INGREDIENTS:

1 (16-oz.) package penne pasta
1 small sweet onion, chopped
1 medium-size fennel bulb, thinly sliced (optional)
2 tablespoons olive oil
3 garlic cloves, minced
1 teaspoon fennel seeds
2 (24-oz.) jars marinara sauce
2 (14-oz.) packages frozen beef meatballs, thawed
1 cup fresh orange juice
3/4 cup organic chicken broth
1 teaspoon firmly packed orange zest
1 medium-size red bell pepper, chopped
1/2 teaspoon kosher salt
1 cup torn fresh basil
1 1/2 (8-oz.) packages fresh mozzarella cheese slices
Garnish: fresh basil leaves

INSTRUCTIONS:

•Preheat oven to 350°F.
•Prepare pasta according to its package directions.
•Sauté onion and fennel bulb in hot oil over medium heat for 8 to 10 minutes or until tender. •Add garlic and fennel seeds, and sauté for 1 minute.
•Stir in marinara sauce, frozen beef meatballs, orange juice, organic chicken broth, orange zest, pepper and kosher salt.
•Increase to medium-high heat, and bring to a boil.

•Reduce heat to medium-low and then cover letting it simmer for 10 minutes.
•Remove from heat.
•Stir in basil, cooked pasta, and salt to taste.
•Transfer to a lightly greased 13- x 9-inch baking dish.
•Place dish on an aluminum foil-lined baking sheet and top it with cheese.
•Bake at 350°F for 25 minutes or until bubbly.

Chicken and Corn Casserole

INNGREDIENTS:

1 kilo chicken breast, cut into chunks
1-1/2 Tbsp. lemon juice
1-1/2 tsp. salt
1 tsp. paprika
1 small onion, chopped
1 tsp. black pepper, ground
2 Tbsp. butter
2 pcs hotdog, finely chopped
1/4 cup water or chicken broth
1-1/2 cup fresh corn, scraped whole from the cob
For the sauce:
1 pc egg yolk
1 Tbsp. kalamansi or lemon juice
2 Tbsp. butter
1/2 tsp. curry powder

INTRUCTIONS:

•Marinate the chicken chunks in lemon juice, salt, paprika, onion and pepper for about half an hour.
•In a saucepan, heat butter and add hotdogs, chicken with marinade, broth and whole corn kernels.
•Cover and simmer until chicken and corn are tender and then set aside.
•Combine egg yolk and lemon juice.
•In a saucepan, melt the butter and slowly stir in the egg yolk until slightly thick.
•Add the curry powder and pour this sauce over the chicken mixture and let it simmer for about 5 minutes.
•Serve hot.

Chicken in Sweet and Sour Flavor

INGREDIENTS:

1 kilo chicken cut into serving pieces
1/4 cup oil
2 tablespoons lemon juice
1/3 cup ketchup
2 tablespoons honey
1 medium onion, sliced
2 celery stalks, sliced
1 medium red pepper, sliced
1 medium zucchini, sliced
1 carrot cut into chunks
1 tablespoon corn starch dissolved in 2 tablespoon water
1 teaspoon salt
1/4 teaspoon pepper

INSTRUTIONS:

- Preheat oven to 300° F.
- Arrange the chicken in a roasting pan.
- Combine oil, lemon juice, ketchup and honey.
- Mix it well and then brush it over chicken.
- Set aside any remaining sauce mixture.
- Cover pan with foil and bake in the preheated oven for 1 hour.
- Remove chicken from pan.
- Place onion, celery, pepper, zucchini, and carrots in the same roasting pan.
- Arrange chicken on top of the vegetables.
- Pour remaining sauce mixture on vegetables.
- Continue baking for 30 minutes.
- Remove chicken from the pan.
- Transfer vegetable to serving dish and set aside.
- Pour pan juice on a saucepan and put the dissolved corn starch.
- Bring to a boil while stirring it constantly until thick.
- Season with salt and pepper.
- Serve chicken with vegetables and sauce on the sides.

Stove Top Stuffing for Healthy Living

INGREDIENTS:

Easy Chicken Casserole
1 pkg. (6 oz.) Stove Top Stuffing Mix for Chicken
1-1/2 lb. boneless skinless chicken breasts, cut into bite-size pieces
1 can (10-3/4 oz.) reduced-fat condensed cream of chicken soup
1/3 cup Reduced Fat or Light Sour Cream
1 pkg. (16 oz.) frozen mixed vegetables, thawed

INTRUCTIONS:

•Preheat oven to 400°F.
•Prepare the stuffing as directed on package.
•Mix the remaining ingredients in 13x9-inch baking dish sprayed with cooking spray and top with the stuffing.
•Bake for about 30 minutes or until chicken is done.

Casserole with Pork Chop and Rice

INGREDIENTS:

2 tablespoons vegetable oil
4 pork chops
1 (10.75 ounce) can condensed cream of chicken soup
1 (10.75 ounce) can condensed cream of celery soup
1 cup milk
1 cup uncooked instant rice
1/2 cup butter

INSTRUCTIONS:

•Preheat oven to 275° F. (135 degrees C).
•Heat vegetable oil in a large skillet over medium heat, and brown the pork chops on both sides for about 5 to 8 minutes per side.
•Place the chops into a 9x13-inch baking dish.
•In a large saucepan, whisk together the cream of chicken soup, cream of celery soup, and milk until smooth.
•Stir in the rice, and add the butter and bring the mixture to a boil over medium heat.
•Stir until the butter has melted.
•Pour the rice mixture over the chops and cover the dish with a foil.
•Bake in the preheated oven until tender and for about 2 hours.

Yummy Cheesy Hamburger Casserole

INGREDIENTS:

2 cups elbow macaroni
1 cup chopped onions
1/2 cup chopped green bell pepper
16 oz. 93% lean ground beef
2 cups shredded cheddar cheese, low fat
1 can diced tomatoes
1 tbsp. oregano
1 tbsp. basil
1 tbsp. ground cumin
salt and pepper to taste

INTRUCTIONS:

•Preheat oven to 350° F.
•Cook macaroni according to its package directions and drain it with the strainer.
•In a skillet, sauté onions and peppers until soft.
•Remove and set aside.
•Brown hamburger and drain.
•Add onions, peppers, meat, tomatoes, oregano, basil, cumin, salt, and pepper. Mix together.
•Add mixture to macaroni and pour in a baking dish coated with cooking spray.
•Heat in oven for 5 minutes.
•Add cheese to the top and bake until cheese melts and dish is bubbly.
•Let set for about 5 minutes before cutting.

Easy Hamburger Casserole

INGREDIENTS:

2 pounds ground beef
1 tablespoon onion, minced
2 cans (10 3/4-ounce) tomato soup
1 teaspoon chili powder
4 cups corn chips
8 ounces package shredded Cheddar cheese

INSTRUCTIONS:

•Preheat oven to 350° F.
•Brown the ground beef and onion together in a large skillet over medium heat and drain.
•Stir in soup and chili powder.
•Spread it in an ungreased 13"x9" baking pan and top it with corn chips.
•Bake, uncovered, at 350°F for about 20 to 25 minutes.
•Remove from oven and then sprinkle it with cheese.
•Bake for an additional 5 minutes until cheese melts.

Tomato Beef in Italian Style Casserole

INGREDIENTS:

1 pound lean ground beef
7 ounces uncooked small elbow macaroni
1 can (14.5 ounce) cut tomatoes, drained
1 can (10.75 ounce) Italian tomato soup or regular tomato soup
1 small onion, chopped or 1 tablespoon dried instant onions
1 clove garlic, minced or 1/8 teaspoon dried minced garlic
1 can (4.5 ounce) sliced mushrooms, drained
1 teaspoon salt
1/2 teaspoon chili powder
1 teaspoon Italian seasonings
1/4 teaspoon pepper

INSTRUCTIONS:

•Warm the oven to 350° F.
•Brown the ground beef and drain.

•Cook macaroni according to package directions.
•Mix beef, macaroni and the remaining ingredients in a 2 quart casserole.
•Cover the casserole.
•Bake at 350° F for 30 minutes.

Baked Beefy Ziti

INGREDIENTS:

16 ounces package Ziti pasta
1 pound lean ground beef
1 onion, chopped
2 27-ounce cans spaghetti sauce
6 ounces provolone Cheese, sliced
6 ounces mozzarella cheese, sliced or shredded
1 1/2 cup sour cream
1/2 cup Parmesan cheese, grated

INSTRUCTIONS:

•Cook pasta as directed on the manufacturer's packaging.
•Drain and set aside.
•In the meantime, sauté the ground beef with the chopped onion in a heavy skillet over medium heat.
•Add spaghetti sauce and let it simmer for about 15 minutes.
•Put about a half of the pasta in a lightly oiled 2-quart baking dish.
•Top with a layer of provolone and mozzarella cheeses.
•Spread on a layer of about half the sour cream and then half the spaghetti sauce mixture. •Cover with the remaining pasta, cheese, sour cream, and sauce.
•Sprinkle the layer with the Parmesan cheese.
•Bake in a preheated 350° F oven for about 30 minutes or until the cheese and sauce are bubbly.
•Serve warm.

Ravioli Lasagna

INGREDIENTS:

1lb lean ground beef
garlic salt
pepper
24oz marinara sauce
1-1/2lbs frozen mini cheese ravioli (Do not thaw. Could use normal sized ravioli)
6oz shredded mozzarella cheese

INTRUCTIONS:

•Preheat oven to 400 degrees.
•Brown the ground beef in a large skillet over medium-high heat.
•Season it with garlic, salt and pepper.
•Drain the dripping and set aside.
•Spread 1/4 cup marinara sauce in the bottom of an 8×8 baking dish.
•Add 1/3 frozen ravioli, ground beef, sauce, and cheese.
•Repeat layers two more times.
•Cover with a sheet of non-stick sprayed foil then bake for 1 hour.
•Remove foil then bake for another 10 more minutes, or until cheese is golden brown and bubbly.

Amish Ground Beef and Noodle Casserole

INGREDIENTS:

2 cups sour cream (a 16-ounce container)
2 cups small-curd cottage cheese (a 16-ounce container)
1/4 cup finely chopped onion
2 Tbsp. minced fresh parsley
1 7- to 8-ounce package medium egg noodles
1 Tbsp. vegetable oil
2 pounds lean ground round or well-trimmed chuck
1 6-ounce cans tomato paste
1 small jar pizza sauce, about 14 oz.
1 Tbsp. minced fresh basil, or 1 tsp. dried
1 Tbsp. minced fresh oregano, or 1 tsp. dried
1 tsp. salt
1/2 tsp. coarsely ground black pepper

INTRUCTIONS:

•In a small mixing bowl, combine the sour cream, cottage cheese, onion, and parsley.
•Set aside.
•In a large saucepan, cook the noodles according to the package directions.
•Drain and set aside.
•Heat the oil in a large sauce pan over medium heat.
•Add the ground beef and stirring it gradually until the meat is no longer pink.
•Drain all liquid and discard.
•Stir in the tomato paste, pizza sauce, basil, oregano, salt and pepper and let it simmer for 5 minutes.
•Preheat the oven to 325° F.
•Grease a 9 x 13-inch pan and begin layering as follows: one-third of the meat sauce, one-half of the noodles, and one-half of the sour cream mixture.
•Repeat these layers, ending with the meat sauce.
•Bake, covered for about 1 hour or until the casserole is bubbly.
•Allow standing for 15 minutes, then served.

Casserole Beef Stroganoff

INGREDIENTS:

5 cups water
1 tablespoon salt
3 cups uncooked egg noodles
1/4 cup butter or margarine
1 cup fine dry bread crumbs
1 pound lean ground beef
1/2 cup onion, finely chopped
1/4 cup green pepper, finely chopped
1/2 teaspoon garlic salt
1 teaspoon salt
1/8 teaspoon pepper
1 cup Swiss cheese, grated
1 can (8-ounce) tomato sauce
1 can (4-ounce) mushroom stems and pieces, drained

INSTRUCTIONS:

•Place 5 cups water, 1 tablespoon salt and 3 cups uncooked noodles in a deep, 3-quart, heat-resistant, non-metallic casserole.
•Put in microwave oven for 12 minutes or until noodles are tender.
•Stir occasionally.
•Drain noodles and set aside.
•In a large, heat-resistant, non-metallic mixing bowl, melt 1/4 cup butter or margarine in microwave oven for 30 seconds.
•Add bread crumbs and cook, uncovered, in microwave oven for 1 1/2 minutes or until bread crumbs are golden brown.
•Add meat to bread crumbs mixture and mix to combine well.
•Cook, uncovered for 5 minutes or until meat is browned while stirring occasionally so that meat crumbles.
•Add onions, green pepper, garlic salt, salt and pepper.
•Blend into meat mixture thoroughly.
•Cook uncovered in microwave oven for 2 minutes.
•In a 2-quart, heat-resistant, non-metallic casserole layer cooked noodles with meat mixture.
•Top with cheese, tomato sauce and mushrooms.
•Cook uncovered in microwave oven for 8 minutes or until cheese melts.

Veggie & Beef Casserole

INGREDIENTS:

1 pound ground beef
1/4 teaspoon salt
1/8 teaspoon black pepper
1 teaspoon oil
8 ounces sliced mushrooms
1 large onion, chopped
3 cloves garlic minced
1/4 cup dry white wine
1 can cream of mushroom soup undiluted
1/2 cup sour cream
1 tablespoon Dijon mustard
4 cups cooked noodles

INSTRUCTIONS:

•Heat oven to 350° F.
•Spray 9x13 pan with non stick cooking spray.
•Brown the beef in skillet.
•Drain the dripping.
•Heat oil dripping in same skillet and brown the onion, mushroom and garlic until tender.
•In a large bowl, mix the soup, white wine, salt, pepper and sour cream.
•Add beef and cooked noodles.
•Mix with onion garlic mixture.
•Pour into greased pan.
•Bake at 350° F, uncovered, for about 30 minutes or until heated through.

Beef Veggies and Hash Brown Casserole

INGREDIENTS:

4 cups frozen hash browns
3 tablespoons vegetable oil
1/8 teaspoon pepper
1 pound ground beef
1 cup water
1 3/4 ounce gravy mix
1/2 teaspoon garlic salt
1 cup shredded cheddar
1 can fried onions
10 ounces frozen mixed vegetables

INSTRUCTIONS:

•Preheat the oven to 400 degrees F.
•Combine hash browns, oil and pepper in a 9x13 inch casserole dish.
•Press around bottom and sides.
•Bake for 15 minutes.
•Brown the beef and then drain.
•Stir in gravy, water and garlic salt and boil.
•Add mixed veggies.
•Reduce heat and cook for 10 minutes.
•Stir in 1/2 cup cheese and 1/2 can onions.
•Place in potato shell.
•Reduce oven heat to 350° F.
•Bake uncovered for 15 minutes.
•Sprinkle with remaining cheese and onion.
•Bake for 5 more minutes.

Chili Meatloaf and Potato Casserole

INGREDIENTS:

1 1/2 pound lean ground beef
3/4 cup onion, finely chopped
1/3 cup Saltine cracker crumbs
1 egg, slightly beaten
3 tablespoons milk
1 tablespoon chili powder
3/4 teaspoon salt
3 cups prepared mashed potatoes
1 cans (11 oz.) whole kernel corn with red and green peppers, drained
1/4 cup thinly sliced green onions
1/2 to 1 cup shredded taco seasoned cheese

INSTRUCTIONS:

•Heat oven to 375 degrees F.
•In large bowl, combine ground beef, onion, cracker crumbs, egg, milk, chili powder and salt.
•Stirring slightly but thoroughly.
•Gently press into bottom of 9 inch square baking pan.
•Bake for about 20 to 25 minutes or until no longer pink and juices run clear.
•Carefully pour off drippings.
•Meanwhile in medium bowl, combine mashed potatoes, kernel corn, red pepper, green peppers and green onions.
•Spread over meatloaf to edges of pan and then sprinkle with cheese.
•Broil 3 to 4 inches from heat for 3 to 5 minutes or until top is lightly browned.
•Cut into 6 rectangular servings.

Beef Cheddar and Bacon Casserole

INGREDIENTS:

1 pound ground beef
1 medium onion, chopped
5 1/4 ounces cheddar and bacon potatoes
15 1/4 ounces can whole kernel corn, drained
10 3/4 ounces can condense cream of potato or cream of mushroom soup
1 cup water
3 tablespoons dry sherry
1/2 cup roasted red peppers
4 ounces can dice green chilies, drained

INSTRUCTIONS:

•In a large skillet, cook the beef and onion over medium-high heat for 6 to 8 minutes.
•Stir often, until the beef is brown and crumbly.
•Drain off excess fat.
•Scatter the dried potatoes over the bottom of slow cooker.
•Sprinkle on the corn.
•In a medium bowl, whisk together the soup with the sauce mix packet from the potatoes, the water, and sherry until thoroughly blended.
•Stir in the roasted red peppers and green chiles.
•Drizzle about 1/3 of soup mixture over the corn and potatoes. (Do not mix.)
•Top with the cooked beef and onion.
•Pour the remaining soup mixture evenly over the top. (Do not mix.)
•Cover and cook on the low setting 4 to 4-1/2 hours or until the potatoes are tender.
•Serve at once.

Easy Beefy Zucchini Stuffin Casserole

INGREDIENTS:

1 1/2 pound ground beef
4 zucchini, sliced
1 small onion, chopped
4 tablespoons butter (as much as desired for your taste)
1 cup grated carrots
1 cup dairy sour cream
1 can cream of chicken soup
1 box Stuffing mix, prepared according to package directions
1 box of herb-seasoned croutons

INSTRUCTIONS:

•Preheat oven to 350° F.
•In a large skillet, brown the ground beef and drain the fat.
•Sauté zucchini and onion in the butter.
•Mix together the beef, zucchini-onion mixture, carrots, sour cream, soup, and stuffing and then place in 9x13-inch casserole dish.
•Top with the croutons and bake for 1 hour at 350° F.

Splendid Beef Taco Casserole

INGREDIENTS:

1 pound extra lean ground beef
1 medium onion, chopped
15 1/2 ounces kidney beans
8 ounces tomato sauce
2 teaspoons chili powder
1/2 teaspoon garlic salt
1 cup tortilla chips, broken
1 cup Cheddar cheese, shredded

INSTRUCTIONS:

•Preheat oven to 350 degrees F.
•Crumble ground beef into a 10-inch skillet and add onion.
•Cook and stir until beef is light brown and onion is tender.
•Drain the fat.
•Add kidney beans (un-drained), tomato sauce, chili powder and garlic salt.

•Heat to boiling.
•Pour half of the meat mixture into ungreased 1 1/2-quart casserole and top with broken tortilla chips.
•Pour remaining beef mixture over top and sprinkle with Cheddar cheese.
•Cover and bake for 25 to 30 minutes or until bubbly.
•Garnish with chopped green pepper and pimento, if desired.

Hamburger Casserole in Slow Cooker

INGREDIENTS:

2 large potatoes, sliced
2 or 3 medium carrots, sliced
1 cans peas
2 medium onion, sliced
Salt & pepper to taste
2 stalks celery, sliced
1 1/2 pound ground beef
1 cans tomato soup
1/2 can water

INSTRUCTIONS:

•Brown the ground beef and drain the dripping.
•Add potatoes, carrots, onion, celery and peas to slow cooker.
•Fill with water and tomato soup.
•Add the beef and spices and mix together.
•Cook on high heat for 3 hours while stirring occasionally.

Beefy Casserole Pie in Amish-inspired Dish

INGREDIENTS:

1 pound ground beef
1 small package cream cheese
1 can mushroom soup
1 cup canned corn with pimento
1 package refrigerated biscuits

INSTRUCTIONS:

•Brown the ground beef in skillet and drain the fats.
•Preheat oven to 350 degrees F.
•Mix cream cheese, soup and corn in a separate bowl.
•Pour into two quart casserole dish and add the beef.
•Top with biscuits.
•Bake at 350 degrees F for about 20 minutes.

Do It Best with Amish Beef Bake Dish

INGREDIENTS:

2 tablespoons vegetable oil
1 medium onion, chopped
1 garlic clove, minced
1 pound lean ground beef
1/2 teaspoon ground coriander
1/4 teaspoon ground ginger
2 medium tomatoes, chopped
1 teaspoon light brown sugar
2 tablespoons fresh parsley, minced
1/2 teaspoon salt
1/8 teaspoon pepper
1 green pepper, chopped

INSTRUCTIONS:

•Preheat oven to 375 degrees F.
•Heat oil in a skillet over moderate heat.
•Add onion and garlic.
•Cook uncovered for 5 minutes.
•Push to one side and add beef.

•Stir occasionally until browned.
•Mix coriander, ginger, tomatoes, brown sugar, parsley, salt, pepper, and peppers in a bowl.
•Add to beef and mix well.
•Transfer the mixture to ungreased 1 quart casserole dish.
•Bake uncovered for 20 minutes.
•Serve over rice.

Cabbage Roll in Slow Cooked Casserole

INGREDIENTS:

1 lb. lean ground beef
1 onion, diced
3 cloves garlic, minced
¼ tsp. ground thyme
1 tsp. dried oregano
¾ tsp. kosher salt
A few grinds of black pepper
¼ tsp. caraway seeds, optional
1 c. brown rice, uncooked (use white rice if following 30-minute instructions)
14 oz. petite diced tomatoes, un-drained
8 oz. tomato sauce
2 c. beef broth
12 oz. bag shredded cabbage (coleslaw mix with carrots and cabbage works great)
1 c. mozzarella cheese
¼ c. grated Parmesan cheese

INSTRUCTIONS:

• Sauté beef and onions in large skillet over medium-high heat oven.
•Stir in oregano, thyme, salt, pepper, and caraway seeds while cooking.
•Add garlic and rice to the beef when the meat is tender and sauté for 3 minutes more.
•Stir in beef broth, tomatoes, and tomato sauce and bring it to boil.
•Reduce heat to let it simmer.
•Cook and cover for another 1 hour, or up to 2 hours.
•Stir in cabbage, and replace lid.
•Let it simmer again over a very low heat for about 10 minutes more.
•Turn broiler to high.
•Remove lid and turn off heat.

•Sprinkle cheeses over the top of the cabbage mixture, and place the pot under broiler for 3-5 minutes or until cheese is bubbly and starting to brown.

Breakfast for Dinner Casserole

INGREDIENTS:

5 c. frozen hash brown potatoes
2 c. ham, diced (asks for ½" slices at the deli and cut into cubes)
½ c. green onion, diced
1 c. shredded cheddar or Colby jack cheese, divided
¼ tsp. garlic powder
½ tsp. kosher salt
Freshly ground black pepper to taste
4 eggs
12 oz. evaporated milk

INSTRUCTIONS:

•Preheat the oven to 375 degrees F.
•Spray 9 x 13" baking dish with cooking spray.
•In a medium bowl, stir together potatoes, ham, ½ c. cheese, and green onions.
•Spread mixture evenly in the prepared baking dish.
•In a small bowl, whisk together eggs, evaporated milk, garlic powder, salt, and pepper. •Pour evenly over potato mixture.
•Cover with foil, and bake for 40 minutes.
•Remove cover, and sprinkle remaining ½ c. cheese over casserole.
•Bake uncovered for another 15 minutes or until hot and bubbly and knife inserted in center comes out clean.

Tortilla Casserole

INGREDIENTS:

1 lb. ground beef
1/2 med. onion, chopped
1 green bell pepper, chopped
1/4 tsp. cumin, or to taste
1 clove garlic (optional)
2 cans (14 oz. each) Rotel Tomatoes and Green Chiles, lightly drained
1/2 cup salsa
2 cans (1 lb. each) Ranch style black beans, drained
1 can (1 lb.) white shoepeg corn
6 to 8 oz. Monterrey Jack cheese, grated
6 to 8 oz. Cheddar cheese, grated
4 to 6 md. (8-inch) flour tortillas
Salad, tomatoes, olives, sour cream, and green onions, to garnish

INSTRUCTIONS:

•Preheat the oven to 350°F.
•Brown the ground beef in a large skillet.
•When meat is half-cooked, add the onion, green pepper and garlic.
•Cook until onions are clear.
•Add Rotel tomatoes, salsa, beans, corn and cumin to taste and bring to a boil. •Simmer for 5 to 10 minutes or until sauce begins to thicken.
•Remove from heat.
•Layer one-third of meat mixture in a 13x9-inch glass pan.
•Cover meat mixture with a singe layer of tortillas and then layer one-third of the cheeses.
•Cover with another third of the meat mixture, tortillas, and one third of the cheese.
•Top casserole with the remaining meat and cheese.
•Bake until sauce bubbles and cheese on top is melted, about 35 to 45 minutes.
•Let stand for 10 minutes before serving.
•Top with salad and desired garnish.

Mexican Ground Beef Tortilla Layer Casserole

INGREDIENTS

1 1/2 lbs. ground beef
1 onion, chopped
1 -2 tablespoon fresh minced garlic
1 large jalapeno pepper, seeded and finely chopped (optional)
2 -4 teaspoons cumin (or to taste)
salt and black pepper
2 (10 ounce) cans red enchilada sauce
1 (15 ounce) can black beans (rinsed and well drained)
2 cups frozen corn
9 corn tortillas
2 cups shredded Mexican blend cheese, divided (can use more or less)
TOPPINGS
2 plum tomatoes, finely chopped
sour cream
green onion
coarsely crushed tortilla chips

INSTRUCTIONS:

•Set oven to 350° F.
•Grease an 11 x 7-inch baking dish.
•In a large skillet, brown the ground beef with onion, garlic, green bell pepper and jalapeno (if using) until the beef is no longer pink.
•Drain any fat then return to skillet and add in one can of enchilada sauce, black beans, corn and cumin.
•Bring the ground beef mixture to a boil and reduce heat to medium-low.
•Let it simmer for 20-25 minutes while stirring occasionally.
•Season with salt and lots of black pepper.
•Arrange 3 corn tortillas in the bottom of the baking dish, cutting as needed to cover bottom of the dish.
•Spread 1/4 cup canned enchilada sauce over the tortillas in the baking dish.
•Cover the sauce with 1/3 of the cooked ground beef mixture, then about 1/3 of the shredded cheese.
•Repeat the layers twice but omitting the final cheese layer on top.
•Drizzle any remaining canned enchilada sauce (from the second can) on top.
•Cover with foil and bake in a 350° F oven for 25 minutes.

•Remove foil and sprinkle with more cheese.
•Bake for another 5 minutes or until the cheese has melted.
•Let stand 10-15 minutes before slicing.
•Top with sour cream and/or tomatoes, green onions and crushed tortilla chips if desired.

Enchilada Casserole

INGREDIENTS:

2 lbs. ground beef
1 small finely chopped yellow onion
1 can corn (can sub. 1 sm bag frozen or fresh, whole kernel)
1/4 c. taco seasoning
1 can cream of mushroom soup
1 can cream of tomato soup
1 can refried beans
2 8oz. cans Old El Paso mild or hot red sauce
34 cups shredded cheese
34 flour tortillas cut into strips chili powder and cumin, to taste

INSTRUCTIONS:

• Preheat oven to 350°F.
•Brown the ground beef with onions and drain the excess fat.
•Place the beef in a large over medium heat oven and add taco seasoning by mixing it well.
•Add corn and refried beans and then mix it well.
• Add and mix well the cream of mushroom, tomato soup, and both cans of enchilada sauce Stir in chili powder and cumin to taste.
• Lightly grease a 9 x 13-inch baking dish, and place a single layer of tortilla strips down (just enough to cover the bottom).
•Place half of the meat mixture over the top of the first layer.
•Add enough cheese to lightly cover the layer and add another layer of tortilla strips (covering the first layer).
•Add the remaining meat mixture and another small amount of cheese.
•Add another layer of tortilla strips (enough to completely cover the mixture).
• Top the last layer of tortillas with enough cheese to completely cover the tortillas.
•Cover dish with foil.

•Bake at 350°F for about 30 minutes.
•Let stand about 5 minutes to cool and enjoy.

Tuna & Mushroom Casserole

INGREDIENTS:

1 can tuna
1 can cream of mushroom soup
1 1/2 cups of grated cheese
1/2 cup frozen peas
1 cup milk 3 cups of macaroni, parboiled

INSTRUCTIONS:

•Combine the tuna with one cup.
•Add the cream of mushroom soup.
•Stir together, then add salt and pepper to taste.
•Mix tuna mushroom soup and milk with parboiled noodles.
•Add peas.
•Bake at 300°F for about an hour.
•Ten minutes before removing from oven, sprinkle with cheese and continue to bake until cheese melts and becomes bubbly.

Easy Assorted Casserole

INGREDIENTS:

1 (10 3/4 oz.) can cream of mushroom soup, undiluted
1 (10 3/4 oz.) can cream of celery soup, undiluted
1 (10 3/4 oz.) can cream of chicken soup, undiluted
1 (10 3/4 oz.) can Cheddar cheese soup, undiluted
2 (14 1/2 oz. each) cans diced tomatoes with basil, garlic, and oregano, un-drained
CHOOSE ONE VEGETABLE:
1 (14 1/2 oz.) can cut green Italian beans, drained
1 (15 1/4 oz.) can sweet peas, drained
1 (10 1/2 oz.) can asparagus cuts and tips, drained
1 (15 1/4 oz.) can whole kernel corn, drained
1 (13 1/2 oz.) can chopped spinach
CHOOSE ONE PASTA/RICE:
2 cups uncooked elbow macaroni
1 cup uncooked regular rice
4 cups uncooked wide egg noodles
3 cups uncooked small pasta shells
CHOOSE ONE MEAT/FISH/POULTRY:
2 (6 oz.) cans solid white tuna in spring water, drained and flaked
2 cups chopped cooked chicken
2 cups chopped cooked ham
2 cups chopped cooked turkey
1 pound ground beef, browned and drained
CHOOSE ONE OR TWO TOPPINGS:
1/2 cup shredded mozzarella cheese
1/2 cup grated Parmesan cheese
1/2 cup shredded Swiss cheese
1/2 cup fine, dry breadcrumbs
1 cup round buttery crackers, crushed
1 cup herb seasoned stuffing mix

INSTRUCTIONS:

•Combine sour cream, milk, water, salt, and pepper with chosen Sauce Maker.
•Stir in selected Vegetable, Pasta or Rice, Meat or Fish and or Poultry.
•Spoon into a lightly greased 13x9inch baking dish.
•Bake, covered, at 350°F for 1 hour and 20 minutes.
•Uncover and sprinkle with selected Toppings and then bake for 10 more minutes.

•Invent your own one dish combinations by switching ingredients for variety.

Chicken & Wild Rice Casserole

INGREDIENTS:

2 to 3 lb. fryers
1 c. water
1 c. dry sherry
1/2 tsp. curry
1/2 c. celery, sliced
1 1/2 tsp. salt
1 med. Onion
12 oz. long grain and wild rice
10 1/2 oz. cream of mushroom soup
Chicken broth
1 c. sour cream

INSTRUCTIONS:

•Mix the ingredients such as fryers, dry sherry, curry, celery, onion, salt and water in deep kettle.
•Simmer for 1 hour.
•Remove chicken and refrigerate.
•Strain broth.
•Cut chicken into small pieces.
•Cook rice in chicken broth and water.
•Combine rice, chicken, sour cream, soup and mushrooms.
•Place in 9 x 13 inch baking dish.
•Refrigerate.
•When ready to use, bake for 1 hour at 350°F.

Layered Fiesta Casserole

INGREDIENTS:

1lb. Extra-lean ground beef
1 green pepper, chopped
1 red pepper, chopped
1 jars (16 oz.) Thick & Chunky Salsa
1 can (14-1/2 oz.) diced tomatoes,
1pkg. (10 oz.) Frozen corn
12 corn tortillas (6 inch)
1-1/2 cups 2% Milk Shredded Sharp Cheddar Cheese, divided

INSTRUCTIONS:

•Heat the oven to 375°F.
•Brown the meat with peppers in large skillet and then drain.
•Return to skillet and stir in salsa, tomatoes and corn.
•Spread 1 cup meat mixture onto bottom of 13x9-inch baking dish.
•Top with 6 tortillas, overlapping as necessary.
•Cover with layers of half each of the remaining meat mixture and cheese.
•Top with remaining tortillas and meat mixture and then cover.
•Bake for about 25 to 30 min. or until heated through.
•Top with remaining cheese.
•Let stand, uncovered for another 5 minutes or until the cheese melted.

Cheesy Tuna Veggie Noodle Casserole

INGREDIENTS:

2 cups medium-size pasta, uncooked
1pkg. (16 oz.) Frozen mixed vegetables, thawed, drained
8 oz. VELVEETA, cut into 1/2-inch cubes
2 cans (5 oz. each) tuna in water, drained, flaked
½ cup milk

INSTRUCTIONS:

•Heat the oven to 350°F.
•Cook the pasta in large saucepan as directed on its package.
•Add vegetables to the boiling water in the last minute.
•Drain the pasta.
•Stir in VELVEETA, tuna and milk with the pasta in a large pan.
•Spoon the pasta mixture into 1-1/2-qt. casserole and then cover.
•Bake for 15 to 20 minutes or until heated through.
•Stir before serving.

Tuna with VELVEETA Cheesy Skillet

INGREDIENTS:

1pkg. VELVEETA cheesy skillet Dinner Kit Tuna Melt
2-1/2 cups water
2 cans (5 oz. each) tuna, drained, flaked
12 round buttery crackers, crushed (about 1/2 cup)

INSTRUCTIONS:

•Combine pasta, vegetables, seasoning mix and water in large skillet.
•Bring it to boil and cover.
•Simmer on medium-low heat for about 9 to 11 minutes or until pasta is tender and most of the water is absorbed.
•Remove from heat.
•Add tuna and mix lightly.
•Stir in VELVEETA Cheese Sauce.
•Top with cracker crumbs.

Shrimp Stroganoff

INGREDIENTS:

3cups egg noodles, uncooked
4cups small broccoli florets
1lb. VELVEETA, cut into 1/2-inch cubes
1can (10-3/4 oz.) condensed cream of shrimp soup
1cup Sour Cream
1lb. Uncooked deveined peeled medium shrimp

INSTRUCTIONS:

•Preheat the oven to 350°F.
•Cook noodles as directed on package.
•Add broccoli to the boiling water in the last 5 minutes.
•For the meantime, cook VELVEETA, soup and sour cream in saucepan on low heat for 8 minutes or until VELVEETA is completely melted and mixture is well blended while stirring it occasionally.
•Drain pasta mixture and put it in a13 x 9-inch baking dish.
•Stir in shrimp.
•Pour VELVEETA sauce over pasta mixture and cover with foil.
•Bake for 25 minutes or until heated through.

Creamy Beef Stroganoff Meatballs

INGREDIENTS:

1 recipe Easy Basic Meatballs
1Tbsp. Oil
1lb. Fresh mushrooms, quartered
1 onion, chopped
2cloves garlic, minced
6cups egg noodles, uncooked
2Tbsp. Flour
1 tube (8 oz.) Chive & Onion 1/3 Less Fat than Cream Cheese
¾ cup fat-free reduced-sodium beef broth
1Tbsp. Dijon Mustard
1/2tsp. Dried thyme leaves
1/4tsp. Paprika

INSTRUCTIONS:

•Prepare and bake Easy Basic Meatballs as directed in the package.

•In the meantime, heat oil in large deep skillet on medium heat.
•Add mushrooms, onions and garlic then cook for 10 minutes while stirring frequently.
•Cook noodles as directed on package while vegetable is in process of cooking.
•Add flour to vegetable mixture.
•Cook and stir for 1 minute.
•Add remaining ingredients and then mix well.
•Bring it to boil then let it simmer on a medium-low heat for 4 minutes while stirring frequently.
•Drain the noodles.
•Add meatballs to sauce and spread to evenly coat.

Fresh Grated Parmesan Spaghetti & Meatballs

INGREDIENTS:

1lb. Extra-lean ground beef
1/3cup seasoned dry breadcrumbs
2 cloves garlic, minced
2 Tbsp. Milk
1 egg
1/3 cup Refrigerated Coarsely Grated Parmesan and Romano Cheeses, divided
1/2lb. Spaghetti, uncooked, broken in half
1jar (24 oz.) spaghetti sauce

INSTRUCTIONS:

•Heat the oven to 375°F.
•Combine the ground beef, bread crumbs, garlic, milk, egg and 1/4 cup cheese.
•Form it into 18 meatballs.
•Place in 15 x 10 x 1-inch pan sprayed with cooking spray.
•Bake 15 min. or until done (160°F).
•Meanwhile, cook the spaghetti as directed on the package but omitting the salt.
•Heat sauce in large saucepan.
•Drain the spaghetti and place it on a platter.
•Add meatballs into sauce.
•Spoon the mixture over the spaghetti.
•Top with remaining cheese.

Leftovers Casserole

INGREDIENTS:

1pkg. (6 oz.) Stuffing Mix for Turkey
4 cups chopped leftover roasted turkey
2 cups frozen mixed vegetables (carrots, corn, green beans, peas), thawed
¾ cup Real Mayo Mayonnaise or Miracle whip Dressing
3 cups leftover mashed potatoes
1 cup Shredded Cheddar Cheese
1/8 tsp. paprika

INSTRUCTIONS:

•Heat the oven to 375°F.
•Prepare stuffing as directed on package.
•Spread onto bottom of 13 x 9-inch baking dish sprayed with cooking spray.
•Combine turkey, mixed vegetables and mayo and spoon over stuffing.
•Mix potatoes and cheese.
•Spread over turkey mixture.
•Sprinkle with paprika.
•Bake for about 30 to 40 min. or until heated through.

Creamy Turkey & Noodles

INGREDIENTS:

1/1pkg. (16 oz.) farfalle (bow-tie pasta), uncooked
4 cup butter
1 onion, chopped
1pkg. (16 oz.) frozen mixed vegetables (carrots, corn, green beans, peas)
6Tbsp. flour
2 cups milk
2pkg. (7.5 oz. each Oven Roasted Turkey Breast, chopped
2cans (10-3/4 oz.) reduced-sodium condensed cream of chicken soup
1cup Sour Cream
1pkg. (8 oz.) Shredded Three Cheese

INSTRUCTIONS:

•Warm the oven to 350°F.
•Cook pasta as directed on package, omitting salt.
•Meanwhile, melt butter in Dutch oven or large deep skillet over a medium heat.
•Add onions and cook for about 4 minutes while stirring or until crisp-tender.
•Add frozen vegetables and cook for another 4 minutes or until thawed while stirring frequently.
•Mix the flour and cook for 1 minute until it blended.
•Gradually pour the milk and then bring to a boil.
•Cook and stir for 2 minutes or until thickened.
•Remove from heat.
•Drain the pasta and set aside.
•Combine turkey, soup and sour cream to make a sauce.
•Put pasta into 2 (13x9-inch) pans sprayed with cooking spray.
•Spoon the sauce over the pasta and spread to evenly coat.
•Top with cheese and cover.
•Bake for about 20 minutes or until heated through.
•Uncovering the pan and bake for another 10 more minutes.

Creamy Ham and Noodle Casserole

INGREDIENTS:

1Tbsp. Butter or margarine
1/2cup sliced celery
1/4cup chopped onion
1/4cup chopped green pepper
1pkg. (8 oz.) Cream Cheese, cubed
1cup milk
1pkg. (12 oz.) Smoked Ham cold cuts, chopped
1/2 cup Grated Parmesan Cheese, divided
2cups (4 oz.) spinach noodles, cooked, drained

INSTRUCTIONS:

•Preheat the oven to 350°F.
•Melt the butter in large skillet over medium heat.
•Add vegetables and cook while stirring occasionally until crisp-tender.
•Add cream cheese and milk and cook on low heat until cream cheese is melted while stirring frequently.
•Add ham and 1/4 cup of the Parmesan cheese and then mix until well blended.
•Stir in sauce and noodles.
•Spoon it into 1-1/2-qt. casserole dish.
•Sprinkle with remaining 1/4 cup Parmesan cheese.
•Bake for about 25 to 30 minutes or until heated through.

Crowd-Pleasing Creamy Casserole

INGREDIENTS:

2cups cubed ham
1pkg. (16 oz.) frozen chopped broccoli, thawed, drained
1pkg. (8 oz.) Shredded Sharp Cheddar Cheese
1pkg. (6 oz.) seasoned croutons
4 eggs
2cups milk
1/2cup MIRACLE WHIP Dressing
2Tbsp. flour
2tsp. dry mustard
2tsp. dried basil leaves

INSTRUCTIONS:

•Combine ham, broccoli, cheese and croutons.
•Place in a 13 x 9-inch baking dish sprayed with cooking spray.
•Whisk eggs and milk in medium bowl until blended.
•Add remaining ingredients and mix well.
•Pour over ham mixture and then refrigerate for 1 hour.
•Heat the oven to 375°F.
•Bake the casserole, uncovered, for 45 minutes or until center is set.

Creamy Garlic-Green Bean Casserole

INGREDIENTS:

1cup Sour Cream
1cup Shredded Mozzarella Cheese
1/2cup Grated Parmesan Cheese
1/2cup Mayo with Olive Oil Reduced Fat Mayonnaise
1/2tsp. garlic powder
2pkg. 16 oz. each) frozen green beans, thawed, drained
26 thin wheat snack crackers, crushed (about 1 cup)
1Tbsp. butter, melted

INSTRUCTIONS:

•Heat the oven to 350°F.
•Combine the sour cream, mozzarella cheese, parmesan cheese, mayo with olive oil and garlic powder in a large bowl.

•Add beans and mix lightly.
•Spoon the mixture into a 13 x 9-inch baking dish.
•Mix cracker crumbs and butter and sprinkle over bean mixture.
•Bake for 25 minutes or until heated through.

Creamy Garlic Chicken

INGREDIENTS:

2 tsp. oil
4 small boneless skinless chicken breasts(1 lb.)
1/4 cup MIRACLE WHIP Dressing
2 cups frozen stir-fry vegetables(broccoli, green beans, mushrooms, red peppers)
1Tbsp. soy sauce
4cloves garlic, minced
3cups hot cooked instant white rice

INSTRUCTIONS:

•Heat oil in a large nonstick skillet over medium heat.
•Add chicken and cook for 4 minutes on each side or until lightly browned on both sides.
•Add dressing, vegetables, soy sauce and garlic and stir altogether.
•Cook and covered for about 7 minutes or until chicken is done (165°F) while stirring occasionally.
•Serve over hot cooked rice.

Eggplant Rollatini

INGREDIENTS:

2 eggplants, ends trimmed, peeled
1 container (16 oz.) 2% Milk or Low Fat Cottage Cheese
2 cups Shredded Mozzarella Cheese, divided
1/3 cup dry bread crumbs
1/4 cup Grated Parmesan Cheese
1/4 cup chopped fresh basil
1 jar (14 oz.) spaghetti sauce

INSTRUCTIONS:

•Remove thinly the opposite long sides of each eggplant and discard.
•Cut each eggplant into 6 lengthwise slices.
•Place in microwaveable bowl.
•Microwave on high heat for about 5 to 6 minutes or until eggplant is very tender.
•Place in a colander and drain well.
•Put the eggplant in a single layer clean kitchen towel and cover it with second towel. •Press gently to remove excess moisture from eggplant.
•Mix cottage cheese, 1-1/2 cups mozzarella, bread crumbs, Parmesan and basil.
•Spoon the mixture about 1/3 cups onto each eggplant slice.
•Roll up by starting at the one short end.
•Place in seam-sides down position to a 13 x 9-inch pan sprayed with cooking spray.
•Cover with spaghetti sauce and the remaining mozzarella.
•Bake for about 30 to 35 minutes or until hot and bubbly.
•Let stand for 5 minutes before serving.

Tortilla Casserole with Swiss chard

INGREDIENTS:

2 teaspoons vegetable oil
2 cups thinly sliced onion, divided
3 garlic cloves, finely chopped
1/2 teaspoon salt
2 (8-ounce) packages button mushrooms, sliced
2 jalapeño peppers, seeded and chopped
4 cups finely chopped Swiss chard (1 bunch)
1/4 cup chopped fresh parsley, divided
1/4 cup water
1 (14.5-ounce) can diced tomatoes, un-drained
12 (6-inch) corn tortillas, quartered
1 cup (4 ounces) shredded reduced-fat sharp cheddar cheese
1/4 cup low-fat sour cream

INSTRUCTIONS:

•Preheat oven to 375°.
•Heat oil in a large nonstick skillet over medium-high heat.
•Add 1 cup onion and garlic, and cook for 1 minute while stirring constantly.
•Stir in the salt, mushrooms, and jalapeños.
•Arrange chard over mushroom mixture.
•Cover and reduce the heat.
•Cook for about 15 minutes or until tender.
•Stir in 2 tablespoons of parsley.
•Combine 1 cup onion, water, and tomatoes in a blender, and process until smooth.
•Pour the tomato mixture into a saucepan.
•Bring to a boil and cook for about 4 minutes or until slightly thick.
•Arrange 16 tortilla quarters in a single layer of a 13 x 9-inch baking dish.
•Spread about 1 cup mushroom mixture over the tortilla pieces.
•Top with 1/2 cup tomato mixture.
•Sprinkle with 1/3 cup cheese.
•Repeat layers twice, ending with 1/3 cup cheese.
•Bake at 375°F for 20 minutes or until cheese melts.
•Top each serving with sour cream and 2 tablespoons parsley.

Southwestern Bean Casserole

INGREDIENTS:

1 teaspoon vegetable oil
Cooking spray
1 cup chopped onion
2 garlic cloves, minced
1 cup canned no-salt-added cream-style corn, divided
1/2 cup drained canned chopped green chilies, divided
1/2 cup bottled salsa
1/2 teaspoon salt
1/4 teaspoon ground cumin
1/4 teaspoon pepper
2 (16-ounce) cans pinto beans, drained
1 (14.5-ounce) can no-salt-added stewed tomatoes, un-drained
1 cup (4 ounces) shredded reduced-fat cheddar cheese, divided
3/4 cup yellow cornmeal
1/4 cup all-purpose flour
1 teaspoon sugar
1/4 teaspoon salt
1/2 cup low-fat buttermilk
1/4 cup vegetable oil
2 egg whites, lightly beaten

INSTRUCTIONS:

•Preheat oven to 375°F.
•Heat 1 teaspoon vegetable oil in a large saucepan over medium-high heat.
•Add onion and garlic, and sauté for 3 minutes.
•Add 1/2 cup corn, 1/4 cup chilies, salsa, salt, cumin, pepper, pinto beans and un-drained stewed tomatoes.
•Bring to a boil.
•Reduce the heat and let it simmer for 15 minutes.
•Pour mixture into a 13 x 9-inch baking dish coated with cooking spray, and sprinkle with 1/2 cup cheese.
•Set mixture aside.
•Combine cornmeal, flour, sugar, and 1/4 teaspoon salt in a medium bowl.
•Combine 1/2 cup corn, 1/4 cup chilies, 1/2 cup cheese, buttermilk, 1/4 cup oil, and egg whites.

•Mix the two combinations of cornmeal mixture and corn mixture, stirring just until moist. •Spread butter evenly over bean mixture. •Bake casserole at 375°F for 25 minutes or until corn bread is lightly browned.

Make-Ahead Cheese-and-Hamburger Casserole

INGREDIENTS:

1 pound ground round
1 cup chopped onion
3 garlic cloves, crushed
1 (8-ounce) package pre-sliced mushrooms
6 tablespoons tomato paste
1 teaspoon sugar
1 teaspoon dried thyme
1 teaspoon dried oregano
1/4 teaspoon pepper
1 (28-ounce) can whole tomatoes, un-drained and chopped
1/3 cup all-purpose flour
2 1/2 cups 2% low-fat milk
1 cup (4 ounces) crumbled feta cheese
3/4 cup (3 ounces) shredded part-skim mozzarella cheese
4 cups uncooked penne (tubular-shaped pasta)
1 tablespoon chopped fresh parsley (optional)

INSTRUCTIONS:

•Combine ground round, onion and garlic in a large nonstick skillet.
•Cook over medium-high heat until browned and stirring to make it crumble.
•Add mushrooms then cook for 5 minutes or until tender.
•Add tomato paste, sugar, thyme, oregano, pepper and chopped un-drained tomatoes.
•Stir well and bring to a boil.
•Reduce heat and let it simmer for 20 minutes, uncovered.
•Set aside.
•Place flour in a medium saucepan.
•Gradually add milk while whisking until it blended.

•Place over medium heat and cook for 10 minutes or until thick while stirring constantly. •Mix in cheeses and cook for 3 minutes or until cheeses melt while stirring constantly. •Reserve 1/2 cup cheese sauce.
•Pour remaining cheese sauce, beef mixture, and pasta into a 13 x 9-inch baking dish, and stir gently.
•Drizzle the reserved cheese sauce over pasta mixture.
•Cover and refrigerate for 24 hours.
•Preheat oven to 350°F.
•Bake at 350°F, covered, for 1 hour and 10 minutes or until thoroughly heated and pasta is tender.
•Sprinkle with parsley, if desired.

Marinara Pasta

INGREDIENTS:

3 tbsp. Olive Oil
8 cloves Garlic(crushed)
1 pc (large)Onion(minced)
100 grams Carrots (chopped)
100 grams Shrimps (shelled and deveined)
¼ kg Squid (ink sac removed and cut into rings)
150 grams Fish Fillet (cut into)
¼ cup Basil Leaves
2 tsp.Calamansi Juice
½ cupCheese(grated)
1 pack (400 grams) Spaghetti (cooked)
1 pouch (560 grams) Italian Style Spaghetti Sauce

INSTRUCTIONS:

•Heat olive oil in a pan.
•Sauté garlic, onion, carrot, squid and shrimps for 2 minutes over high heat.
•Sprinkle with lemon or calamansi juice, salt and pepper to taste.
•Remove from pan. Set aside.
•In the same pan with 2 tablespoon olive oil, stir-fry fish and half of the basil.
•Add Spaghetti Sauce.
•Cover and let it simmer for 5 minutes while stirring it occasionally.
•Add shrimp-squid mixture and the remaining chopped basil.
•Season with salt and pepper to taste.

•Allow to simmer.
•Mix with or pour over cooked Spaghetti.
•Top with cheese.

Carbonara con Tuna

INGREDIENTS:

4 tbsp. Butter
2 cans (155 grams each) Tuna Chunks in Oil, drained, reserve oil
⅓ tbsp. Grated Cheddar Cheese
⅔ cup Canned sliced Mushroom
4 tsp. Lemon Juice
1 tsp. Grated Lemon Rind, optional
1 pack (400 grams) Spaghetti, cooked, reserve ⅓ cup pasta broth
2 pouches (200 grams each) Carbonara Sauce

INSTRUCTIONS:

•Sauté mushrooms in butter or margarine for 3 minutes, (if using tuna with oil, include oil in sautéing).
•Add tuna and lemon juice and then cook for 2 minutes.
•Add Carbonara Sauce and pasta broth.
•Season with salt and pepper to taste.
•Cover and let it simmer over low heat for 5 minutes.
•Add cheese and lemon rind.
•Pour over cooked Spaghetti.
•Top with extra cheese if desired.

Seafood & Sausage Pasta Casserole

INGREDIENTS:

2 tbsp. Olive Oil
4 cloves Garlic, chopped
1 pc medium Onion, chopped
1 pc Hungarian Sausage, sliced
¼ kg Clams
2 tbsp. White Wine
350 grams Maya-Mayaor labahita, cubed
1 tsp. fresh Thyme
225 grams Spaghetti, cooked
1 pouch (200 grams) Carbonara Sauce

INSTRUCTIONS:

•Heat olive oil in pan.
•Sauté garlic, onion, sausage, clams and white wine.
•Simmer it for about 2 minutes.
•Add fish, Carbonara Sauce, 1/3 cup water and ½ tsp. iodized fine salt (or ½ tbsp. iodized rock salt).
•Simmer it for another 5 minutes.
•Add thyme.
•Pour over or mix with cooked Spaghetti.

Mushroom Pasta Soup

INGREDIENTS:

6 cloves Garlic(crushed)
1 pc (medium)Onion(sliced)
3 tbsp Butter
150 grams Chicken Breast Fillet(cut into strips)
½ cup Canned Button Mushroom(sliced)
1½ pc Chicken Bouillon Cube
1½ tbsp. All-Purpose Flour
⅓ cup Squash(coarsely grated)
½ tsp. Dried Basil(or 6-8 pc fresh basil leaves, shredded)
⅓ cup Frozen Mixed Vegetables
1 pouch (250 grams)
Italian Style Spaghetti Sauce
⅔ cup
Salad Macaroni

INSTRUCTIONS:

•Sauté garlic and onion in butter for 2 minutes.
•Add chicken, mushrooms, bouillon cubes and flour.
•Sauté for 2 minutes.
•Add squash and basil.
•Sauté again for 2 minutes.
•Add 3½ cups water and Spaghetti Sauce.
•Allow to boil then add Macaroni.
•Simmer for 8 minutes.
•Add mixed vegetables, ¼ teaspoon iodized fine salt (or ¼ tablespoon iodized rock salt) and ⅛ teaspoon pepper.
•Simmer for 2 minutes.

Pineapple Cracker Casserole

INGREDIENTS:

54 ounces pineapple chunks, drained
¼ cup granulated sugar
¼ cup all purpose flour
1 cup shredded sharp cheddar cheese
1 sleeve Ritz crackers
3 tablespoons melted butter

INSTRUCTIONS:

•Preheat the oven to 350 degrees Fahrenheit.
•In a large mixing bowl, combine pineapple, sugar, flour, and cheese.
•Pour mixture into a greased 8 x 8 casserole dish.
•Crush crackers and sprinkle over the top of the pineapple mixture.
•Pour melted butter evenly over cracker layer.
•Bake casserole for 25 minutes or until golden brown and slightly bubbly.

Cheese Pineapple Casserole

INGREDIENTS:

30 oz. pineapple chunks (drained)
1 cup white sugar
3/4 cup all-purpose flour
2 cups shredded sharp cheddar cheese
25 crackers (buttery round, crumbled)
1/2 cup melted butter

INSTRUCTIONS:

•Preheat oven to 350 degrees Fahrenheit (175 degrees C).
•Spread pineapple in the bottom of a 2 quart casserole dish.
•In a small bowl, stir together the sugar, flour and cheese.
•Add to casserole dish.
•Sprinkle crackers over the top of pineapple and cheese mixture.
•Pour melted butter over the top and bake for 30 minutes.

Sweet Potato with Pecans Casserole

INGREDIENTS:

4 1/2 cups cooked and mashed sweet potatoes
1/2 cup butter, melted
1/3 cup milk
1 cup white sugar
1/2 teaspoon vanilla extract
2 eggs, beaten
1 cup light brown sugar
1/2 cup all-purpose flour
1/3 cup butter
1 cup chopped pecans

INSTRUCTIONS:

•Preheat oven to 350 degrees Fahrenheit (175 degrees C).
•Grease a 9x13 inch baking dish.
•In a large bowl, mix together mashed sweet potatoes, 1/2 cup butter, milk, sugar, vanilla extract, and eggs.
•Spread sweet potato mixture into the prepared baking dish.
•In a small bowl, mix together brown sugar and flour.
•Cut in 1/3 cup butter until mixture is crumbly, and then stir in pecans.
•Sprinkle pecan mixture over the sweet potatoes.
•Bake for 25 minutes in the preheated oven, or until golden brown.

Grandma Ginger's Fish Casserole

INGREDIENTS:

4 teaspoons extra-virgin olive oil, divided
1 medium onion, very thinly sliced
1/2 cup dry white wine
8 ounces cod or tilapia, cut into 2 pieces
1 teaspoon chopped fresh thyme or 1/4 teaspoon dried
1/4 teaspoon kosher salt
1/4 teaspoon freshly ground pepper
3/4 cup finely chopped whole-wheat country bread, (about 1 slice)
1/4 teaspoon paprika
1/4 teaspoon garlic powder
1/2 cup finely shredded Gruyère or Swiss cheese

INSTRUCTIONS:

•Preheat the oven to 400°F.
•Heat 2 teaspoons oil in a medium ovenproof skillet over medium-high heat.
•Add onion and cook for 4 to 6 minutes while stirring often or until starting to soften.
•Add wine and then increase heat to high and cook for 2 to 4 minutes while stirring often or until the wine is slightly reduced.
•Place fish on top of the onion and sprinkle with thyme, salt and pepper.
•Cover the pan tightly with foil and transfer to the oven and then bake for 12 minutes.
•Toss the bread with the remaining 2 teaspoons oil, paprika and garlic powder in a small bowl.
•Uncover the fish and top with the bread mixture and cheese.
•Bake, uncovered, until the fish is just cooked through in about 8 to 10 minutes.

Cheesy Baked Fillet of Fish Casserole

INGREDIENTS:

1 cup sour cream
2 tablespoons butter
2 tablespoons lemon juice
1 -1 1/2 lb. of firm white fish fillet (halibut, or ling cod work well)
salt pepper
1/2 medium onion, thinly sliced and separated into rings
1 -1 1/2 cup grated cheddar cheese

INSTRUCTIONS:

•Preheat oven to 350 degrees Fahrenheit.
•Melt butter and blend with the lemon juice and sour cream.
•Salt and pepper the fish to taste and place it in a casserole dish.
•Spread the onion rings evenly on top.
•Pour the sour cream mixture over fish and spread evenly.
•Top with the cheese.
•Bake for 35 minutes or until fish flakes with a fork.

Tomato & Spinach Dinner Strata

INGREDIENTS:

4 teaspoons extra-virgin olive oil, divided
1 medium onion, chopped
8 ounces mushrooms, thinly sliced
1/2 teaspoon freshly ground pepper, divided
1/4 teaspoon salt
1 15-ounce container part-skim ricotta cheese
1 10-ounce package frozen chopped spinach, thawed and squeezed dry,
1 1/2 pounds fresh spinach, cooked, squeezed dry and chopped
1/8 teaspoon freshly grated nutmeg
2 cups prepared marinara sauce, divided
6 slices whole-grain sandwich bread, preferably day-old
1 cup shredded part-skim mozzarella cheese
3 large eggs
1 cup low-fat milk
1/4 cup freshly grated Parmesan cheese
2 tablespoons chopped fresh parsley

INSTRUCTIONS:

•Coat a 7-by-11-inch baking dish with cooking spray.
•Heat 2 teaspoons oil in a large nonstick skillet over medium heat.
•Add onion and cook while stirring often, until softened but not browned for about 5 to 8 minutes and transfer it to a bowl.
•Add the remaining 2 teaspoons oil to the pan and then increase heat to medium-high.
•Add mushrooms and cook while stirring for 4 to 5 minutes or until the moisture has evaporated.
•Transfer to the bowl with the onions, add 1/4 teaspoon pepper and salt and then stir to combine.
•Combine ricotta, spinach, nutmeg and the remaining 1/4 teaspoon pepper in another bowl.
•Spoon 1 cup marinara sauce into the prepared baking dish.
•Break each slice of bread into 4 roughly equal pieces and arrange half the bread on the sauce (the bread doesn't have to completely cover the sauce).
•Spoon the ricotta mixture over the bread.
•Arrange the remaining bread over the ricotta and then scatter the mushroom mixture over the bread, topping it with mozzarella cheese.

•Spoon the remaining marinara sauce over the top until the pan become very full.
•Whisk eggs and milk in a small bowl and pour slowly over the casserole, poking the filling gently with the tip of a knife until the egg mixture is evenly distributed and the bread is saturated.
•Coat a piece of foil with cooking spray on one side and cover the casserole, sprayed-side down.
•Refrigerate for at least 2 hours or up to 1 day.
•Preheat oven to 375°F.
•Bake the strata, uncovered, for 40 minutes.
•Sprinkle with Parmesan and bake until puffed and golden brown, 10 minutes more.
•Let stand for 10 minutes. Serve sprinkled with parsley.

Baked Tortellini Casserole

INGREDIENTS:

1 tablespoon extra-virgin olive oil
2 tablespoons all-purpose flour
2 1/2 cups low-fat milk, heated
1/2 cup grated fontina cheese, divided
1/2 teaspoon ground nutmeg
Salt & freshly ground pepper, to taste
1 pound fresh or frozen cheese tortellini, preferably low-fat
1/4 cup fine dry breadcrumbs
2 tablespoons freshly grated Parmesan cheese

INSTRUCTIONS:

•Preheat oven to 350°F.
•Coat 6 individual gratin dishes or a 1 1/2-quart shallow baking dish with cooking spray.
•Cook pasta according to package directions.
•Heat oil in a large saucepan over medium heat.
•Add flour and cook, whisking constantly, for 1 to 2 minutes.
•Add hot milk and bring to a simmer, whisking, until smooth and slightly thickened for 3 to 4 minutes.
•Remove from heat and add 1/4 cup fontina and nutmeg, stirring it to melt the cheese.
•Season with salt and pepper.

•In the meantime, cook tortellini until just tender for about 6 to 8 minutes or according to package directions.
•Drain and rinse well.
•Combine the tortellini with the cheese sauce and toss.
•Transfer to the prepared dishes or baking dish.
•Top with the remaining 1/4 cup fontina.
•Combine breadcrumbs and Parmesan and sprinkle evenly over the tortellini.
•Bake the tortellini until golden and bubbly for about 15 to 25 minutes.
•Serve immediately.

Cheesy Potato Casserole

INGREDIENTS:

Canola oil cooking spray
2 pounds red potatoes, diced
1 cup low-fat milk
2 tablespoons cornstarch
8 ounces sharp Cheddar cheese, shredded (about 2 cups)
1 cup nonfat Greek yogurt
1 medium onion, chopped
1/2 teaspoon plus a pinch of salt, divided
1/2 teaspoon freshly ground pepper
2 cups crushed unsweetened corn flake

INSTRUCTIONS:

•Preheat oven to 350°F.
•Coat a 9-by-13-inch (or similar-size) baking dish with cooking spray.
•Place potatoes in a large pot and add water to cover.
•Bring it to a boil.
•Immediately drain and rinse with cold water when cooked and return it to the pot.
•For the meantime, whisk milk and cornstarch in a large saucepan.
•Bring to a boil over medium-high heat, whisking often until bubbling and thickened enough to coat the back of a spoon in about 2 to 4 minutes.
•Remove from the heat and stir in Cheddar, yogurt, onion, 1/2 teaspoon salt and pepper until combined.
•Pour the sauce over the potatoes and mix well.
•Spread evenly in the prepared pan.

•Sprinkle the casserole with corn flakes.
•Using short bursts coat the corn flakes with cooking spray and sprinkle with the remaining pinch of salt.
•Bake until browned and bubbling at the edges for about 1 hour.
•Let it cool for 20 minutes before serving.

Shrimp Chili Cornbread Casserole

INGREDIENTS:

2 teaspoons canola oil
1 large onion, chopped
1 medium green bell pepper, chopped
4 cloves garlic, minced
3 medium zucchini, diced (about 5 cups)
1 1/2 tablespoons chili powder
1 1/2 teaspoons ground cumin
1 teaspoon ground cinnamon
1 teaspoon salt
2 14-ounce cans no-salt-added diced tomatoes
1 1/2 pounds raw shrimp, (41-50 per pound), peeled and deveined
1/2 cup chopped fresh cilantro
CORNBREAD TOPPING
1 cup yellow cornmeal
1 cup all-purpose flour
2 teaspoons baking powder
1/2 teaspoon salt
3/4 cup nonfat milk
1/4 cup canola oil
1 large egg
1 tablespoon honey

INSTRUCTIONS:

•To prepare filling, heat 2 teaspoons oil in a Dutch oven over medium heat.
•Add onion and bell pepper and then cook by stirring often for about 3 minutes or until softened.
•Add garlic and cook, stirring for 30 seconds.
•Stir in zucchini and cook by stirring often for 3 minutes.
•Stir in chili powder, cumin, cinnamon and 1 teaspoon salt and cook for 20 seconds.
•Pour in tomatoes and their juices and bring it to a simmer.

•Remove from the heat.
•Stir in shrimp and cilantro.
•Pour into a 9-by-13-inch baking pan.
•Preheat oven to 350°F.
•To prepare cornbread topping, whisk cornmeal, flour, baking powder and 1/2 teaspoon salt in a large bowl.
•Whisk milk, 1/4 cup oil, egg and honey in a medium bowl until smooth.
•Add the wet ingredients to the dry ingredients and stir just until moistened.
•Drop by heaping tablespoons over the shrimp mixture.
•Bake the casserole, uncovered, until the top is browned and the filling is bubbling in about 40 to 45 minutes.
•Let it stand for 10 minutes before serving.

Stuff Rice Zucchini Casserole

INGREDIENTS:

1 1/2 cups long-grain brown rice
3 cups reduced-sodium chicken broth
4 cups diced zucchini, and/or summer squash (about 1 pound)
2 red or green bell peppers, chopped
1 large onion, diced
3/4 teaspoon salt
1 1/2 cups low-fat milk
3 tablespoons all-purpose flour
2 cups shredded pepper Jack cheese, divided
1 cup fresh or frozen (thawed) corn kernels
2 teaspoons extra-virgin olive oil
8 ounces turkey sausage, casings removed
4 ounces reduced-fat cream cheese, (Neufchâtel)
1/4 cup chopped pickled jalapeños

INSTRUCTIONS:

•Preheat oven to 375°F.
•Pour rice into a 9-by-13-inch baking dish.
•Bring broth to a simmer in a small saucepan.
•Stir hot broth into the rice along with zucchini (and/or squash), bell peppers, onion and salt. •Cover with foil.
•Bake for 45 minutes.

•Remove foil and continue baking until the rice is tender and most of the liquid is absorbed, in about 35 to 45 minutes more.
•In the meantime, whisk milk and flour in a small saucepan.
•Cook over medium heat until bubbling and thickened in about 3 to 4 minutes.
•Reduce heat to low.
•Add 1 1/2 cups Jack cheese and corn and cook, stirring, until the cheese is melted.
•Set aside.
•Heat oil in a large skillet over medium heat and add sausage.
•Cook, stirring and breaking the sausage into small pieces with a spoon, until lightly browned and no longer pink in about 4 minutes.
•When the rice is done, stir in the sausage and cheese sauce.
•Sprinkle the remaining 1/2 cup Jack cheese on top and dollop cream cheese by the teaspoonful over the casserole.
•Top with jalapeños.
•Return the casserole to the oven and bake until the cheese is melted, about 10 minutes.
•Let stand for about 10 minutes before serving.

Buffalo Chicken Casserole

INGREDIENTS:

12 oz. whole-wheat elbow noodles
2 tbsp. canola oil
3 med. carrots, sliced
3 med. stalks celery, sliced
1 large onion, chopped
1 tbsp. minced garlic
2 lbs. boneless, skinless chicken breast, trimmed and cut into 1-inch cubes
1/3 cup cornstarch
4 cups low-fat milk
1/8 tsp. salt
5 tbsp. hot sauce, preferably Frank's Red Hot
3/4 cup (4 oz.) crumbled blue cheese

INSTRUCTIONS:

•Preheat oven to 400°F.
•Bring a Dutch oven of water to a boil.

•Cook noodles until barely tender in about 2 minutes less than the package directions. •Drain, rinse and set aside.
•Heat oil in the pot over medium heat.
•Add carrots, celery, onion, garlic and then cook until beginning to soften in about 5 minutes.
•Add chicken and cook for 5 to 7 minutes or until brown and no longer pink on the outside. •Whisk cornstarch and milk in a medium bowl.
•Add to the pot along with salt.
•Bring to a boil over medium-high heat and stirring it often, until bubbling and thick enough to coat the back of a spoon, for about 4 minutes.
•Remove from the heat and stir in hot sauce.
•Spread the noodles in a 9-by-13-inch (or similar 3-quart) baking dish.
•Top with the chicken mixture and sprinkle with blue cheese.
•Bake the casserole for about 30 minutes or until it is bubbling.
•Let stand for 10 minutes before serving.

Brussels Sprout Gratin

INGREDIENTS:

2 1/2 lbs. Brussels sprouts, trimmed and halved (quartered if large; about 8 cups)
2-3 tbsp. extra-virgin olive oil, divided
1 medium onion, thinly sliced
3 tbsp. all-purpose flour
3/4 teaspoon salt
1/4 teaspoon white or black pepper
2 1/2 cups low-fat milk
1 1/2 cups fresh whole-wheat breadcrumbs or 1/2 cup shredded or crumbled cheese

INSTRUCTIONS:

•Position racks in upper and lower third of the oven and then preheat to 425°F.
•Toss Brussels sprouts in a large bowl with 1 tablespoon oil until well coated.
•Divide it between 2 baking sheets and spread in an even layer.
•Roast and stirring once then rotating the pans top to bottom about halfway through or until tender and beginning to brown in about 20 to 25 minutes.

•Meanwhile, heat 1 tablespoon oil in a large saucepan over medium heat.
•Add onion and cook for 5 to 8 minutes while stirring frequently or until very soft and golden brown.
•Add flour, salt and pepper and then cook while stirring it for 1 minute more.
•Add milk and continue to stir, scraping up any browned bits.
•Cook for about 4 minutes and stirring constantly until the sauce bubbles and thickens enough to coat the back of a spoon.
•Remove from the heat.
•When the Brussels sprouts are done, remove from the oven.
•Preheat the broiler.
•Transfer half of the Brussels sprouts to a 2-quart, broiler-safe baking dish.
•Spread half the sauce over the Brussels sprouts.
•Add the remaining Brussels sprouts and top with the remaining sauce.
•Combine breadcrumbs and the remaining 1 tablespoon oil in a small bowl (skip this step if you are topping with cheese).
•Sprinkle the breadcrumb mixture (or cheese) over the gratin.
•Place under the broiler and broil for 1 to 5 minutes, watching it closely, until the gratin is bubbling and beginning to brown on top.
•Let stand for 10 minutes before serving.

Creamy Hamburger Noodle Casserole

INGREDIENTS:

2 bunches scallions, trimmed
8 oz. Ground beef, 90%-lean
1 1/2 tsp. canola oil
1/2 cup bulgur,
2 cloves garlic, minced
2 8-oz. cans tomato sauce
1/2 cup water
1/4 tsp. salt, divided
Ground pepper, fresh to taste
6 oz. Whole-wheat egg noodles, No-yolk
1 cup cottage cheese, low-fat
1 cup sour cream, reduced-fat
1/4 cup shredded extra-sharp Cheddar cheese

INSTRUCTIONS:

•Heat oven to 350°F.
•Coat a 2-quart baking dish with cooking spray.
•Put a large pot of water on to boil.
•Separate white and green parts of scallions and then thinly slice and reserve separately.
•Cook beef in a large skillet over medium-high heat for about 3 to 5 minutes or until color is no longer pink.
•Break clumps with a wooden spoon and transfer to a plate lined with paper towels.
•Wipe out the pan, add oil and reduce heat to medium-low.
•Add bulgur, garlic and the reserved scallion whites.
•Cook for 5 to 7 minutes, stirring constantly, until the scallions soften.
•Add tomato sauce, water and the beef and then bring to a simmer.
•Cover and simmer gently until the bulgur is tender and the sauce is thickened for about 15 to 20 minutes.
•Season with 1/8 teaspoon salt and pepper.
•In the meantime, cook noodles for 6 to 8 minutes or according to package directions.
•Drain and rinse under cold water.
•Puree the cottage cheese in a food processor until smooth.
•Transfer to a medium bowl and fold in sour cream.
•Reserve some scallion greens.
•Season with the remaining 1/8 teaspoon salt and pepper.
•Spread half the noodles in the prepared pan.
•Top with half of the cottage cheese mixture and half of the meat sauce.
•Repeat procedure with the remaining noodles, cottage cheese and sauce.
•Sprinkle Cheddar over the top.
•Bake the casserole for 30 to 40 minutes or until bubb
•Let stand for 10 minutes before serving.

Quick Shrimp Enchilada Bake

INGREDIENTS:

1 lbs. peeled cooked shrimp, tails removed, diced
1 cup corn, thawed, frozen
2 (4-oz.) cans chopped green chilies, not drained
2 cups canned green enchilada sauce, or green salsa, divided
12 corn tortillas
1 (15-oz.) can beans, nonfat refried
1 cup cheese, shredded, reduced-fat
1/2 cup cilantro, fresh, chopped
1 lime, cut into wedges

INSTRUCTIONS:

•Warm oven to 425°F.
•Coat a 9-by-13-inch glass baking dish with cooking spray.
•Combine shrimp, corn, chilies and 1/2 cup enchilada sauce (or salsa) in a microwave-safe medium bowl.
•Cover and microwave on high heat for about 2 1/2 minutes or until heated through.
•Spread 1/4 cup enchilada sauce (or salsa) in the prepared baking dish.
•Top with a layer of 6 overlapping tortillas.
•Spread refried beans evenly over the tortillas.
•Top the beans with the shrimp mixture, followed by the remaining 6 tortillas.
•Pour the remaining sauce (or salsa) over the tortillas.
•Cover with foil.
•Bake the casserole for about 20 minutes or until it begins to bubble on the sides.
•Remove the foil and sprinkle cheese on top.
•Continue baking until heated through and the cheese is melted in about 5 minutes more. •Top with cilantro and serve with lime wedges.

Veggie Pies

INGREDIENTS:

1 lb. Yukon Gold or white potatoes, peeled and cut into 1-inch chunks
1/2 cup buttermilk
1 tbsp. butter
3/4 tsp. salt, divided
1/2 tsp. freshly ground pepper, divided
1 tbsp. Olive oil, extra-virgin
1 large onion, finely diced
1/2 cup finely diced carrot
1tbsp. water
3/4 cup frozen corn kernels, thawed
1 tsp. chopped fresh thyme or 1/2 teaspoon dried
3 tbsp. all-purpose flour
1 (14-oz.) can vegetable broth
1 1/2 cups lentils, cooked or canned)

INSTRUCTION:

•In a large saucepan, put potatoes covered with water and then bring it to simmer over medium-high heat.
•Reduce heat to medium, partially covered and cook until tender for about 10 to 15 minutes. •Drain and return the potatoes to the pot.
•Add buttermilk, butter and 1/4 teaspoon each salt and pepper.
•Mash the potato with a potato masher until smooth.
•Position rack in upper third of oven and preheat broiler.
•Coat four 10- to 12-ounce broiler-safe ramekins with cooking spray.
•Place ramekins on a broiler-safe baking sheet.
•Heat oil in a large skillet over medium-high heat.
•Add onion, carrot and water.
•Cover and cook while stirring occasionally for 3 to 5 minutes or until softened.
•Stir in corn, thyme and the remaining 1/2 teaspoon salt and 1/4 teaspoon pepper.
•Cook by stirring occasionally for 2 minutes.
•Sprinkle with flour and mix to coat and add the broth.
•Bring to a simmer.
•Stir in lentils and cook while stirring constantly for 2 minutes.
•Divide the hot lentil mixture among the prepared ramekins (or spread in the baking dish). •Top with the mashed potatoes.

•Broil, rotating halfway through, until the potato is lightly browned in about 6 to 10 minutes.

Chili Hot Relleno Casseroles

INGREDIENTS:

2 (4-oz.) cans diced green chilies, drained and patted dry
3/4 cup frozen corn, thawed and patted dry
4 scallions, thinly sliced
1 cup shredded reduced-fat Cheddar cheese
1 1/2 cups milk, nonfat
6 large egg whites
4 large eggs
1/4 tsp. salt

INSTRUCTIONS:

•Heat up oven to 400°F.
•Coat eight 6-ounce or four 10-ounce heatproof ramekins with cooking spray and place on a baking sheet.
•Equally divide green chilies, corn and scallions among the ramekins. Top each with cheese.
•Whisk milk, egg whites, eggs and salt in a medium bowl until combined. Divide the egg mixture evenly among the ramekins.
•Bake the mini casseroles until the tops begin to brown and the eggs are set, about 25 minutes for 6-ounce ramekins and about 35 minutes for 10-ounce ramekins.

Skillet Tuna Noodle Casserole

INGREDIENTS:

8 oz. whole-wheat egg noodles
1 tbsp. extra-virgin olive oil
1 medium onion, finely chopped
8 oz. mushrooms, sliced
1/2 tsp. salt
1/2 cup dry white wine
6 tbsp. all-purpose flour
3 cups nonfat milk
1/2 tsp. freshly ground pepper
12 oz. canned chunk light tuna drained
1 cup frozen peas, thawed
1 cup finely grated Parmesan cheese, divided
1/2 cup coarse dry whole-wheat breadcrumbs

INSTRUCTIONS:

•Boil a large pot of water.
•Cook noodles according to package its directions.
•Drain and rinse.
•Position rack in upper third of oven and preheat broiler.
•For the meantime, heat oil in a large ovenproof skillet over medium-high heat.
•Add onion, mushrooms and salt and then cook while stirring often for about 5 minutes or until the onion is softened but not browned,
•Add wine and cook for 4 to 5 minutes or until evaporated.
•Sprinkle flour over the vegetables and stir to coat.
•Add milk and pepper and bring to a simmer by stirring constantly.
•Stir in tuna, peas and 1/2 cup Parmesan until evenly incorporated.
•Then, stir in the noodles until the pan will be very full.
•Remove from the heat.
•Sprinkle the casserole with breadcrumbs and the remaining 1/2 cup Parmesan.
•Broil for 3 to 4 minutes or until bubbly and lightly browned on top.

Scalloped Potatoes

INGREDIENTS:

2 lb. Yukon Gold potatoes cut into 1/4-inch-thick slices (about 8 cups)
2-3 tbsp. Extra-virgin olive oil, divided
1 medium onion, thinly sliced
3 tbsp. All-purpose flour
3/4 tsp. salt
1/4 tsp. white or black pepper
2 1/2 cups low-fat milk
1 1/2 cups fresh whole-wheat breadcrumbs or 1/2 cup shredded or crumbled cheese

INSTRUCTIONS:

•Position racks in upper and lower third of oven; preheat to 425°F.
•Toss potatoes in a large bowl with 1 tablespoon oil until well coated.
•Divide between 2 baking sheets and spread in an even layer.
•Roast, stirring once and rotating the pans top to bottom about halfway through, until tender and beginning to brown, 20 to 25 minutes.
•Meanwhile, heat 1 tablespoon oil in a large saucepan over medium heat.
•Add onion and cook, stirring frequently, until very soft and golden brown, 5 to 8 minutes. •Add flour, salt and pepper; cook, stirring, for 1 minute more. Add milk and continue to stir, scraping up any browned bits.
•Cook, stirring, until the sauce bubbles and thickens enough to coat the back of a spoon, about 4 minutes.
•Remove from the heat.
•When the potatoes are done, remove from the oven.
•Preheat the broiler.
•Transfer half the potatoes to a 2-quart, broiler-safe baking dish.
•Spread half the sauce over the potatoes. Add the remaining potatoes and top with the remaining sauce.
•Combine breadcrumbs and the remaining 1 tablespoon oil in a small bowl (skip this step if you are topping with cheese).
•Sprinkle the breadcrumb mixture (or cheese) over the gratin.
•Place under the broiler and broil, watching closely, until the gratin is bubbling and beginning to brown on top, 1 to 5 minutes, depending on your broiler.

•Let stand for 10 minutes before serving.

Sweet Potato Casserole Topped with Meringue

INGREDIENTS:

SWEET POTATO CASSEROLE
2 1/2 pounds sweet potatoes (about 3 medium), peeled and cut into 2-inch chunks
2 large eggs
2 tbsp. s brown sugar
1/4 teaspoon ground cinnamon
1 tablespoon canola oil
1 cup low-fat evaporated milk
1 teaspoon vanilla extract
1/2 teaspoon salt
1 8-ounce can of crushed pineapple, un-drained
1/2 cup chopped pecans, toasted
MERINGUE TOPPING
4 teaspoons dried egg whites reconstituted according to package directions, or 2 large pasteurized egg whites, at room temperature
1/4 cup granulated sugar

INSTRUCTIONS:

•Put the sweet potatoes in a large saucepan and cover with water.
•Bring it to a boil.
•Reduce the heat to simmer and cook for 10 to 15 minutes or until tender,.
•Drain well and transfer to a food processor and process until smooth.
•Preheat oven to 350°F.
•Coat an 8-inch-square broiler-safe baking dish with cooking spray.
•Whisk whole eggs, brown sugar, cinnamon, and oil, evaporated milk, vanilla and salt in a large bowl until smooth.
•Add the sweet potato and whisk until smooth.
•Blend the pineapple and its juice.
•Spread the mixture in the prepared baking dish.
•Sprinkle with pecans.
•Bake the casserole until heated through and the edges are bubbling, 35 to 45 minutes. Set aside while you make the topping.

•To prepare meringue topping just position rack in top third of oven and preheat broiler. •Beat egg whites in a medium bowl with an electric mixer at high speed until soft peaks form.
•Beat in granulated sugar in a slow, steady stream.
•Continue beating until stiff peaks form.
•Spoon the meringue into a gallon-size sealable bag.
•Seal the bag, pressing out as much air as possible. Cut a 1/2-inch hole in one corner.
•Pipe the meringue onto the casserole, making marshmallow-size dots.
•Broil until lightly browned, watching carefully to prevent burning for a bout 30 to 90 seconds.
•To make soft peaks, beat egg whites with an electric hand mixer until they are stiff, but still soft enough to curl over when beaters are turned upside down.

Lemon Chicken Potato Casserole

INGREDIENTS:

2.5 cups condensed cream of mushroom or cream of chicken soup
1/2 cup milk
1.5 lbs. Yukon gold potatoes, very thinly sliced
2 cloves garlic, minced
1 small white onion, peeled and thinly sliced
1.5 lbs. boneless, skinless chicken breasts
Salt and freshly-ground black pepper
1 lemon, thinly sliced and halved
(Optional garnish: chopped fresh parsley or fresh thyme)

INSTRUCTIONS:

•Heat oven to 420° F.
•Add condensed soup and milk to a saucepan and whisk to combine.
•Heat over medium-high heat until simmering while stirring frequently.
•When it reaches a simmer, remove from heat and set aside.
•In the meantime, in a separate large mixing bowl, add potatoes, onion, garlic, and chicken. •Pour in the condensed soup mixture, along with a generous pinch of salt and pepper, and gently toss to combine until the potato and chicken mixture is evenly coated.
•Transfer mixture to a 9 x 13 baking dish.

•Gather lemon wedges into the mixture randomly.
•Then cover the top of the pan with aluminum foil.
•Bake for 1 hour or until the potatoes are tender.
•Carefully remove the foil, and change oven to the high "broil" setting.
•Broil the casserole for an extra 2-3 minutes to crisp up the top, watching very carefully so that it does not burn.
•Remove the pan from oven and serve warm.

Quinoa and Cajun Shrimp Casserole

INGREDIENTS:

¾ lb. large shrimp, peeled and deveined
4 medium tomatoes cut into chunks
1 jalapeno, seeded and chopped
½ C chopped sweet onion
2 cloves of garlic, minced
1 tbsp. tomato paste
3 tbsps. olive oil
2½ tsps. cajun seasoning
Salt and pepper to taste
2½ Cup cooked quinoa
1 Cup fontina cheese, shredded
Fresh cilantro for garnish

INSTRUCTIONS:

•Toss the shrimp and 1 teaspoon Cajun seasoning together and then set aside.
•Toss the tomatoes with 1 tablespoon olive oil and 1 teaspoon Cajun seasoning and set aside again.
•Heat 1 tablespoon olive oil over medium heat in a cast iron skillet (or any oven-safe skillet.) •Cook the shrimp until opaque, about 2-3 minutes per side.
•Take away from the pan and set aside.
•Add the remaining 1 tablespoon of olive oil to the pan along with the onion, jalapeno and garlic.
•Cook until the onion and jalapeno is tender while stirring often.
•Blend in the quinoa, tomato paste, ½ tsp. Cajun seasoning and tomato chunks.
•Top with the shrimp and then sprinkle with the fontina cheese.
•Place in the oven and bake at 350° F for 15 minutes.

•During the last 2 minutes, turn on the broiler to high and broil until the cheese is slightly brown and bubbly.
•Garnish with fresh cilantro.

Cheesy Grit Casserole

INGREDIENTS:

1/12 cups grits
6 cups water (salted)
1 ½ cups shredded cheddar, plus a little to sprinkle on the top
1 stick butter
garlic (1 ½ tsp. minced fresh or ½ tsp. granulated) optional
3 eggs
1 and 1/4 cup milk

INSTRUCTIONS:

•Sprig a 9 x 13 in casserole dish with Pam.
•Warm oven to 350 degrees Fahrenheit.
•Cook grits in boiling salted water in about 12-15 minutes or until done.
•Add butter and cheese while stirring it until melted.
•Gradually beat eggs and milk together, and then add to grits.
•Transfer into the prepared pan and sprinkle with extra cheese.
•Bake in prepared oven for about 45-60 minutes.

Egg Cheese Casserole

INGREDIENTS:

5 eggs, beaten
1 cup small curd cottage cheese
¼ cup butter, melted and cooled
1 (4 oz.) can green chilies, diced
¼ cup all purpose flour
½ tsp. baking powder
2 cups Colby jack cheese, grated or shredded

INSTRUCTIONS:

•Mix the eggs, cottage cheese, butter, green chilies and all purpose flour.
•Add 2 cups grated Colby jack cheese while mixing gradually.
•Pour the mixture into a nine inch square baking dish olive with cooking spray.
•Sprinkle top of mixture with cayenne pepper, black pepper, onion powder, garlic powder and parsley flakes.
•Bake at 350 degrees Fahrenheit or until lightly browned on top and the center is puffed and firm.

Blackberry French Toast

INGREDIENTS:

1 cup blackberry jam
1 (12 oz.) French bread loaf, cut into 1 1/2-inch cubes
1 (8 oz.) package 1/3-less-fat cream cheese, cut into 1-inch cubes
4 large eggs
2 cups half-and-half
1 tsp. ground cinnamon
1 tsp. vanilla extract
1/2 cup brown sugar, firmly packed
Toppings: maple syrup, whipped cream

INSTRUCTIONS:

• In a small saucepan, cook blackberry jam over medium heat in about 1 to 2 minutes or until melted and smooth, stirring once.
•Place half of bread cubes in bottom of a lightly greased 13- x 9-inch baking dish.
•Top with cream cheese cubes, and drizzle with melted jam.

•Top with remaining bread cubes.
•Whip together eggs, half- and –half, cinnamon and vanilla extract.
•Pour over bread mixture.
•Sprinkle with brown sugar.
•Cover tightly, and chill for about 8 to 24 hours.
•Preheat oven to 325°F.
• Cover and bake for 20 minutes.
•Uncover and bake for another 10 to 15 minutes or until bread is golden brown and mixture is set.
•Serve with desired toppings.

Breakfast Brie-and-Veggie Strata

INGREDIENTS:

1 large sweet onion, halved and thinly sliced
1 large red bell pepper, diced
1 large Yukon gold potato, peeled and diced
2 tbsp. Olive oil
1 (8 oz.) Brie round
1 (12 oz.) package sourdough bread loaf, cubed
1 cup (4 oz.) shredded Parmesan cheese
8 large eggs
3 cups milk
2 tbsp. Dijon mustard
1 teaspoon seasoned salt
1 teaspoon pepper

INSTRUCTIONS:

•Stir-fry sweet onion, bell pepper and potato in hot oil for about 10 to 12 minutes or just until vegetables are tender and onion begin to turn golden.
•Sleek and discard rind from Brie.
•Cut cheese into 1/2-inch cubes.
•Layer a lightly greased 13- x 9-inch baking dish with half of each of the bread cubes, onion mixture, Brie cubes, and Parmesan cheese.
•Whisk together eggs, milk, mustard, salt and pepper.
•Pour half of egg mixture evenly over cheeses.
•Repeat layers once.
•Cover and chill at least for 8 hours or up to 24 hours.

•Bake at 350°F for 45 to 50 minutes or until lightly browned on top and set in center.

Tomato-Herb Frittatas with Italian Cheese

INGREDIENTS:

12 large eggs
1 cup half-and-half
1/2 teaspoon salt
1/4 teaspoon freshly ground pepper
2 tbsp. chopped fresh chives
1tbsp. chopped fresh parsley
1 teaspoon chopped fresh oregano
1 pt. grape tomatoes, halved
1 1/2 cups (6 oz.) shredded Italian three-cheese blend

INSTRUCTIONS:

•Turn on oven to 450°F.
•Put the eggs, half-and-half, salt and ground pepper in a blender and start to blend until all ingredients are blended well.
•Stir together chives, parsley and fresh oregano in a small bowl.
•Place 8 lightly greased 4-inch (6-oz.) ramekins on 2 baking sheets and layer it with tomatoes, 1 cup cheese, and chive mixture in ramekins.
•Pour egg mixture over top, and sprinkle with remaining 1/2 cup cheese.
•Bake at 450°F for 7 minutes, placing 1 baking sheet on middle oven rack and other on lower oven rack.
•Switch baking sheets, and bake 7 to 8 more minutes or until set.
•Remove top baking sheet from oven and transfer bottom sheet to middle rack, and bake 1 to 2 more minutes or until lightly browned.
•Cook Tomato-Herb Frittata recipe as directed, substituting a lightly greased 13- x 9-inch baking dish for ramekins and increasing bake time to 18 to 20 minutes or until set.

Tuna Noodle Casserole

INGREDIENTS:

6 oz. egg noodles
2 tbsps. Butter
1 (10 3/4 ounce) can condensed cream of mushroom soup, undiluted
1/2-1 tsp. garlic powder
3 -4 tbsp. grated parmesan cheese
3/4 cup milk (or can use half-and-half cream)
1/2 cup sour cream (can increase to to 3/4 cup)
1/4-1/2 tsp. seasoning salt (or to taste, or use white salt)
1/2 tsp. fresh ground black pepper (or to taste)
1 small onion, finely chopped (can use 2 green onions)
1/4 cup pimiento, chopped
1 small green bell pepper, finely chopped
1 large celery rib, diced
1 (6 1/2 ounce) can tuna, drained and flaked (can add another 3 ounces for a meatier casserole if desired, or use cooked chicken or turkey)
12 -15 butter flavored crackers, broken in pieces

INSTRUCTIONS:

•Heat oven to 375 degrees Fahrenheit.
•Grease a 2-quart casserole dish.
•Cook the egg noodles in boiling salted water and drain.
•Toss with 2 tablespoons butter.
•In a large saucepan, mix the undiluted mushroom soup, garlic powder, Parmesan cheese (if using) milk or half and half, sour cream, salt, pepper, chopped onion, pimiento, bell pepper and celery.
•Cook over low heat, stirring frequently for 15 minutes.
•Add in the tuna or chicken and then mix to combine.
•Combine the mixture with the cooked egg noodles.
•Transfer to a prepared greased baking dish.
•Sprinkle top with the broken crackers.
•Bake for about 25 minutes.

Quinoa Enchilada Casserole

INGREDIENTS:

1 cup quinoa
1 (10 oz.) can mild enchilada sauce
1 (4.5 oz.) can chopped green chilies,
1/2 cup corn kernels, drained, frozen, canned or roasted
½ cup canned black beans, drained and rinsed
2 tbsps. Chopped fresh cilantro leaves
½ tsp. cumin
½ tsp. chili powder
½ tsp. salt
½ tsp. ground black pepper
¾ cup shredded cheddar cheese, divided
¾ cup shredded mozzarella cheese, divided
1 avocado, halved, seeded, peeled and diced
1 Roma tomato, diced

INSTRUCTIONS:

•In a large saucepan of 2 cups water, cook quinoa according to package and then set aside. •Heat oven to 375 degrees Fahrenheit.
•Lightly grease an 8x8 or 2 quart baking dish or coat with nonstick spray.
•In a large bowl, combine quinoa, enchilada sauce, green chilies, corn, black beans, cilantro, and cumin and chili powder.
•Season with salt and pepper, to taste.
•Stir in ½ cup cheddar cheese and ½ cup mozzarella cheese.
•Spread quinoa mixture into the prepared baking dish.
•Top with remaining cheeses.
•Place into oven and bake for about 15 minutes or until bubbly and cheeses have melted. •Serve immediately, garnished with avocado and tomato, if desired.

Sausage Casserole

INGREDIENTS:

1 1/2 pounds ground pork sausage
1 (8 oz.) package refrigerated crescent roll dough
2 cups mozzarella cheese
4 eggs, beaten
3/4 cup milk
Salt and pepper to taste

INSTRUCTIONS:

•Put sausage in a large, deep skillet.
•Cook over medium high heat until evenly brown.
•Drain, crumble and set aside.
•Warm oven to 425 degrees Fahrenheit (220 degrees C).
•Lightly grease a 9x13 inch baking pan.
•Arrange crescent rolls flat in the bottom of the pan.
•Combine cooked sausage, cheese, eggs, milk, salt and pepper and then pour over crescent rolls.
•Bake in heated oven for 15 minutes or until bubbly and rolls are baked.

Brunch Pork Sausage Casserole

INGREDIENTS:

2 box's hash brown potatoes(I used Betty Crocker)
1 ½ lb. bulk spicy pork sausage
2 medium (2 cups) red bell peppers, chopped
8 medium (1/2 cup) green onions, chopped
1 cup (4 oz.) shredded Cheddar cheese
1 cup (4 oz.) shredded pepper Jack cheese
2 cups milk
½ tsp. salt
½ tsp. pepper
6 eggs
Chopped fresh cilantro, if desired

INSTRUCTIONS:

•Spray a 3-quart casserole dish with cooking spray.
•In 4-quart bowl, cover the potatoes with 10 cups of boiling water.
•Let stand for 3 minutes.
•Drain well and return potatoes to bowl.
•In 12-inch skillet, cook sausage over medium heat for 5 minutes.
•Add bell peppers and cook for 4 minutes while stirring frequently or until sausage is no longer pink and peppers are tender.
•Drain and add sausage mixture to potatoes in bowl.
•Stir in onions and ½ cup of each of the cheeses.
•Spread it in the baking dish.
•In a medium bowl, beat milk, salt, pepper and eggs until blended.
•Pour over sausage-potato mixture and sprinkle with remaining ½ cup of each cheese. •Cover and refrigerate for 8 hours or overnight.
•Heat oven to 375°F.
•Uncover baking dish.
•Bake for 50 minutes or until light golden brown and cheese is melted.
•Let stand for 10 minutes before serving.
•Dusting with cilantro.

Luscious Yellow Squash Casserole

INGREDIENTS:

6 cups yellow squash, sliced
1 to 2 tbsp. vegetable oil
1 large onion, sliced
4tbsp. butter
1/2 cup sour cream
1 tsp. House Seasoning (salt, pepper, garlic powder)
1 cup Cheddar cheese, grated
1 cup butter crackers, crushed

INSTRUCTIONS:

•Sauté squash in vegetable oil for about 15-20 minutes or until broken down.
•Drain.
•Sauté onions in butter for 5 minutes.
•Mix squash and onions together.
•Add sour cream, seasoning, and cheddar cheese.
•Mix well until all ingredients blended.
•Pour into casserole dish.
•Top with cracker crumbs.
•Bake at 350 degrees Fahrenheit for 25-30 minutes.

Yellow Squash Au Gratin

INGREDIENTS:

2 pounds sliced yellow summer squash
1/2 teaspoon sugar
1 teaspoon salt
4 ounces butter
1- 1/2 cups shredded mild Cheddar cheese or Monterey Jack
1 cup buttery crackers, crumbled
1/2 cup evaporated milk
2 eggs, beaten
Black pepper to taste

INSTRUCTIONS:

•Boil water with salt and sugar.
•Add the sliced squash and let it simmer until it become tender.

•Drain well.
•Add the butter, 1 cup of the cheese, 3/4 cup cracker crumbs, milk, eggs, and pepper.
•Mix well and pour it into a buttered 2-quart casserole or baking dish.
•Sprinkle the remaining cheese and cracker crumbs over the top.
•Bake this yellow squash casserole for 30 to 45 minutes at 325 degrees Fahrenheit.

Skillet Summer Squash

INGREDIENTS:

1/4 cup butter or margarine
4 cups summer squash, thinly sliced
1 onion, sliced
1 tsp. salt
Dash of pepper
1/4 cup water
1/2 cup cheese, grated

INSTRUCTIONS:

•Thaw butter in saucepan.
•Add squash, onion, salt, pepper and water.
•Sous-chef, covered for 10 to 15 minutes or until squash is tender.
•Sprinkle with cheese.

Mug-Style French Toast

INGREDIENTS:

2 slices bread, cut into 1/2-inch cubes
1/4 cup milk
1 egg
1/2 tsp. vanilla extract
1 tbsp. sugar
1/2 tsp. cinnamon
1/8 tsp. salt

INSTRUCTIONS:

•Covering a 12-ounce microwavable coffee mug with cooking spray.
•Put bread cubes in mug and press down lightly.
•In a small bowl, whisk milk, egg, vanilla, sugar, cinnamon and salt.
•Pour egg mixture over bread cubes and let soak in for 1 minute.
•Microwave on high 1 minute, and then add another 10 seconds at a time till its set.

Dump Pumpkin Pie

INGREDIENTS:

1 cup white sugar
2 (15-oz.) cans pumpkin puree (I used one 29-ounce can)
1 tbsp. pumpkin pie spice
½ tsp. salt
1 (18.25-oz.) white or yellow cake mix
1/2 cup butter
Cinnamon

INSTRUCTIONS:

•In the bottom of a slow cooker combine the sugar, pumpkin puree, pumpkin pie spice and salt.
•Stir constantly.
•In a separate bowl, combine the cake mix and the butter.
•Use a fork or a pastry blender to cut the butter into the cake mix until butter is pea sized and cake mix is crumbly.
•Scatter the cake mix on top of the pumpkin puree.
•Sprinkle cinnamon on top of the cake mix.
•Place a double layer of paper towels on top of your slow cooker.

•Place the lid over the paper towel and make sure it is secure.
•Cover and cook on low heat for 3 to 4 hours or on high for 90 minutes to 2 hours.
•Remove the lid and turn to warm.
•Let sit on warm for 20-30 minutes and then serve with vanilla ice cream.

Hash Brown Potato Casserole

INGREDIENTS:

5 cups frozen hash brown potatoes
2 cups ham, diced (asks for ½" slices at the deli and cut into cubes)
½ cup green onion, diced
1 cup shredded cheddar or Colby jack cheese, divided
¼ tsp. garlic powder
½ tsp. kosher salt
Freshly ground black pepper to taste
4 eggs
12 oz. evaporated milk

INSTRUCTIONS:

•Heat oven to 375 degrees Fahrenheit.
•Grease a 9 x 13 - inch baking dish with cooking spray.
•In a medium bowl, stir together potatoes, ham, ½ cup cheese, and green onions.
•Spread mixture evenly in prepared baking dish.
•In a small bowl, whisk together eggs, evaporated milk, garlic powder, salt, and pepper.
•Pour evenly over potato mixture.
•Cover with foil, and bake for 40 minutes.
•Remove cover, and sprinkle remaining ½ cup cheese over casserole.
•Bake uncovered for about 15 minutes more or until hot and bubbly and knife inserted in center comes out clean.

Low and Slow Cabbage Roll Casserole

INGREDIENTS:

1 lb. lean ground beef
1 onion, diced
3 cloves garlic, minced
¼ tsp. ground thyme
1 tsp. dried oregano
¾ tsp. kosher salt
a few grinds of black pepper
¼ tsp. caraway seeds, optional
1 c. brown rice, uncooked
14 oz. petite diced tomatoes, un-drained
8 oz. tomato sauce
2 cup beef broth
12 oz. bag shredded cabbage
1 cup mozzarella cheese
¼ cup grated parmesan cheese

INSTRUCTIONS:

•In an oven-safe Dutch oven or large skillet over medium-high heat, sauté beef and onions. •Mixing in oregano, thyme, salt, pepper, and caraway seeds while cooking.
•When meat is cooked through and onions are tender, add garlic and rice, and sauté 3 minutes longer.
•Stirring in beef broth, tomatoes, and tomato sauce.
•Bring to a boil, and then reduce heat to simmer and cover.
•Cook at least one hour, or up to 2 hours.
•Add the cabbage, and replace lid.
•Simmer over very low heat about 10 minutes longer.
•Turn broiler to high.
•Remove lid and turn off heat.
•Sprinkle cheeses over the top of the cabbage mixture, and place the pot under broiler for 3-5 minutes or until cheese is bubbly and starting to brown.

Spinach & Cheese Casserole

INGREDIENTS:

10 ounces fresh spinach, whole (or 12 ounces of frozen chopped spinach)
1/4 cup onion, chopped
4 egg whites, well beaten
2 tablespoons low-fat Parmesan cheese, grated
1 cup 1% milk
1/2 tsp. salt
1/3 cup celery, chopped
1/2 tsp. nutmeg, ground

INSTRUCTIONS:

•Wash fresh spinach and remove the stems.
•Steamed in a covered saucepan over low heat until the leaves are wilted.
•Drain in a colander or sieve, press out liquid and chop spinach.
•Mix the onion, egg whites, cheese, milk, salt, celery and nutmeg by stirring it gradually.
•Folding in the spinach and then pour mixture into a well greased 9 inch pie plate.
•Bake at 375 degrees Fahrenheit for 45 minutes or until a knife inserted in the middle comes out clean.
•Cut into 6 wedges and serve warm.

Quick & Easy Tuna Noodle Casserole

INGREDIENTS:

2 cans reduced fat cream of celery soup
1/3 cup dry sherry
2/3 cup skim milk
2 tbsp. parsley flakes
10 oz. frozen mix vegetables
2 cans light tuna in water, drained
10 oz. whole grain egg noodles, cooked
2 tbsps. Margarine
1/2 cup toasted almonds

INSTRUCTIONS:

• Thoroughly combine soup, sherry, milk, and parsley flakes in a lightly greased slow cooker.
•Stirring until well-blended and texture is consistent.
•Mixing in vegetables and drained tuna.
•Fold in whole grain noodles until evenly distributed.
•Top with almonds and butter substitute.
•Cover and cook on low heat for about 7 to 9 hours, high for 2 to 3 hour or until noodles are tender but not overdone.

Meatloaf Casserole

INGREDIENTS:

1 ½ lb. 97% lean ground beef
¾ cup onion, chopped finely
1/3 cup whole wheat cracker crumbs
2 egg whites, slightly beaten
3 tbsps. Skim milk
1 tbsp. chili powder
¾ tsp. salt
3 cups mashed potatoes
1 (11-oz.) whole kernel corn with red and green peppers, drained and rinsed
1/4 cup green onions, thinly sliced
1/2 cup reduced fat Mexican-style cheese blend

INSTRUCTIONS:

•Preheat oven to 375 degrees Fahrenheit.
•In large bowl, combine ground beef, onions, cracker crumbs, egg whites, milk, chili powder and salt.
•Mix lightly but thoroughly.
•Gently press into bottom of 9-inch square baking pan.
•Bake meatloaf for 20 to 25 minutes or until no longer pink and juices run clear.
•Carefully pour off drippings.
•For the meantime, combine potatoes, corn, and onions.
•Spread over meatloaf to edges of pan and then sprinkle the top with cheese.
•Broil 3 to 4 inches from heat for 3 to 5 minutes or until top is lightly browned.

•Cut into 6 rectangular servings.

Much Love Chicken Casserole

INGREDIENTS:

3 turkey bacon strips
1/2 cup chopped onion,
1/2 cup celery, sliced thinly
4 oz. can slice mushrooms, drained
10 3/4 oz. can condensed reduced sodium cream of celery soup, undiluted
1 cup fat free sour cream
Salt, to taste
1/8 tsp. pepper
2 tsps. Worcestershire sauce
2 oz. jar diced pimientos
4 cups diced cooked chicken, removed of excess skin and fat
1 1/2 cup whole wheat flour
1 1/2 tsp. baking powder
1/4 tsp. baking soda
1/2 tsp. salt
1 cup reduced fat cheddar cheese, shredded
1 tsp. dried parsley
1/4 cup light salad oil
6 tbsps. Skim milk plus 1 teaspoon lemon juice
Paprika, to taste
Fresh parsley, if desired

INSTRUCTIONS:

• Cook turkey bacon in a large skillet.
•Crumble and set aside.
•Sauté onion, celery and mushrooms in bacon drippings until tender.
•Add soup, sour cream, salt, pepper, Worcestershire sauce, pimientos, chicken and turkey bacon and then mix it well.
•Spread into a greased 13 x 9 x 2-inch baking dish.
•Bake at 350 degrees F for 25 minutes.
•Meanwhile, to make the topping, combine flour, baking powder, soda and salt.
•Add cheese and parsley.
•Blend in oil and buttermilk to moisten mixture.
•With floured fingers, shape dough into 24 mini biscuits.

•Arrange over partially baked casserole and sprinkle lightly with paprika.
•Return to oven and bake for 20-25 minutes more.
•Garnish with fresh parsley if desired.

Spinach Artichoke Chicken Casserole

INGREDIENTS:

12 ounces chicken, chopped into small pieces
8 ounces short pasta, such as ziti
10 ounces frozen spinach, defrosted and drained
1 can quartered artichoke hearts (14 ounces), drained
2 cloves garlic, finely chopped
1/3 cup pecorino Romano cheese
1/2 cup sour cream
1/2 cup cheddar cheese
1/2 cup cream cheese softened
2 tablespoons light mayonnaise
1 cup milk
1 tablespoon olive oil
Salt and black pepper, to taste

INSTRUCTIONS:

•Cook the pasta according to package instructions, then toss it with olive oil or nonstick spray and set it aside.
•In a large nonstick skillet add the chicken spiced with oil, salt and pepper over a medium high heat.
•Sauté for about 5 minutes or until the chicken just starts to brown on all sides then push the chicken to one side of the pan.
•Add the spinach and garlic to the empty space in the pan and sauté for another 2 minutes. •If the pan gets too dry, add a few tablespoons of water as needed.
•Add the artichokes and stir to combine.
•Add the milk, sour cream, cheddar, cream cheese, mayo, and pecorino Romano cheese while stirring until the cheeses melt and blend together.
•Simmer slowly for 2 minutes, then stir in the cooked pasta and simmer for another minute to blend all the ingredients.
•Pour the contents of the pan into a greased baking dish and top with grated cheese and paprika.

•Place under the broiler for 2 to 5 minutes or until the top is golden and crispy.

Rotisserie Chicken and Wild Rice Casserole

INGREDIENTS:

1/4 cup all-purpose flour
1/4 cup light butter
1 cup Sunrich Sol Unsweetened
1 chicken bouillon cube
1 whole rotisserie chicken
4 garlic cloves, minced
2 cups cooked wild rice
3 tbsps. Bread crumbs
½ cup Cheddar cheese

INSTRUCTIONS:

•Preheat oven to 325 degrees Fahrenheit.
•Combine the butter, flour, and Sunrich SōL Unsweetened in a small saucepan.
•Cook and stir over low heat or until slightly thickened and bubbly.
•Allow the sauce to reduce until it begins to coat the sides of the saucepan.
•Add the garlic and rotisserie chicken to the Sol sauce.
•Toss until well combined.
•Fold in the cooked wild rice.
•After thoroughly combining the wild rice to the mixture, transfer to a baking dish.
•Sprinkle with bread crumbs and top with cheddar cheese.
•Bake in the oven for 25 minutes, or until the cheddar cheese is a golden brown.

White Rice, Chicken and Mushroom Casserole

INGREDIENTS:

2/3 cup dry lentils
1/2 cup basmati white rice
1/4 cup onion, diced
4 chicken breasts, boneless and skinless (about 1.5 pounds), each breast cut into strips
1 cans (10 oz.) cream of mushroom soup
3/4 cup fat free sour cream
2 cups low sodium chicken broth
2 cups mushrooms, sliced (can use wild for earthier flavor)
1/2 cup sliced almonds, toasted in nonstick pan until golden brown
2 tsps. Fresh parsley, finely chopped (or dried)

INSTRUCTIONS:

•Heat oven to 350 degrees.
•Combine lentils, rice, and onion and mix in the bottom of a 9 x 13-inch baking dish.
•Arrange chicken breast strips evenly on top of the mixture.
•In medium bowl, combine condensed cream of mushroom soup, fat-free sour cream, chicken broth, and sliced mushrooms.
•Spread on top of the chicken and barley mixture.
•Cover pan with foil and bake for 1 hour.
•Remove foil, sprinkle almonds and parsley over the top, and bake 15 minutes more.
•Serve hot!

Corn and Chicken Noodle Casserole

INGREDIENTS:

2 skinless boneless chicken breasts cut into cubes
1/2 can reduced fat cream of chicken soup
1 tbsp. olive oil
1/4 lb. Velveeta cheese, cut into cubes
1/2 a bag egg noodles
1 can corn
1 tbsp. seasoned salt
1/2 tbsp. parsley flakes
1 tsp. pepper

INSTRUCTIONS:

•Cook egg noodles in boiling water till chewy.
•Cook chicken and salt in olive oil until chicken is tender and color is not pink in the middle.
•Drain the oil.
•Combine cream of chicken soup and egg noodles with the chicken and let it simmer until reaches to boiling.
•Reduce heat, and add Velveeta cheese, corn, and pepper.
•Cook and let the Velveeta melt all over the chicken.
•Remove from heat and sprinkle with parsley flakes.

Chicken Cowboy Casserole

INGREDIENTS:

8 chicken drumsticks
8 oz. low fat smoked sausage, sliced
32 oz. fat free barbecued baked beans
15 oz. frozen whole kernel corn, thawed
15 oz. can black beans, well rinsed and drained
1 3/4 cup frozen baby lima beans, thawed
1 1/2 cup onions, chopped
1 cup your favorite tomato sauce
1 1/2 cup baked corn tortilla chips, crushed

INSTRUCTIONS:

•Preheat oven to 375 degrees Fahrenheit.

•Have a shallow 3-quart baking dish ready.
•Remove skin and fat from chicken.
•In the baking dish, mix together the chicken, sausage, baked beans, corn, black beans, lima beans, onions and tomato sauce.
•Cover and bake for 1 hour.
•Uncover and sprinkle with chips.
•Bake uncovered for 15 minutes longer or until the chicken is cooked through.

Apple, Chicken and Mushroom Casserole

INGREDIENTS:

8 chicken drumsticks
1 onion
2 apples
1 package mushroom soup mix
1 tsp. dried thyme
2 tsps. Whole grain mustard
1 1/2 cup water
1 cup plain yogurt
8 brown button mushrooms
Salt and pepper

INSTRUCTIONS:

•Remove skin from chicken.
•Peel and finely slice onion.
•Peel, core and dice apples.
•Place chicken, onion and apple in a casserole dish with the mushroom soup mix, thyme, mustard and water.
•Place a tight fitting lid on top.
•Bake at 350 degrees F for 1 hour or until chicken is tender. Stir in yogurt.
•Clean mushrooms and cut in half.
•Mix through chicken in casserole and bake a further 15 minutes.
•Season with salt and pepper.

Turkey Bacon and Ground Beef Casserole

INGREDIENTS:

1/2 lb. extra lean ground beef
1/2 lb. turkey bacon, diced
1 small onion, diced
1 can kidney beans, drained and rinsed well
1 can navy beans, drained and rinsed well
1 can butter beans, drained and rinsed well
1/3 cup SPLENDA brown sugar substitute
1/4 cup reduced sugar ketchup
1/2 tsp. dry mustard
2 tbsps. Maple syrup

INSTRUCTIONS:

•Brown the ground beef in a skillet over medium-high heat.
•Add turkey bacon and onion, and drain any excess grease.
•In large baking dish, add to the hamburger mix the kidney beans, navy beans, butter beans, brown sugar substitute, ketchup, dry mustard and maple syrup.
•Make sure everything is thoroughly combined.
•Bake at 350 degrees Fahrenheit for 1 hour or until everything is thoroughly heated.

Simple Burger Casserole

INGREDIENTS:

1 pound extra lean ground beef
1 can low fat cream of mushroom soup
3/4 cup skim milk
1/2 cup onion, chopped
1 pinch salt
1 pinch black pepper
3 cups raw potatoes, sliced
1/2 pound reduced fat Cheddar cheese, grated
1/4 cup margarine

INSTRUCTIONS:

•Brown the ground beef and drain off fat.
•Set aside.
•Preheat oven to 350 degrees Fahrenheit.
•Mix low fat cream of mushroom soup, skim milk, onion, salt and pepper in a separate bowl.
•Layer the potatoes in large casserole dish with the soup mixture and hamburger.
•Repeat the layering until the last of the ingredient is place.
•Top layer with hamburger and dot of margarine.
•Cover and bake for 1 1/4 to 1 1/2 hours.
•Sprinkle with grated low fat Cheddar cheese and bake just until cheese is melted.

Beef Macaroni Casserole

INGREDIENTS:

1 1/2 cup whole grain macaroni
2 lbs. extra lean ground beef
1 onion, chopped
1 clove garlic, crushed
1 tsp. salt, or to taste
1 tsp. Worcestershire sauce
1 dash Tabasco
1 can (28-oz.) tomatoes
1 can (10-oz.) low sodium tomato soup
1 cup low fat cheddar cheese, shredded

INSTRUCTIONS:

•Heat oven to 350 degrees F.
•Boil whole grain macaroni according to package directions.
•Drain the pasta.
•Brown the extra lean ground beef, onion and garlic.
•Add salt, Worcestershire sauce, Tabasco, tomatoes, and tomato soup.
•Combine with cooked macaroni pasta and pour into 2-1/2 quart casserole.
•Sprinkle low fat cheddar cheese over top of casserole.
•Cover and bake for 30 minutes.
•Uncover and continue baking for an additional 20 to 25 minutes.

Italian Beef and Mushroom Casserole

INGREDIENTS:

1 lb. extra lean ground beef
7 oz. whole wheat small elbow macaroni, uncooked
1 can (14.5 ounce) cut tomatoes, drained
1 can (10.75 ounce) low sodium tomato soup
1 onion, chopped
1 clove garlic, minced
1 can (4.5 ounces) sliced mushrooms, drained
1 pinch salt
1/2 tsp. chili powder
1 tsp. Italian seasonings
1 pinch black pepper

INSTRUCTIONS:

•Heat oven to 350 degrees Fahrenheit.
•Brown the extra lean ground beef and remove the fats.
•Boil whole wheat elbow macaroni according to its package directions.
•Mix ground beef, whole wheat macaroni, tomatoes, tomato soup, chopped onion, garlic, sliced mushrooms, salt, pepper, chili powder, and Italian seasoning in a 2 quart casserole dish.
•Cover and bake for 30 minutes.

Stove Top Veggie and Beef Casserole

INGREDIENTS:

1 1/2 lb. extra lean ground beef
4 zucchini, sliced
1 onion, chopped
4 tbsps. Margarine
1 cup carrots, grated
1 cup light sour cream
1 cans Cream of chicken soup
1 box Stove Top Low Sodium Stuffing mix, prepared according to package directions
1 box of herb-seasoned croutons

INSTRUCTIONS:

•Heat oven to 350 degrees F.

•In a large skillet, brown the extra lean ground beef and drain the fat.
•Sauté zucchini and onion with the margarine.
•Mix together the ground beef, zucchini –onion mixture, carrots, light sour cream, cream of chicken soup, and Stove Top Lower Sodium stuffing.
•Place in a 9x13 inch casserole dish.
•Top with croutons and bake for 1 hour.

Beef with Spud Puppiesa Casserole

INGREDIENTS:

1 pound extra lean ground beef
1 medium onion, chopped
10 3/4 ounces organic cream of mushroom soup
10 ounces frozen peas
Garlic powder, to taste
Black pepper, to taste
1 1/2 cup reduced fat cheddar cheese
1 pound Cascadian Farms Spud Puppiesa

INSTRUCTIONS:

•Preheat oven to 325 degrees F.
•Brown the ground beef with the onions.
•Remove the drippings or the extra fats.
•Add the soup and peas.
•Sprinkle generously with garlic powder and pepper.
•Spray a casserole dish with cooking spray and spread the hamburger mixture over the bottom of the pan.
•Toss the cheese with the frozen Spud Puppiesa, and spread over the casserole.
•Bake for approximately one hour, until cheese is bubbly.

Three in One Casserole

INGREDIENTS:

1 lb. & 2 oz. boned shin of beef, trimmed weight
1 lb. & 2 oz. boned shin of pork, trimmed weight
1 lb. & 2 oz. boned shoulder of lamb, trimmed weight
3 cups dry white Alsace wine
2 3/4 lbs. potatoes, sliced (1/2 in thick)
1 3/4 lbs. leeks
3 oz. butter or margarine
1 1/2 lb. onions, thinly sliced
1 bouquet garni, with plenty of thyme
10 peppercorns, crushed
2 garlic cloves, crushed
2 cups (18 fluid ounce) chicken stock
1 calf's foot, blanched and cut into 3 pieces
2 tbsps. Flour
Salt
Pepper, freshly ground

INSTRUCTIONS:

•In day 1, trim leeks and discard the greenest parts.
•Split the leeks lengthways, wash and dice.
•Cut each type of meat into 6 even pieces.
•Put them into 3 separate bowls and sprinkle generously with white wine.
•Cover the bowls and refrigerate for at least 12 hours.
•In day 2, preheat oven to 325 degrees Fahrenheit.
•Heat the butter in a flameproof earthenware casserole over low heat.
•Put in the onions and simmer for several minutes.
•Lay the leek on top of the onions, and then the potatoes.
•Add the bouquet garni, peppercorns and garlic.
•Arrange the 3 meats separately on top, one type to the left, one in the middle, one in the right.
•Pour over the marinade and the remaining wine.
•Salt lightly, add the chicken stock and lay the pieces of calf's foot on top.
•Set the lid on the casserole.
•Combine the flour with a little cold water to make a soft paste.
•Spread this paste between the top of the casserole and the lid to make an airtight seal.

•Cook in the low oven for 4 hours.
•Present the casserole at the table just as is.
•Break the seal and lift off the lid.

Turkey Tater Tots Casserole

INGREDIENTS:

1 1/2 lb. lean ground turkey
1/2 medium onion, chopped
1 to 2 garlic cloves, minced
1 can fat free cream of chicken soup
2 cups 2 percent cheddar cheese, shredded
1/2 cup skim milk
4 tbsps. Plain yogurt
1 bag frozen tater tots (the smaller round)
Salt and black pepper, to taste

INSTRUCTIONS:

•Heat oven to 350 degrees Fahrenheit.
•Grease a 9x13 inch baking dish.
•In a large skillet, brown the ground turkey, onions and garlic.
•Drain the drippings and set aside.
•Mix together the soup, milk and yogurt in a medium bowl until smooth.
•Add meat mixture and 1 cup of cheese and stirring to combine.
•Layer half of the tater tots on the bottom of the greased baking dish.
•Pour the meat & cheese mixture over the top.
•Place the other half of the tater tots on top of the meat.
•Sprinkle remaining cheese on top and bake uncovered for 25 to 30 minutes, or until golden brown and bubbly.

It's Almost A Healthy Casserole

INGREDIENTS:

1 pound 97% lean ground beef, browned and drained
1 medium onion, minced
1 16-ounce can diced tomatoes
1 tablespoon Worcestershire sauce
1 teaspoon salt
2 potatoes, sliced
1/3 cup flour
10 ounces frozen corn
1 bell pepper, seeded and cut into strips
1 1/2 cup low-fat cheddar cheese, shredded

INSTRUCTIONS:

•Heat oven to 375° F.
•Brown the beef and drain the drippings.
•Combine the beef, onion and tomatoes in a bowl with water, Worcestershire sauce and salt.
•Spoon into a 3-quart casserole greased with cooking spray.
•Layer the potatoes, flour, corn and green peppers on top.
•Cover and bake at 375° F for 45 minutes.
•Sprinkle with cheese.
• Uncovered and bake for 30 minutes longer.

Layered Casserole

INGREDIENTS:

4 white potatoes, sliced
1 16-oz. can peas, drained, 1/3 cup of the liquid reserved
1/2 head red or white cabbage, shredded
2 large sweet potatoes, sliced
1 lb. fresh mushrooms, sliced
1 large Bermuda onion, sliced thin
1 large red onion, sliced thin
4 8-oz pork or lamb chops
garlic powder, salt, and pepper to taste
16 oz. marinara or catsup

INSTRUCTIONS:

•Warm oven to 350° F.
•Spray lightly the bottom of a casserole dish with cooking spray.
•Layer the sliced white potatoes and sprinkle with garlic powder.
•Layer peas, sweet potatoes, cabbage and sprinkle with salt and pepper.
•Layer mushrooms and sprinkle with pepper.
•Layer both onions and sprinkle with pepper.
•Garnish the top of the onions with garlic, salt, and pepper
•Mix the reserved pea water with the marinara or catsup and pour over the casserole.
•Cover with a tight lid or foil and bake at 350° F degrees for 40-45 minutes.
•Remove cover and bake another 15 minutes or so, until top is browned.

Vegetable Loaded Casserole

INGREDIENTS:

1 package frozen whole wheat dough
1 large head of broccoli, chopped
1 small onion, chopped
2 large carrots, diced
1 cans organic cream of mushroom soup
Whole wheat breadcrumbs, to taste
1/4 cup skim milk
1/2 lb. reduced fat cheese, grated

INSTRUCTIONS:

•Heat oven to 350 degrees Fahrenheit.
•Spread out your frozen dough at the bottom of a baking dish, and bake for about 10 minutes.
•Cook broccoli, onion and carrots in saucepan.
•Add 3 tablespoons water and cook about 10 to 12 minute.
•Drain.
•Put the cooked vegetables on top of the dough.
•Mix together the soup and milk then pour over the vegetables.
•Sprinkle cheese and bread crumbs on top.
•Bake for about 25 minutes.

Spaghetti Cheesy Casserole

INGREDIENTS:

1 1/2 lb. lean ground chuck
1 green bell pepper, chopped
1 onion, chopped
1/2 cup chopped celery
2 cloves garlic, crushed
1 10.75-oz. cans low fat condensed cream of mushroom soup, undiluted
3/4 cup water
1 16-oz. cans tomatoes, un-drained & chopped
2 tablespoons chili powder
Pinch salt
1/4 teaspoon pepper
8 oz. whole wheat spaghetti, uncooked
2 oz. reduced fat cheddar cheese, cut into 1/2-inch cubes
1 5-oz. jar pimiento-stuffed olives, drained
3/4 cup reduced fat shredded cheddar cheese

INSTRUCTIONS:

•Cook meat, green pepper, onion, celery, and garlic in a Dutch oven while stirring gradually until meat crumbles.
•Drain well and return mixture to Dutch oven.
•Mixing in soup, water, tomatoes, chili powder, salt and pepper.
•Bring to a boil over medium heat.
•Cover, reduce heat, and simmer for 1 hour while stirring occasionally.
•Preheat oven to 325 degrees Fahrenheit.
•Cook spaghetti according to package directions and drain.
•Mix spaghetti, cheese cubes, and olives into meat sauce.
•Spoon mixture into a lightly greased 11x7x1.5-inch baking dish.
•Cover and bake at 325° F for 20 minutes or until thoroughly heated.
•Sprinkle with 3/4 cup reduced fat shredded cheese.
•Uncovered and bake for another 10 minutes.

Cheesy Mushroom Broccoli Loaded Casserole

INGREDIENTS

1 package frozen whole wheat dough
1 large head of broccoli, chopped
1 small onion, chopped
2 large carrots, diced
1 can organic cream of mushroom soup
Whole wheat breadcrumbs, to taste
1/4 cup skim milk
1/2 pound reduced fat cheese, grated

INSTRUCTIONS

Pre-heat oven to 350 degrees F.
Spread out your frozen dough at the bottom of a baking dish, and bake for about 10 minutes.
Cook broccoli, onion and carrots in saucepan. Add 3 tablespoons water. Cook about 10 to 12 minute then drain. Put the cooked vegetables on top of the dough.
Mix together the soup and milk, then pour over the vegetables.
Sprinkle cheese and bread crumbs on top, and bake for about 25 minutes.

Turkey, Potato and Herbs Casserole

INGREDIENTS

1 1/2 lb. turkey breast filets
1 egg (optional)
1 tbsp. crushed garlic
1/4 cup skim milk
3/4 cup plain fine breadcrumbs
2 tbsp. olive oil
1 stalk celery
1 small onion
1/2 large green pepper
1 tsp. crushed garlic
1 tsp. herb's d'Provence
1 tsp. salt
3 large red potatoes, sliced paper thin
3/4 cup reduced fat shredded cheese
Fresh ground pepper to taste

1 1/2 cup skim milk
1/4 cup white flour for sauces,

INSTRUCTIONS

•Pat dry the turkey breast filets.
•Combine egg, milk, and crushed garlic in one plate.
•On another plate, put bread crumbs.
•Heat olive oil in a frying pan over medium-high heat.
•Dip and coat filets in garlic-milk mixture and bread crumbs.
•Cook the filets with margarine until become lightly brown.
•Put celery, onion, green pepper, and crushed garlic in a food processor and process for 1-5 seconds, until mixture is chopped roughly, but not pureed.
•Stir in herb's de Provence and salt, and then set mixture aside.
•Slice potatoes paper thin.
• Spray bottom of a 9" X 13" casserole with nonstick spray, or coat lightly with margarine.
•Arrange casserole as follows: Layer one-half of potato slices in bottom of casserole.
•Layer all of the browned turkey filets on top of potatoes.
•Spread herb mixture atop each turkey filet.
•Sprinkle one-half of the cheese over turkey and vegetables.
•Grind some pepper on top.
•Lay the rest of the potato slices on top of the turkey.
•Whisk together the remaining milk and flour.
•Pour it slowly over the casserole.
•Top the casserole with the rest of the grated cheese and ground pepper.
•Cover the casserole dish with aluminum foil and bake in a preheated 375°F oven for 45 minutes.
•Remove foil and bake for another 10-minutes, or until sauce is thick and potatoes are completely tender.
•Let casserole rest for 10 minutes before serving.

Red Bean and Tomato Casserole

INGREDIENTS:

3 cups red beans, soaked in water overnight
2 medium onions, chopped
2 cups Pomi Chopped Tomato
1 garlic cloves, minced
2 medium green peppers, sliced
2 tsp. paprika
1 tbsp. olive oil

INSTRUCTIONS:

•Boil beans for one hour in salted water.
•Pour 1 cup of Pomi tomato into a large skillet and then add the onion, oil and paprika.
•Cook for 5 minutes until the ingredients are well blended.
•Drain the cooked beans.
•Stir into the sauce and add 1 cup of Pomi.
•Cover tightly and bake in the oven at 350 degrees Fahrenheit for 1 hour.
•Add a little more Pomi, previously diluted in water or broth if the sauce seems too thick.
•Serve piping hot.

Sweet Potato Casserole

INGREDIENTS:

1 cup pecans
3 cups sweet potatoes, peeled and chopped
1/2 cup water, barley water or almond milk
1/2 cup dates, soaked for about 20 minutes
1 tsp. cinnamon
1 dash vanilla powder
1 banana, 1/2 an apple or pear, 1 cup pineapple or mango, or 2-3 dates chopped

INSTRUCTIONS:

•Prepare a casserole dish with your choice of fruit.
•Put potatoes, water or milk, soaked dates, cinnamon and vanilla in processor and puree till smooth.
•Pour over fruit into a casserole dish.
•Sprinkle pecans over the potato mixture.
•Warm in the dehydrator at 105 degrees F for 2 hours.

Cajun Cornbread Casserole

INGREDIENTS:

15 oz. diced tomatoes, un-drained
1 small onion, diced
2 celery stalks, minced
3 garlic cloves, minced
1 bell pepper, seeded and diced
2 tbsps. Cajun seasoning
15 oz. kidney beans, drained and rinsed
1 cup cornmeal
1 1/2 tsp. baking powder
1 pinch salt
1 1/2 tbsp. raw sugar (optional)
3/4 cup nondairy milk
1/4 cup unsweetened applesauce

INSTRUCTIONS:

•Heat oven to 400 degrees Fahrenheit.
•Grease a square 8 or 9-inch baking pan or casserole dish.

•Ditch tomato juices into a skillet and chop tomatoes into smaller pieces, and set aside.
•Add water as necessary until a thin layer of liquid covers the skillet.
•Sauté onion, celery, garlic and bell peppers over high heat until onions are translucent, bell peppers are tender and all of the water has evaporated in about 4 minutes.
•Mix in 1 to 2 tablespoons of Cajun seasoning, tomatoes and kidney beans, stirring to combine, and then set side.
•Whisk cornmeal, baking powder, salt and additional Cajun seasoning if desired (several dashes so the flour looks speckled when stirred) in a small mixing bowl.
•Add 1 to 2 tablespoons of sugar for a sweet cornbread topping.
•Then mixing in nondairy milk and applesauce.
•It should be thick, but spreadable like hummus and not dry.
•Pour bean mixture into your baking dish and pat down firmly with a spatula.
•Spread cornbread mixture on top and bake 30 to 35 minutes, or until the cornbread is deep golden, cracked and firm to the touch.
•Let set out for about 15 minutes before serving.

Kelly's Sweet Potato Casserole

INGREDIENTS

2 lbs. sweet potatoes, peeled and cut into 1-inch cubes
3/4 cup brown sugar
1/4 cup maple syrup
1/4 cup milk
2 eggs
1/4 cup butter
1/4 tsp. cinnamon
1 tsp. vanilla extract
1/2 tsp. salt
1/4 cup flour
3 tbsps. Butter, melted
1/2 cup pecans, coarsely chopped

INSTRUCTIONS

•Boil the sweet potatoes in water until tender for about 20 to 30 minutes.
•Once cooked, drain and mash.

•Combine 1/4 cup of the sugar, maple syrup, milk, eggs, room temperature butter, cinnamon, vanilla extract and salt to make a mixture.
•Pour the mixture into a baking dish.
•Mix 1/2 cup brown sugar, flour, melted butter and pecans.
•Mixing until the mixture forms crumbs.
•Sprinkle it on top of the sweet potatoes.
•Bake in a preheated 375 degrees Fahrenheit oven for about 30 minutes or until golden brown on top.

Turkey Sausage Casserole

INGREDIENTS:

1 1/2 lb. lean turkey sausage
1 lb. frozen corn kernels
6 eggs
1 pouch cornbread mix
2 cans light creamed corn
3 oz. frozen green chilies
Pepper
Garlic powder
2/3 lb. reduced fat cheddar cheese
Skim milk

INSTRUCTIONS:

•Sous-chef the turkey sausage in a griddle or pan until completely browned.
•Get rid of any excess fat from the pan and evenly spread the turkey sausage in a casserole dish.
•Scatter the frozen corn kernels over the sausage.
•Mix the eggs, cornbread mix, creamed corn, green chilies, pepper, garlic powder and 1/2 a pound of cheese.
•Add the milk to the mixture.
•Pour mixture over the corn and sausage.
•Sprinkle the top with more cheese.
•Bake at 350° F until barely set.

Hot Pumpkin Casserole

INGREDIENTS

14 oz. Frozen cut corn, fully thawed
12 oz. Frozen sweet potato fries
10 oz. Frozen cut leaf spinach, fully thawed
1 can pumpkin, about 1 1/2 cups
1 can black beans, thoroughly rinsed and drained (about 2 cups)
2 tsp. hot sauce
3 tsp. chili powder
4 tsp. salt-free seasoning mix
1 1/2 cup soymilk
Garlic powder, to taste
Salt, to taste
8 tortillas

INSTRUCTIONS

•Put the thawed corn and sweet potato fries on a baking sheet.
•Roast in a preheated 425 degree F oven for about 45 minutes, or until both vegetables are crispy.
• Place a saucepan over medium heat while the vegetables are roasting.
•Then, add in your pumpkin, hot sauce, chili powder, salt free seasoning, garlic powder, and salt and soy milk.
•Mixing together and then for about 5 to 10 wait until the mixture is thoroughly combined.
•Turn off the heat and set aside.
•Once the vegetables are done roasting, combine them with the fully thawed spinach and black beans in a large bowl.
•Lower the oven's temperature to 375 degrees Fahrenheit.
•Pour about a third to half of the pumpkin sauce on the bottom of a casserole dish.
•Take about one to three tablespoons of the vegetable mixture and place in one of the tortillas.
•Roll the tortilla around the mixture until it takes on a log-like shape.
•Place the tortilla roll-up into the casserole dish.
•Repeat until all of the tortillas and the vegetable mixture have been used up.
•Pour the remaining pumpkin sauce over top of the casserole and spread to coat evenly. •Bake the casserole dish in a 375 degree

Fahrenheit oven until everything is completely warmed through, about 20 minutes.

Polenta Chili Corndog Casserole

INGREDIENTS:

For the chili:
2 hot dogs, sliced into half-inch pieces
1/2 lb. lean ground beef
1 large onion, diced
1 small zucchini, grated
1 carrot, peeled and grated
2 Serrano peppers, minced
2 garlic cloves, minced
16 oz. jar of Chi Chi's mild salsa
8 oz. water
1 cans red kidney beans, rinsed and drained
2 tbsps. Brown sugar
2 tbsps. Chili powder
Salt and black pepper, to taste
For the Polenta:
2 cups water
1 cup milk
2 tbsps. Butter
1/2 tsp. salt
1 cup instant polenta
2 oz. extra sharp cheddar cheese

INSTRUCTIONS

•Heat the oven to 375 degrees F or 190 degrees C.
•Sauté the ground beef, onion, zucchini, carrot, peppers and garlic in a large skillet over a medium heat.
•Add with some salt and pepper to taste and sauté until the meat is browned and the veggies are wilted.
•Add the hotdogs to the pan and sauté just until they begin to develop a slight color.
•Add the salsa, water, beans, brown sugar, and chili powder, stir it together and let it simmer uncovered for 10 minutes while you make the polenta.
•Add the water, milk, butter and salt to a medium saucepan and bring up to a boil.

•Lower the heat then add the polenta while whisking to avoid lumps and simmer for 3 minutes.
•Turn off the heat, stir in the cheese and set aside.
•Spoon the chili into a greased 9x12-inch casserole dish.
•Top with the polenta and bake at 375 degrees F or 190 degrees C for 25 minutes.

Baked Potato Cheese Casserole

INGREDIENTS:

1/4 cup margarine or the butter substitute of your choice
3 large baking potatoes, rinsed well
Salt and black pepper, to taste
2 tbsps. Reduced fat Parmesan cheese, grated

INSTRUCTIONS:

•Heat up oven to 475 degrees F.
• Melt the margarine in a small pan or in the microwave.
•Cut potatoes in half lengthwise, and then slice them crosswise about 18-inch thick slices.
•Arrange by lining up in buttered 13x9-inch baking pan, with the slices overlapping.
•Pour melted margarine over potatoes.
•Season with salt and pepper.
•Bake for 20 minutes.
•Remove from the oven and sprinkle with reduced fat Parmesan cheese.
•Bake for another 5 to 7 minutes, or until cheese is melted and slightly brown.

Chicken Egg Noodle with Spinach Casserole

INGREDIENTS:

6 tbsps. Unsalted butter
1/4 cup all-purpose flour
4 cups whole milk
1 cup sour cream kosher salt and black pepper
12 oz. egg noodles
4 slices sandwich bread
2 cups shredded cooked chicken or rotisserie chicken

5 oz. baby spinach, chopped
2 tsps. Dried thyme

INSTRUCTIONS:

•Preheat oven to 400° F.
•Melt 4 tablespoons of the butter in a large saucepan over medium heat.
•Add the flour and cook while stirring for 1 to 2 minutes or until foamy.
•Gradually whisk in the milk.
•Bring to a simmer and cook, whisking often for 3 to 5 minutes or until thickened.
•Remove from heat and whisk in the sour cream, 1 teaspoon salt, and ¼ teaspoon pepper.
•For the meantime, cook the noodles according to the package directions.
•Drain and return them to the pot.
•Pulse the bread in a food processor until coarse crumbs form.
•Melt the remaining 2 tablespoons of butter in a microwave-safe bowl.
•Add the milk mixture, chicken, spinach, and thyme to the noodles and toss to combine. •Spoon out to a 9-by-13-inch or some other 3-quart baking dish and then sprinkle with the bread crumbs, and drizzle with the melted butter.
•Bake for 8 to 10 minutes or until the bread crumbs are golden and the filling is bubbling. •Let cool for 5 minutes before serving.

Potato Nuggets Casserole

INGREDIENTS

1/4 cup extra-virgin olive oil
1 medium yellow onion, finely chopped (about 2 cups)
1 lb. 80-percent lean ground beef
Kosher salt and freshly ground black pepper
2 cups frozen cut green beans, thawed (8 oz.)
1 3/4 cups frozen corn kernels, thawed (8 oz.)
2 10-oz. cans cream of mushroom soup
1 lb. frozen shredded potato nuggets

INSTRUCTIONS

•Heat the oven to 350 degrees Fahrenheit.
•Boil oil and sauté onions for about 15 minutes or until soft and begin to brown.

•Add the beef to the onions and cook until the meat is brown, stirring and scraping the bottom of the skillet to release the yummy brown bits, about 10 minutes.
•Season with salt and pepper.
•Transfer the beef and onion mixture from the skillet into a 9-by-13-inch baking dish.
•Sprinkle the green beans and corn evenly on top.
•Spread the cream of mushroom soup over top.
•Add frozen potato nuggets on top.
•Uncovered and bake for 1 hour or until the potato nuggets should be golden brown.

Buttered Corn Casserole

INGREDIENTS:

1 cans whole kernel yellow corn, un-drained
1 can cream style yellow corn
1 (8 oz.) carton sour cream
2 eggs, beaten
1 box Jiffy corn muffin mix
1 stick butter, melted

INSTRUCTIONS:

•Combine all together the ingredients and pour into large, lightly greased casserole dish.
•Bake at 350°F for 55 to 60 minutes.

French Toast with Pecans Casserole

INGREDIENTS:

1/4 cup butter
3/4 cup brown sugar
4 eggs
1 1/2 cups milk
1 tsp. vanilla
1 tbsp. powdered sugar
Brown sugar
White sugar
Cinnamon French
1 loaf toast bread

Butter
Pecans

INSTRUCTIONS:

•Melt butter and add brown sugar, stirring constantly till mixed.
•Spread butter/ brown sugar mix into bottom of 9x13the pan
•Beat eggs, milk, vanilla & powdered sugar
•Lay down a layer of French toast bread (cut off crusts if desired)
•Ladle on half of egg mixture
•Sprinkle with brown sugar and cinnamon (and pecans if you like nuts)
•Spread thin layer of butter on one side of French toast bread for next layer (cut crusts if desired)
•Lay down second layer of bread, butter side up
•Ladle rest of egg mixture over the top
•Sprinkle with white sugar and cinnamon
•Cover and refrigerate overnight
•In the morning remove from refrigerator uncover and preheat oven to 350
•Once preheated cook for 45 minutes and enjoy!

Creamy Scalloped Potatoes

INGREDIENTS:

10-11 small red potatoes
2 (5.2 oz.) packages Boursin cheese
1 pint heavy whipping cream
Grated Parmesan Cheese
Salt

INSTRUCTIONS:

•Brush potatoes and remove the end part.
•Slice the potatoes thinly.
•Combine together Boursin cheese and heavy whipping cream until evenly blended.
•Spread a layer of potatoes in 9x13 baking dish.
•Salt lightly and pour some of the cream-cheese mixture over the potatoes.
•Mash the potatoes so that the cream-cheese mixture gets in the cracks and spaces of the potatoes.

•Sprinkle lightly with parmesan cheese.
•Continue this layering process with the salt, cream-cheese mixture and parmesan cheese- mashing between each layer.
•Bake at 350 degrees Fahrenheit for about 1 hour to 1 hour and 20 minutes or until done.

Chicken Broccoli Cracker Casserole

INGREDIENTS

1 (16 oz.) bag frozen broccoli
1-2 cups cooked and shredded chicken
2 (8 oz.) blocks cream cheese
2 cups milk
1½ tsp. garlic salt
¾ cup Parmesan Cheese, separated
Ritz Crackers, crushed

INSTRUCTIONS

•Boil broccoli in salted water according to package directions.
•Lay the broccoli in a greased 9x13 casserole dish.
•Heat the milk, cream cheese, garlic salt and ½ cup Parmesan cheese over low heat while stirring constantly until the mixture is smooth.
•Pour 1 cup of sauce over the broccoli.
•Add the chicken into the pan and pour the rest of the sauce over it.
•Sprinkle the top with ¼ cup Parmesan cheese and Ritz cracker crumbs.
•Bake at 350 degrees Fahrenheit for 15-20 minutes.

Cheese Tater Baked Ziti

INGREDIENTS

cooking spray or oil mister
1 tbsp. olive oil
1 medium onion, thinly sliced
1 large zucchini, halved lengthwise and thinly sliced
8 oz. button or baby bella mushrooms, sliced
8 oz. whole wheat pasta (penne and rotini work well), cooked al dente according to package
1 large jar marinara sauce (about 24 ounces)
1-15 oz. container of fat-free ricotta cheese
Salt and pepper to taste
1 c. reduced-fat Italian blend cheese (or mozzarella)
1 tbsp. chopped parsley (optional)

INSTRUCTION

•Heat oven to 350 degrees Fahrenheit.
•Spray a 9 x 13 baking dish with cooking spray or oil mister.
•Simmer olive oil in a large skillet over medium heat.
•Add onion and cook until softened for about 4 minutes.
•Mix in the zucchini and mushrooms.
•Cook until softened and liquid has boiled off for about 7 minutes more.
•Remove from heat.
•Add pasta, marinara sauce, ricotta, salt, and pepper to skillet with vegetables.
•Blending it until well combined.
•Pour pasta mixture into baking dish.
•Top with cheese.
•Bake for 30 minutes.
•Sprinkle with parsley before serving, if desired.

Spinach and Potato with Feta Cheese Gratin

INGREDIENTS

Butter
5-6 medium-sized red potatoes, washed, peeled, and sliced ⅛-inch thick, divided
4 bags (10-oz.) fresh baby spinach

3 cans (13.5-ounces) spinach, washed and drained, dry with paper towel
½ cup crumbled feta cheese
2 cups heavy cream
3 eggs
salt and pepper to taste

INSTRUCTIONS

- Heat oven to 375 degrees Fahrenheit.
- Brush a 13x9 baking dish with butter.
- Layer half of the potato slices in dish by overlapping slightly.
- Spread the spinach on top of the potato slices.
- Add the crumbled feta cheese over the spinach.
- Layer the rest of the potato slices on top.
- In a separate mixing bowl, whisk together the heavy cream, eggs, and salt and pepper.
- Pour the cream mixture into dish to cover potatoes and then cover with foil.
- Bake for 40 minutes, or until potatoes are tender when pierced with a fork.
- Remove foil and continue to bake for 35 to 40 minutes or until top of gratin is golden.

Chicken Burrito Casserole

INGREDIENTS:

5 burrito style flour tortillas
1 can (12.5 oz.) chicken in water, drained
2 cans (10.5 oz.) cream of chicken soup
1 container (8 oz.) sour cream
1 can (10 oz.) diced tomatoes & green chilies, drained
3/4 cups salsa
2 cups shredded cheese

INSTRUCTIONS:

- Heat the oven to 350 degrees Fahrenheit.
- Smear a 9×13 inch casserole dish with cooking spray.
- Pile all 5 tortillas on top of each other.
- Roll the tortillas up & then slice them into strips, about 1/4 – 1/2 inch thick.

•Combine the tortilla strips, chicken, soup, sour cream, rootle, salsa & 1 & 1/2 cups of the cheese in a large bowl.
•Stirring constantly to make sure it's well mixed.
•Pour the mixture into your prepared casserole dish & cover with foil.
•Bake for 45 minutes.
•Remove the foil & add the remaining 1/2 cup of cheese to the top of the casserole.
•Bake for an additional of 10-15 minutes or until the cheese is melted and the casserole is hot and bubbling.

Pork Chops with Curry Casserole

INGREDIENTS:

4 pork chops
Kosher salt
Pepper
1 large onion, sliced thin
3 large green tomatoes, sliced a bit thicker than the onions
Curry powder

INSTRUCTION:

•Heat the oven to 350 degrees Fahrenheit.
•Prepare the pork chops seasoned with a pinch of salt and a couple grinds of pepper.
•Heat the skillet to medium-high heat.
•Put the pork chops seasoned side down in the skillet.
•Repeat the seasonings on the other side, and brown the chops for 3-4 minutes per side.
•Butter a casserole dish and put half of the onions in a layer across the bottom.
•Sprinkle the entire layer with a pinch of salt and a pinch of curry powder.
•Top with a layer of half of the tomatoes.
•Repeat salt and curry seasoning.
•Repeat with the rest of the onions, more salt & curry powder and then the rest of the tomatoes and salt and curry powder.
•Top the vegetables with the browned pork chops.
•Bake at 350 degrees Fahrenheit for 30-45 minutes, uncovered.
•Flip over the chops and nestle them down into the veggies.
•Cover the casserole and continue baking until tender.

Spicy Lasagna Casserole

INGREDIENTS

1 package of lasagna noodles, cooked al dente
3 jars of pasta sauce (650 ml)
1 to 1 1/2 lbs. of ground beef
1/4 cup sugar
3 tbsps. Dried basil
4 tbsps. Dried oregano
1 tbsp. chili powder
1 tbsp. garlic powder
Salt and pepper to taste
4 bay leaves, to be discarded after simmering sauce
3 to 4 shallots, diced, cook in the microwave for about 30- 40 seconds till soft
1/2 large sweet onion, diced, cook in the microwave for about 1 to 1 1/2 minutes till soft
4 to 5 cloves of garlic, pressed
1/2 to 1 cup of parmesan cheese, grated
5 to 6 cups of mozzarella cheese, grated

INSTRUCTIONS

•Heat oven to 375°F to 400°F depending on how your oven works.
•Fill a large stock pot with water and bring to a boil on the stove.
•Add some salt when boiling.
•Toss in the noodles.
•Allow to cook according to the package.
•Drain, pat dry and line the pan.
•In the meantime, brown the ground beef in a skillet until juices runs clear.
•In a large Dutch oven combine the sauce, sugar, cooked ground beef, spices, bay leaves, shallots, onions and garlic.
•Stir and cook over medium heat till it boils while stirring for about 3 or 4 minutes.
•Reduce heat to simmer and allow to cook until the noodles are done.
•Putting all the prepared noodles and sauce.
•Spray your casserole dish with non stick spray.
•Scoop about 2 tablespoons of sauce into each pan to line the bottom thinly and then put some noodles.
•Toss a bit of mozzarella cheese on top of the noodles.

•Spoon 1/4 of the sauce over that layer.
•Spread evenly
•Toss one fourth of the parmesan cheese over top.
•Toss about 1/4 of the cheese over top.
•Repeat the layering of the lasagna with second casserole dish
•Cook uncovered for about 15 to 20 minutes in the preheated oven.

Blueberry French Toast Casserole

INGREDIENTS

French toast
12 slices bread, cut into cubes
1 (8-oz.) package cream cheese, cut in cubes
1 cup blueberries (fresh or frozen)
12 large eggs
⅓ cup maple syrup
2 cups milk or cream
1 teaspoon vanilla
Syrup
1 cup sugar
1 cup water
2 tbsps. Cornstarch
1 cup blueberries (fresh or frozen)
1 tbsp. butter

INSTRUCTIONS

•Arrange ½ of the bread cubes in a smeared 9 x 13 pan.
•Scatter cream cheese cubes and blueberries evenly over the bread cubes.
•Top and evenly sprinkle with remaining bread cubes.
•Blend together eggs, syrup, milk and vanilla in a large bowl.
•Pour over bread cubes.
•Press the bread cubes slightly down to absorb the milk/egg mixture.
•Cover pan with foil.
•Let it chill in the refrigerator for overnight.
•Bake covered with foil at 350 degrees for 30 minutes.
•Remove the foil and bake for another 30 minutes or until fluffy and golden.
•Top with blueberry syrup.

•Preparing the syrup by heating the following water, sugar, and cornstarch in a saucepan over medium heat.
•Stir in blueberries and simmer for 10 minutes.
•Add butter and stir until melted.
•Serve over the French toast.

South of the Border Casserole

INGREDIENTS:

6 poblano chili peppers
1 t. butter
1 1/2 lbs. chorizo, removed from casings
1 cup chopped onion
1/2 cup chopped red bell peppers
4 t minced garlic
4 t chili powder
7 - 8 corn tortillas, cut into quarters
10 large eggs
3 cup half and half
1/2 tsp. Tabasco
1/2 tsp. salt
1/2 tsp. black pepper
1/2 cup chopped green onion tops
1/4 cup chopped cilantro plus some for garnish
1 1/2 cup grated pepper jack
1 1/2 cup grated cheddar
Sour cream for garnish
Tapatio or other picante sauce for garnish

INSTRUCTIONS:

•Roast the poblanos lining up in the baking sheet in a broil.
•Turning them when they turn black.
•Put the roasted poblanos in a plastic or paper bag and let them rest for 15 minutes.
•Peel the chilies, cut to spread open, and remove the stems and seed pod.
•Butter or spray a 9 x 13 inch baking dish.
•Line the bottom of the baking dish with the chilies.
•Cook the chorizo in a large skillet.
•Add the onions and bell peppers, and cook for four minutes while continuing to stir.

•Add the garlic and chili powder and cook for one minute more. Set aside.
•Whip together the eggs, half and half, Tabasco, salt, and black pepper.
•Combine the cheeses with the green onions and cilantro and toss together to evenly distribute.
•Spread 1/3 of the chorizo over the poblanos in the baking dish.
•Place a layer of the tortilla quarters on top of the meat with 1/3 of the cheese mixture.
•Repeat layering two more times.
•Pour the eggs over the whole casserole.
•Cover, and refrigerate overnight or at least 6 hours.
•Bake uncovered at 350° F for one hour and 15 minutes or until an inserted knife comes out clean.
•Let rest for 10 minutes.
•Serve with sour cream, hot sauce, and chopped cilantro.

Chicken Mushroom Ravioli Casserole

INGREDIENTS

2 cups frozen spinach, not thawed
2 cups cooked shredded chicken
8 ounces sliced mushrooms
2 cups shredded Italian cheese
1 ½ cups Alfredo sauce,
1 pkg (19-25 oz.) frozen ravioli, cooked

INSTRUCTIONS

•Heat oven to 350 degrees Fahrenheit.
•In a large bowl mix spinach, chicken, mushrooms, and 1 cup of cheese.
•Spread ½ cup of Alfredo sauce on the bottom of a 3 qt baking dish, half the ravioli, half of the chicken mixture and repeat (begin with Alfredo sauce) until all are layered.
•Top with remaining ½ cup of Alfredo sauce, 1 cup shredded cheese.
•Bake for 30-35 minutes until cheese is bubbly.

Beef, Lamb and Artichoke Casserole

INGREDIENTS:

2 tbsps. Olive oil
6 lamb forequarter chops, trimmed
2 brown onions, halved,
2 carrots, sliced
2 garlic cloves, sliced, crushed 1 teaspoon dried oregano
1/2 tsp. dried rosemary
1 tbsp. plain flour
2 cups salt-reduced beef stock
2 x 400g cans cherry tomatoes in juice
170g jar marinated artichoke pieces, drained
400g can cannellini beans, drained, rinsed
2 tbsp. lemon juice
1/4 cup fresh flat-leaf parsley leaves, to serve Steamed white rice, to serve

INSTRUCTIONS

•Heat oven to 350 F.
•Heat oil in a 10-cup-capacity flameproof baking dish over medium heat.
•Roast lamb chops, in batches, for 2 to 3 minutes each side or until browned all over. •Transfer to a plate.
•Add onion and carrot to dish.
•Cook, stirring, for 5 minutes or until onion is softened.
•Cook for 1 minute.
•Slowly add stock, stirring constantly, until smooth.
•Add tomato, artichoke, beans and lemon juice.
•Return chops to pan.
•Cover tightly with foil.
•Bake for 50 minutes.
•Remove foil and bake for another 20 minutes or until thickened.

Chicken Tetrazzini Casserole with Cauliflower

INGREDIENTS

Kosher salt
1 small head cauliflower
8 oz. extra-wide egg noodles, cooked
1 stick (8 tbsp.) butter
8 oz. assorted fresh mushrooms or white mushrooms, sliced
4 cloves garlic, finely chopped
1 large or 2 medium shallots, finely chopped
3 tbsp. all-purpose flour
1/2 cup dry sherry
2 cups chicken stock
1 cup heavy cream
Freshly ground pepper
Freshly grated nutmeg
3 to 4 cups shredded Poached Chicken Breasts, recipe follows
1 cup panko
1 cup grated Parmigiano-Reggiano
1/4 cup chopped fresh flat-leaf parsley
4 whole bone-in, skin-on chicken breasts (for all white meat) or 3 whole 4-pound chickens (for a mix of white and dark meat)
1 tbsp. whole black peppercorns
8 cloves garlic, smashed
4 large bay leaves
4 carrots, coarsely chopped
4 stalks celery, coarsely chopped
2 lemons, sliced
2 onions, quartered
Herb bundle of fresh parsley, rosemary and thyme tied with kitchen string

INSTRUCTIONS:

•Heat the oven to 400°F.
•Boil 1 1/2 cups of water with salt in a pot and then add the cauliflower, cover and steam until just tender for about 7 to 8 minutes. Drain and cut into florets.
•Heat 4 tablespoons butter in a large skillet over medium heat and then add the mushrooms and cook until tender and browned.
•Add the garlic and shallots and cook, stirring, for 2 to 3 minutes.
•Add the flour and cook, whisking, for 1 minute.

•Deglaze with the sherry, stirring and scraping up any browned bits with a wooden spoon. •Whisk in the chicken stock and bring to a boil.
•Reduce the heat to a simmer and cook for a few minutes, then stir in the heavy cream.
•Season with salt, pepper and a few grates of nutmeg.
•Combine the cauliflower, noodles, chicken and sauce and transfer to a casserole dish.
•Melt the remaining 4 tablespoons butter in small pan, then drizzle over the panko in a bowl and toss to combine.
•Add the Parmigiano-Reggiano, toss and sprinkle the breadcrumbs over the casserole.
•Bake until hot, bubbling and golden in about 40 to 45 minutes and then sprinkle with parsley.

Breakfast Casserole

INGREDIENTS

8 oz. spicy or sweet turkey sausage links, casings removed, meat crumbled
2 scallions, sliced
6 large eggs and 6 large egg whites
1 3/4 cups 1-percent milk
Kosher salt and freshly ground black pepper
One 9-oz. package frozen chopped spinach, thawed and drained of excess liquid
3/4 cup shredded Cheddar
1/2 cup grated Parmesan
1/2 whole wheat baguette, cut into 3/4-inch cubes (about 4 cups)
Cooking spray

INSTRUCTIONS

•Heat a large nonstick skillet over medium heat.
•Put the turkey and scallions and cook, stirring to break up any large chunks, until browned and cooked through, about 10 minutes.
•Take away from heat and let cool slightly.
•Beat the eggs, egg whites, milk and 1/2 teaspoon each salt and pepper in a large bowl until combined.
•Add the cooked sausage, spinach, cheeses and bread and toss to distribute ingredients evenly.
•Spray a 3-quart casserole dish with cooking spray.
•Spread the egg mixture evenly in the dish.

•Cover and refrigerate for at least 6 hours or preferably overnight.
•Heat the oven to 350 degrees Fahrenheit.
•Bake the casserole, uncovered, until set and lightly browned on top, about 30 minutes.

Chickpea Pumpkin Casserole

INGREDIENTS

1 cup dried chickpeas
1 tbsp. olive oil
2 medium red onions, cut into wedges
600g butternut pumpkin, chopped
1 garlic clove, crushed
4 sprigs fresh lemon thyme
1 1/2 cups Vegetable Stock Reduced Sodium
200g cherry tomatoes
100g baby spinach
4 slices mixed-grain low-GI bread and lemon wedges

INSTRUCTIONS

•Place chickpeas in a bowl and cover with cold water.
•Stand overnight in a cool place.
•Drain and rinse under cold water.
•Preheat oven to 350 F
•Place chickpeas in a saucepan and cover with cold water.
•Bring to the boil over high heat.
•Reduce heat to medium and let it simmer, covered, for 30 minutes or until tender.
•Drain and set aside.
•Heat oil in a large, heavy-based flameproof casserole dish over medium-high heat.
•Add onion and pumpkin and cook, stirring, for 10 minutes or until soft.
•Add garlic and thyme and stir to combine.
•Add chickpeas, stock and tomatoes.
•Bring to the boil.
•Roast for 30 minutes or until pumpkin and chickpeas are tender.
•Remove from oven.
•Stir in spinach.
•Serve with bread and lemon wedges.

Drumstick Pasta Casserole

INGREDIENTS

1 leek
1 onion
8 anchovy fillets (optional)
1 tbsp. picked rosemary leaves
1 tbsp. picked oregano leaves
1 red bird's-eye chilli
1/2 cup plain flour
8 chicken drumsticks
1/2 cup olive oil
5 sage leaves
3 cloves garlic
1 cup pitted kalamata olives
1/4 cup capers 2 bay leaves
1 cup dry white wine
2 cans diced tomatoes
1/3 cup tomato paste
1/2 bunch flat-leaf parsley, leaves picked,
Torn 500g risoni

INSTRUCTIONS

•Cut ingredients and take off the green part of the leek and discard.
•Cut lengthwise the remaining leek, then wash well in a bowl of cold water to remove any dirt.
•Thinly slice widthwise,
•Place flour and drumsticks in a large bowl and toss well to coat.
•Season with salt and pepper.
•Heat 2 tablespoons oil in a large, heavy-based frying pan over medium–high heat.
•Shake excess flour from 4 drumsticks.
•Add drumsticks to pan and cook, turning frequently, for 3 minutes or until browned all over.
•Place on a plate and set aside until needed.
•Repeat the process with another 2 tablespoons oil and remaining 4 drumsticks.
•Season drumsticks with salt and pepper.
•Heat remaining 2 tablespoons oil in a large casserole over high heat.
•Add chopped ingredients and sage.

•Crush garlic into pan, then stir for 5 minutes or until onion is softened.
•Add olives, capers, bay leaves and wine.
•Stir for 5 minutes or until liquid is reduced by half.
•Add (2 cups) water, chicken, tomatoes, paste and half the parsley.
•Stir to coat chicken. Bring to the boil.
•Reduce heat to low and stir occasionally for 40 minutes or until chicken is cooked through. •On the other hand, cook pasta by putting it in a boiled water and then add risoni and cook for 8 minutes or until al dente.
•Drain pasta through a large colander.
•Stir the remaining parsley into casserole.
•To serve, divide the risoni and drumsticks among bowls, then spoon over sauce.

Hot & Spicy Sausage Casserole

INGREDIENTS

2 packages (12 oz., each) Hot & Spicy Breakfast sausage
1 cup chopped green onions
1 sweet red bell pepper, chopped
1 can (4 oz.) diced mild green chilies
1/4 cup chopped fresh cilantro
1 package (30 oz.) frozen shredded hash brown potatoes
1 -1/2 cups shredded Cheddar cheese
12 eggs
1 cup milk
1/2 tsp. salt
1/8 tsp. pepper

INSTRUCTIONS

•Cook sausage according to package directions.
•Cut into ¼-inch slices and set aside.
•In a bowl, combine green onions, red pepper, chilies and cilantro and then set aside.
•Spray the interior of a 5 to 6 quart slow cooker with vegetable cooking spray.
•Layer one-third of the hash browns, sausage, green onion mixture and cheese into crock.

•Repeat layers twice.
•In a bowl, beat the eggs, milk, salt and pepper and pour over layered ingredients.
•Cover and cook on low heat for 7-8 hours or until thermometer inserted into the center reads 160°F.

Chicken with Bacon Casserole

INGREDIENTS

2 tbsps. Olive oil
40g butter
8 chicken thigh cutlets
2 medium leeks, trimmed, halved, washed, sliced
4 rashers middle bacon, trimmed, chopped
2 garlic cloves, crushed
2 tbsps. Fresh thyme leaves
1/2 cup dry white wine
1/4 cup plain flour
2 cups chicken stock
200g button mushrooms, quartered
Mashed potato, to serve

INSTRUCTIONS

•Heat oven to 350 F
•Cook 1 tablespoon oil and 20 g butter in a heavy-based, flameproof casserole dish over medium-high heat.
•Simmer chicken, in batches, for 5 to 6 minutes or until golden.
•Transfer to a bowl.
•Heat remaining oil and butter in dish.
•Add leek, bacon, garlic and thyme.
•Stirring and cook for 3 minutes or until leek has softened.
•Add wine and bring to a boil.
•Stir in flour and cook for 1 minute.
•Slowly add stock while stirring constantly.
•Return chicken to a dish and add mushrooms.
•Cover dish and bring to a boil.
•Transfer to oven and bake for 1 hour.
•Remove lid and bake, uncovered, for 30 minutes or until chicken is tender.
•Serve with mashed potato.

Yummy Lamb Casserole

INGREDIENTS:

1 tbsp. olive oil
4 lamb leg chops
1 small bunch spring onions, trimmed
200g small button mushrooms
400g can chopped tomatoes
1/4 cup dry red wine
2 tbsp. tomato paste
2 tbsp. chopped fresh flat-leaf parsley leaves
1/3 cup pitted black olives
Soft polenta, to serve

INSTRUCTIONS:

•Heat oil in a saucepan over medium-high heat.
•Cook lamb, in 2 batches, for 2 minutes each side or until browned.
•Remove from pan.
•Add onions and mushrooms to pan.
•Cook and stirring it for 2 minutes or until lightly browned.
•Return lamb to pan and then add tomato, wine and tomato paste.
•Bring to the boil and reduce heat to low.
•Simmer, covered, for 5 minutes.
•Remove lid and let it simmer, uncovered, for 5 minutes or until sauce has thickened slightly.
•Stir through parsley and olives.
•Serve with soft polenta.

Mexican Chili Beef Rice Casserole

INGREDIENTS

2 tbsps. olive oil
750g gravy beef, trimmed, cut into 3cm cubes
1 large brown onion, finely chopped
2 garlic cloves, crushed
1 medium red capsicum, thinly sliced
2 tbsps. Plain flour
1 tbsp. Mexican chili powder
1/2 teaspoon ground coriander
1 cup Beef Stock
400g can no-added-salt chopped tomatoes
400g can no-added-salt red kidney beans, drained, rinsed
Steamed doongara rice and fresh
Coriander leaves, to serve

INSTRUCTIONS

•Heat oven to 350 F.
•Heat half the oil in a large, heavy-based, flameproof casserole dish over medium-high heat. •Brown the beef, in batches, for 5 to 6 minutes and transfer to a bowl.
•Heat remaining oil in dish and then add onion, garlic and capsicum.
•Cook and stirring it for 5 minutes or until onion has softened.
•Return beef to dish and add flour, chili and ground coriander.
•Cook and stirring it for another 1 minute.
•Blending in stock, tomato and 1 cup cold water and then cover the dish.
•Bring to a boil.
•Transfer to oven and then bake for 1 hour and 30 minutes.
•Remove from oven.
•Stir in kidney beans.
•Bake for 30 minutes or until beef is tender.
•Serve with rice and coriander.

Hot & Spicy Pork Meatball Casserole

INGREDIENTS

500g pork mince
1 egg
1/2 cup fresh breadcrumbs
1/2 teaspoon smoked paprika
Olive oil cooking spray
1 medium brown onion, finely chopped
1 medium red capsicum, chopped
2 garlic cloves, crushed
1 long red chili, finely chopped
2 tsp. ground cumin
400g can chopped tomatoes
100g baby spinach
Couscous, to serve

INSTRUCTIONS

•Combine pork mince, egg, breadcrumbs and paprika in a bowl.
•Roll into 16 balls.
•Grease saucepan with oil and then heat over medium-high heat.
•Put and meatballs, in batches, for 4 to 5 minutes or until browned.
•Transfer to a plate.
•Add onion to pan and cook while stirring for 3 to 4 minutes or until softened.
•Add capsicum, garlic and chili and then cook by stirring it for 2 to 3 minutes or until capsicum has softened.
•Stir in the cumin for 1 minute or until fragrant.
•Add tomato and 3/4 cup cold water and return meatballs to pan.
•Bring it to a boil by reducing the heat to low.
•Simmer, uncovered, for 15 to 20 minutes or until meatballs are cooked through.
•Stir in spinach and cook, covered, for 2 to 3 minutes or until spinach wilts.
•Serve with couscous.

Chicken with Saffron Rice Casserole

INGREDIENTS

1.8kg whole fresh chicken, rinse and pat dried
2 tablespoons olive oil
2 (about 180g) chorizo, thinly sliced
1 large red capsicum, halved, deseeded, cut into 2cm pieces
1 red onion, coarsely chopped
80ml (1/3 cup) dry sherry
2 x 400g cans diced tomatoes
185ml (3/4 cup) chicken stock
2 tsp. dried oregano leaves
Saffron rice, to serve
Fresh oregano leaves, to serve

INSTRUCTIONS

- Warm oven to 250 F
- Place the chicken, breast-side down, on a clean work surface.
- Use poultry shears to cut along either side of the backbone and discard.
- Cut the breast in half along the breastbone.
- Use a sharp knife to cut around the legs, between the thigh and the breast.
- Cut the drumsticks from the thighs.
- Cut the wings from the breasts and cut the breasts in half diagonally.
- Remove any excess skin.
- Heat the oil in a flameproof casserole dish or large frying pan over medium heat.
- Add half the chicken and cook for 4 minutes each side or until golden.
- Transfer to a large plate.
- Repeat with remaining chicken, reheating the dish between batches.
- Add the chorizo, capsicum and onion to the dish.
- Cook, stirring often, for 10 minutes or until chorizo is golden.
- Add the sherry and cook, stirring, for 2 minutes or until reduced by half.
- Transfer the chorizo mixture to a casserole dish, if necessary.
- Add the chicken, tomato, stock and dried oregano.
- Cover and bake in oven for 1 hour or until the chicken is tender.
- Divide the rice among serving dishes and top with the chicken mixture.

•Sprinkle with fresh oregano to serve.

Lambcashire Casserole

INGREDIENTS:

1 tablespoon olive oil
20g butter
4 (200g each) lamb forequarter chops
2 medium brown onions, sliced
2 medium carrots, peeled, sliced
4 sprigs fresh thyme
2 tbsps. Plain flour
2 dried bay leaves
3 cups Beef Stock
1 tbsp. Worcestershire sauce
2 medium Desiree potatoes, peeled, thinly sliced
20g butter, melted
Parsley leaves, freshly cut

INSTRUCTIONS:

•Heat oven 350 F.
•Boil oil and butter in a 24cm (base) round, heavy-based, flameproof casserole dish over medium-high heat.
•Cook lamb chops, in batches, for 2 to 3 minutes each side or until browned.
•Transfer to a plate.
•Add onion, carrot and thyme.
•Cook, stirring, for 4 to 5 minutes or until onion has softened.
•Add flour and cook while stirring for 1 minute.
•Add bay leaves.
•Stir in stock and Worcestershire sauce.
•Return lamb chops to pan.
•Remove it from heat.
•Arrange potatoes in an overlapping pattern on top.
•Cover the dish and bake for 1 hour and 30 minutes.
•Remove from oven.
•Increase temperature to 420 F.
•Brush potatoes with melted butter.
•Bake, uncovered, for 30 minutes or until potatoes are golden and lamb chops are tender. •Discard bay leaves and thyme sprigs.

•Serve sprinkled with parsley.

Yellow Fin Tuna Casserole

INGREDIENTS

2 tbsps. Olive oil
1 leek (white part only), thinly sliced
1 carrot, finely chopped
1 celery stalk, finely chopped
400g can chopped tomatoes
2 x 400g cans cannellini beans, rinsed
200g chicken or vegetable stock
1 tbsp. Dijon mustard
2 x 200g yellow fin tuna fillets
1 cup (50g) panko breadcrumbs
1 garlic clove, crushed
1 tbsp. finely chopped flat-leaf parsley

INSTRUCTIONS

•Heat 1 tablespoon oil in a pan over medium-low heat.
•Cook leek, carrot and celery for 10 minutes while stirring it until softened.
•Add tomato, beans and stock and let it simmer over medium heat for 20 minutes.
•Slightly reduced heat and then stir in mustard.
•Preheat the oven to 420 F.
•Lightly oil 4 individual baking dishes or ramekins.
•Heat it over high heat.
•Sear tuna for 1 minute each side.
•Cut into bite-sized pieces.
•Layer beans, then tuna, then more beans in the dishes.
•Mix panko, garlic, parsley and 1 tablespoon oil, then sprinkle on top.
•Bake for 20 minutes or until golden and bubbling.
•Serve with a salad.

Speedy Chicken And Mushroom Casserole

INGREDIENTS

2 tsps. Alfa One rice bran oil
400g diced chicken breast
1 medium brown onion, chopped
2 rashers middle bacon, trimmed, chopped
250g button mushrooms, quartered
1/4 cup plain flour
1 tbsp. Dijon mustard
1 cup chicken stock
1/2 cup thickened cream
2 tbsps. Chopped fresh flat-leaf parsley

INSTRUCTIONS

• In a large frying pan, boil oil over medium-high heat.
•Add chicken and cook while stirring slowly for 5 minutes or until golden.
•Transfer to a plate.
•Add onion and bacon to pan and stirring for 3 to 4 minutes or until onion has softened.
•Add mushroom and cook for another 2 minutes or until mushroom has started to soften. •Stir in flour and mustard and cook for 2 minutes.
•Gradually stir in stock and bring to a boil.
•Return chicken to pan.
•Cover and reduce heat to low.
•Simmer for 15 minutes or until chicken is cooked through.
•Add cream and season with salt and pepper.
•Cook, without boiling, for 3 minutes or until heated through.
•Sprinkle some parsley and serve.

Port And Orange Braised Beef

INGREDIENTS:

1 1/2 tbsp. olive oil
800g chuck steak, trimmed, cut into 4cm pieces
1 brown onion, halved, cut into thin wedges
2 garlic cloves, thinly sliced
1 cup port
1 1/2 cups salt-reduced chicken stock
3 large sprigs fresh rosemary
3 dried bay leaves
2 strips orange rind, pith removed
1/4 cup chopped fresh flat-leaf parsley leaves
Mashed potato, to serve

INSTRUCTIONS:

•Heat 1 tablespoon oil in a large, heavy-based flameproof casserole dish over high heat. •Season and brown the beef, in batches, stirring for 5 minutes.
•Transfer to a bowl.
•Add remaining oil to the dish and add onion.
•Cook, stirring, for 5 minutes or until onion has softened.
•Add garlic and cook while stirring it for 1 minute.
•Add port and simmer, stirring, for 3 minutes.
•Return beef to dish.
•Add chicken stock, rosemary, bay leaves and orange rind.
•Reduce heat to low.
•Cook, partially covered, for 2 hours or until beef is tender and the liquid is reduced.
•Remove and discard rosemary and bay leaves.
•Season with salt and pepper.
•Stir in parsley and serve with mashed potato.

Beef and Lamb with Veggies Casserole

INGREDIENTS

2 tbsps. Olive oil
1.5kg diced lamb
2 medium brown onions, chopped
2 medium carrots, peeled, chopped
2 celery stalks, chopped
2 garlic cloves, crushed
2 cups Beef Stock
2 x 400g cans diced tomatoes
500g orange sweet potato, peeled, cut into 2cm pieces
250g cauliflower florets
1 1/2 cups couscous
20g butter, chopped
1 1/2 cups boiling water
1/4 cup chopped fresh flat-leaf parsley leaves

INSTRUCTIONS

•Heat half of the oil in a large heavy-based saucepan over medium-high heat.
•Sous-chef lamb, in batches, rousing, for 3 minutes or until browned.
•Transfer to a bowl.
•Heat the remaining oil in a pan and then add onion, carrot and celery.
•Stirring it for 5 minutes or until vegetables are just tender.
•Add garlic and let it simmer for 1 minute or until fragrant.
•Stir in stock, tomatoes, lamb and other juices to pan.
•Bring it to a boil and then reduce heat to make it simmer for 1 hour.
•Add sweet potato and cook for 10 minutes or until almost tender.
•Add cauliflower and cook for another 10 minutes or until tender.
•Season the casserole.
•Place couscous and butter in a large heatproof bowl.
•Stir in boiling water.
•Cover and set aside for 5 minutes.
•Use a fork to fluff and separate grains.
•Spooned half of the casserole and sprinkle over couscous with some parsley.
•Allow remaining casserole to cool.
•Spoon into an airtight container and refrigerate until required.

Tasty Vegetable and Fish Fillet Casserole

INGREDIENTS:

Olive oil cooking spray
1 brown onion, halved, thinly sliced
350g orange sweet potato, peeled, cut into 2cm pieces
2 small zucchini, cut into 1cm pieces
200g broccoli, trimmed, cut into florets
1 small (250g) eggplant, diced
800g can diced tomatoes
1/3 cup fresh oregano leaves
500g white fish fillets, cut into large pieces
1 small white bread stick, sliced, toasted

INSTRUCTIONS:

•Heat oil in a heavy-based saucepan over medium heat.
•Add onion while stirring it for 2 minutes or until golden.
•Add sweet potato and cook while stirring for 3 minutes.
•Add zucchini, broccoli, eggplant, tomatoes and 1/4 cup oregano.
•Bring to boil.
•Cover and cook for 8 to 10 minutes or until sweet potato is tender.
•Stir in fish and simmer, uncovered it for 4 to 5 minutes or until fish is cooked through.
•Sprinkle with remaining oregano.
•Serve casserole with toasted bread.

Beef with Parsley Dumplings Casserole

INGREDIENTS:

1/4 cup plain flour
1kg beef chuck steak, diced
1/4 cup olive oil
3 pickling onions, quartered
2 garlic cloves, crushed
2 cups Beef Stock
410g can crushed tomatoes
2 carrots, peeled, sliced
2 parsnips, peeled, halved, cut into 2cm pieces
1 swede, peeled, cut into 2cm pieces
3 celery stalks, sliced
Parsley dumplings
1 1/2 cups self-rising flour, sifted
1/2 cup plain flour, sifted
2 tablespoons finely chopped fresh flat-leaf parsley leaves
3/4 cup milk
60g butter, melted

INSTRUCTIONS:

•Heat oven to 325 F
•Place flour and beef in a snap-lock bag.
•Season with salt and pepper.
•Shake to coat.
•Heat 2 tablespoons oil in a heavy-based, ovenproof casserole dish over medium-high heat. •Cook beef, in batches, for 3 to 4 minutes or until browned and transfer to a plate.
•Add remaining oil to dish.
•Add onions and garlic.
•Cook for 4 to 5 minutes or until tender.
•Return beef to dish with stock, tomato, carrot, parsnip, swede and celery and bring it to a boil.
•Cover with lid and transfer to oven.
•Bake for 1 hour and 30 minutes or until meat is tender.
•Meanwhile, make dumplings by combining flours and parsley in a jug.
•Make a hole in the center and then add milk and butter.
•Stir to form a soft dough.
•Roll mixture into 12 dumplings.

•Arrange dumplings over beef mixture.
•Bake, covered, for 20 to 25 minutes or until dumplings are cooked through.

Steamed Rice, Bok-Choy and Beefy casserole

INGREDIENTS:

1 tbsp. olive oil
1 kg beef chuck steak, cut into 3cm pieces
1 bunch spring onions, ends trimmed, green ends reserved
2 garlic cloves, crushed
4 cups Beef Stock
1/2 cup (125ml) shaoxing wine (or dry sherry)
1/4 cup (60ml) dark soy sauce
1/4 cup (60ml) light soy sauce
4 whole star anise
2 cinnamon quills
4 strips orange rind
1/4 cup (60g) white sugar
150g pun net oyster mushrooms, ends trimmed, coarsely torn
1 bunch baby bok choy, quartered lengthways
5cm piece fresh ginger, peeled, cut into matchsticks
1 tsp. sesame oil
Steamed Sun Rice and Jasmine Fragrant Rice, to serve

INSTRUCTIONS:

•Heat oven to 300 F.
•Boil half the oil in a large flameproof casserole pan over medium-high heat.
•Add one-quarter of the beef and cook, turning occasionally, for 5 minutes or until brown all over.
•Transfer it to a bowl.
•Repeat in 3 more batches with remaining beef, reheating pan between each batch.
•Heat remaining oil in pan and add the spring onions and garlic and cook, stirring, for 5 minutes or until onion softens.
•Add the beef, beef stock, shozing wine, combined soy sauces, star anise, cinnamon, orange rind and sugar and bring to a simmer.
•Remove from heat.
•Bake in preheated oven, loosely covered and stirring occasionally, for 1 1/2-2 hours or until beef is tender and sauce thickens slightly.

•Add the mushrooms and cook for a further 10 minutes or until mushrooms are tender.
•Add the bok choy and ginger and remove from heat.
•Meanwhile, use a small sharp knife to diagonally thinly slice the reserved green onion tops.
•Spoon the beef casserole among serving bowls.
•Top with green onion and drizzle with sesame oil.
•Serve with steamed jasmine rice, if desired.

Simple Beef Casserole

INGREDIENTS:

1 tbsp. olive oil
1kg beef chuck steak, cut into 3cm pieces
2 brown onions, coarsely chopped
2 celery sticks, coarsely chopped
1 carrot, peeled, coarsely chopped
2 garlic cloves, crushed
2 tbsp. plain flour
1 cup (250ml) dry red wine
2 cups (500ml) Beef Stock
1 x 400g can chopped tomatoes
1 bouquet garni

INSTRUCTIONS:

•Preheat oven to 300 F
•Heat half the oil in a large flameproof casserole pan over medium-high heat.
•Add one-quarter of the beef and cook, turning occasionally, for 5 minutes or until brown all over.
•Transfer it to a bowl.
•Repeat in 3 more batches with remaining beef, reheating pan between each batch.
•Heat remaining oil in pan and add the onion, celery, carrot and garlic and cook, stirring, for 5 minutes or until onion softens.
•Scatter the flour over the vegetable mixture and stir to combine.
•Cook, stirring, for 2 minutes or until well combined.
•Add the beef and red wine and bring to a boil.
•Cook while stirring it for 2 minutes or until wine reduces by half.

•Add the beef stock, tomatoes and bouquet garni and bring to a simmer.
•Remove from heat.
•Bake in preheated oven, loosely covered, stirring occasionally, for 1 1/2-2 hours or until beef is tender and sauce thickens slightly.
•Taste and season with salt and pepper.
•Serve with mashed potato, if desired.

Crispy Pontiac Potato Topping in Beef and Bacon Casserole

INGREDIENTS:

1/4 cup (40g) plain flour
1kg beef chuck steak, cut into 3cm pieces
50g butter
1 tbsp. olive oil
12 pickling onions, peeled
250g button mushrooms
100g piece speck, cut into 1cm pieces
4 garlic cloves, crushed
2 cups (500ml) dry red wine
2 cups (500ml) Beef Stock
2 tbsp. tomato paste
4 sprigs thyme
1 dried bay leaf
80g butter, melted
2 garlic cloves, crushed
2 tsp. thyme leaves
4 Pontiac potatoes, thinly sliced
Steamed green beans, to serve

INSTRUCTIONS:

•Preheat oven to 325 F
•Put the flour in a large bowl and season with salt and pepper.
•Add the beef and gently toss to lightly coat.
•Heat half the butter and oil in a flameproof casserole dish over high heat.
•Add one-quarter of the meat and coo, turning, for 5 minutes or until brown all over. •Transfer to a plate.
•Repeat in batches with the remaining beef.
•Boil the remaining butter and oil in the pan.

•Add onions and mushrooms and then cook, stirring occasionally for 5 minutes or until onions are golden brown.
•Add speck and garlic, then cook for 2 more minutes or until heated through.
•Return beef to the pan and pour over the wine, stock and tomato paste.
•Bring to a simmer and remove from heat.
•Add the thyme and bay leaf.
•Bake, covered, for 2 hours or until beef is tender.
•Remove from oven and increase heat to 400 F.
•Season with salt and pepper.
•Combine butter, garlic and thyme in a bowl.
•Add the potato and toss to combine.
•Season with salt and pepper.
•Arrange potato evenly over the beef mixture.
•Bake, uncovered, for 30 minutes or until potato is golden brown and tender.
•Serve immediately with green beans.

Delicious Lamb and Chicken Stock Casserole

INGREDIENTS:

2.2kg leg of lamb, boned, fat trimmed, cut into 6cm pieces
2 tablespoons olive oil
3 garlic cloves, thinly sliced
185ml (3/4 cup) white wine
250ml (1 cup) chicken stock
125ml (1/2 cup) red wine vinegar
4 large fresh sage sprigs
4 large fresh rosemary sprigs
1/4 teaspoon dried chili flakes
3 drained anchovy fillets, finely chopped
300g (2 cups) frozen broad beans, thawed, peeled
Roast potatoes, to serve

INSTRUCTIONS:

•Season the lamb with salt.
•Heat the oil in a flameproof casserole dish over high heat and cook the lamb, in 2 batches, for 5 minutes or until browned.
•Transfer to a plate.
•Add the garlic to the dish.
•Cook and stirring it for 1 minute or until aromatic.
•Add wine and cook, scraping the dish with a flat-edged wooden spoon to dislodge any bits that have cooked onto the base, for 1 minute.
•Add the lamb, chicken stock and vinegar.
•Bring to a boil and then reduce heat to low.
•Add the sage, rosemary and chili flakes.
•Season with pepper and then cover and cook for 1 1/2 hours while stirring occasionally until the lamb is tender.
•Transfer the lamb to a plate by using a slotted spoon.
•Increase heat to high and add the anchovy.
•Let it simmer for 7 minutes or until the liquid reduces by a quarter.
•Add the lamb and broad beans.
•Cook for 3 minutes or until warmed through.
•Serve with potatoes.

Chili Beef Casserole with Mashed Potato

INGREDIENT:

40g (1/4 cup) plain flour
Salt & freshly ground black pepper
800g gravy beef or casserole steak, cut into 3cm cubes
60ml (1/4 cup) vegetable oil
1 brown onion, halved, coarsely chopped
1 garlic clove, crushed
250ml (1 cup) dry red wine
375ml (11/2 cups) Beef Stock
375ml (11/2 cups) tomato pasta sauce
100g pitted kalamata olives
2 tsp. finely grated orange rind
1/4 tsp. allspice
1/4 tsp. dried chili flakes
1/4 cup loosely packed coarsely chopped fresh continental parsley
Mashed potato
1kg Sebago (washed) potatoes, peeled, cut into 2cm cubes
160ml (2/3 cup) milk
50g butter
Pinch of salt

INSTRUCTIONS:

•Heat oven to 350 F.
•Put the flour in a large bowl, mix with salt and pepper.
•Add the beef and gently toss in the flour mixture to evenly coat.
•Heat 1 tablespoon of oil in a 2L (8-cup) capacity flame-proof, ovenproof casserole dish over medium heat.
•Add half of the beef and cook while stirring occasionally for about 5 minutes or until brown.
•Transfer the browned beef to a bowl.
•Repeat with another 1 tablespoon of oil and the remaining beef.
•Boil the remaining oil in the same dish over medium-high heat.
•Add the onion and garlic and then cook by stirring it for 4-5 minutes or until onion softens.
•Mix the beef and stir to combine.
•Add the wine, stock, tomato pasta sauce, olives, orange rind, allspice and chili, and bring to a boil.
•Remove from heat and cover with a tight-fitting lid.
•Bake in heated oven for 2 hours or until beef is tender.

•Remove from oven.
•Put in the parsley and taste, season with salt and pepper.
•In the meantime, to make mashed potato, place potato in a large saucepan and cover with cold water.
•Bring to a boil over medium-high heat.
•Cook, uncovered, for 25 minutes or until tender.
•Drain and return to pan.
•Add milk and butter.
•Use a potato masher or fork to mash until smooth and then add seasoning to taste.
•Serve the casserole with the mashed potato.

Bacon Beef topped with Mashed Potato Casserole

INGREDIENTS:

2 tbsp. olive oil
4 bacon rashers, rind and excess fat trimmed, chopped
1 large brown onion, chopped
2 garlic cloves, finely chopped
1kg beef chuck steak, trimmed, cut into 3cm cubes
2 tbsps. Plain flour
250ml (1 cup) dry red wine
375ml (1 1/2 cups) Beef Stock
1 x 400g can peeled whole tomatoes, un-drained, mashed
3 (about 300g) carrots, peeled, diagonally sliced
Salt & freshly ground black pepper
1/2 cup chopped fresh continental parsley
Boiled potatoes or mashed potato, to serve

INSTRUCTIONS:

•Heat oven to 325 F.
•Burn oil in a large, heavy-based ovenproof saucepan or flameproof casserole dish with a lid over medium-low heat.
•Put the bacon and onion and then cook, uncovered while stirring occasionally for 5 minutes or until the onion is softened.
•Stir in the garlic for a minute or until it gives fragrance.
•Transfer the bacon mixture to a plate and set aside.
•Heat half of the remaining oil in the pan over medium-high heat.
•Brown half of the beef and cook, tossing occasionally for 1-2 minutes.
•Sprinkle the beef with half of the flour and cook for another minute.

•Transfer the beef to a plate and set aside.
•Repeat with the remaining oil, beef and flour.
•Add the wine to the pan and bring to a boil over medium-high heat.
•Cook, using a flat-bottomed wooden spoon to scrape the base of the pan to dislodge any bits that have cooked onto it for 1 minute (this is called deglazing and will add color and flavor to the casserole).
•Return the bacon mixture and the beef to the pan.
•Add the stock, mashed tomatoes and carrots, and stir to combine.
•Bring to a boil over high heat.
•Cover the pan and cook in preheated oven for 2 hours or until the beef is very tender. •Remove the pan from the oven and use a large metal spoon to skim any excess fat from the surface of the casserole.
•Season with salt and pepper, and stir in the parsley.
•Serve with boiled potatoes or mashed potato.

Cabbage Rolls with Beef

INGREDIENT

2/3 cup long-grain rice, cooked (2 cups)
1 tbsp. (20g) butter
1 medium brown onion, finely diced
2 cups diced celery
4 middle bacon rashers, finely diced (about 1 cup)
1 tbsp. finely diced garlic (about 4 cloves)
2 x 500g packets beef mince
1 tablespoon chopped fresh thyme
1/2 cup chopped parsley
1/4 cup pine nuts
1 cup grated parmesan cheese
2 tsps. Sea salt
1 tsp. black pepper
1 large green drumhead cabbage
1400ml tomato Passata
2 tbsps. Sour cream

INSTRUCTIONS

•Place large frying pan over medium heat.
•Add butter and let it melt.
•Add onion, celery and bacon and cook for 5 minutes.
•Add garlic and cook for another 2 minutes and set aside.

•Mix tomato passata with about 2 cups of boiling water, mix and pour over the cabbage rolls, immersing them completely in the liquid.
•Top with extra cabbage leaves.
•Place lid on casserole dish, place in oven and bake for at least 60 minutes to around 90 minutes.
•The cabbage leaves should be really soft when they are ready.
•Place beef mince in a large mixing bowl, add thyme, parsley, pine nuts, parmesan, rice, the onion and bacon mixture, then season with the salt and pepper.
•Mix until combine well.
•Set mixture aside.
•Heat fan-forced oven to 350 F.
•Place a large stockpot filled 2/3rds with water over high heat and bring to the boil.
•Place cabbage on flat surface and remove core by taking a paring knife and deeply cutting around the edge of the core in a square shape and then remove core.
•Blanch cabbage in boiling water.
•Reserve the tough outer leaves to line a large casserole dish.
•Line large casserole dish with tough outer leaves.
•Place a cabbage leaf on a flat surface, take about 1/2 cup of mince mixture and form a log at the base of the leaf then roll in edges and roll the leaf onto itself to enclose mixture completely.
•Make 12 rolls and then place in the casserole dish.
•To serve, mix 2 cups of tomato juice with sour cream.
•Pour a little tomato juice over cabbage rolls, garnish with extra parsley and serve warm.

Chive Dumplings in Beef Burgundy

INGREDIENTS:

2 tbsp. olive oil
1.5kg diced beef chuck steak
200g shortcut rindless bacon, halved lengthways, cut into 1cm strips
2 garlic cloves, finely chopped
3 medium brown onions, quartered
1 cup red wine
1/2 cup Beef Stock
1 tbsp. tomato paste
300g button mushrooms, halved
Chive dumplings
1 cup self-rising flour
50g butter, softened
2 tsp. chopped fresh chives
2 tsp. chopped fresh flat-leaf parsley leaves
1/2 cup buttermilk

INSTRUCTIONS:

•Warm oil in a large heavy-based, flameproof casserole dish over medium-high heat.
•Cook beef, in batches, for 5 to 6 minutes or until browned and then transfer to a bowl.
•Reduce heat to medium and boil remaining oil in dish.
•Add bacon and garlic and then cook, stirring, for 5 minutes or until bacon is golden.
•Return the beef and juices to dish and add onion and wine.
•Bring to a boil and then add stock and paste.
•Reduce heat to low and let it simmer, covered, for 1 hour and 15 minutes.
•Add mushrooms and then cook with cover for a further 15 minutes or until meat and mushrooms are tender.
•Season with salt and pepper.
•Meanwhile, prepare the Chive dumplings by putting the flour in a bowl.
•Add butter into flour until mixture resembles fine breadcrumbs. Make a small hole in the center of mixture.
•Put chives, parsley and buttermilk.
•Season with salt and pepper.

•Stir until just combined.
•Place a little of the mixture, 2cm apart with the beef mixture.
•Cook, covered, for another 15 minutes or until dumplings are puffed and cooked through.

Beef Brisket in Whipped Horseradish

INGREDIENTS:

2 tbsp. olive oil
1.5kg corned beef brisket, uncooked
2 onions, sliced
2 garlic cloves, finely chopped
2 tbsps. Tomato paste
100ml tomato sauce (ketchup)
100g dark brown sugar
1 tsp. onion powder
2 tsp. smoked paprika (pimenton)
2 cups (500ml) chicken stock
6 carrots, roughly chopped
1 tbsp. chopped chives
50g unsalted butter
800g Desiree potatoes, chopped
1/2 cup (125ml) milk
1 1/2 tbsp. horseradish cream

INSTRUCTIONS:

•Preheat the oven to 325 F
•Heat oil in a casserole over medium-high heat.
•Season the brisket and then cook by turning both sides for about 8-10 minutes or until browned.
•Remove from pan and set aside.
•Cook onion in the heated pan with oil by stirring it for 3-4 minutes or until softened. •Reduce heat to medium and then add the garlic to make aromatic flavor.
•Add the tomato paste, tomato sauce, brown sugar, onion powder and paprika, then cook, stirring, for a further 1-2 minutes until well combined.
•Add the stock and bring to a simmer.
•Return brisket to the casserole, fat-side up.
•Cover surface with baking paper, then cover with a lid and bake for 3-3 1/2 hours until tender.

•Meanwhile, place the carrot in a pan of cold, salted water and let it boil.
•Simmer for another 10-15 minutes or until tender.
•Drain, then toss with chives and half of the butter.
•Set aside and keep warm.
•Place potato in a separate pan of cold, salted water.
•Bring to the boil, then simmer for 15-20 minutes until tender.
•Drain and return to pan.
•Heat gently, stirring, to remove any excess water and mash potato until smooth.
•Add the milk, horseradish cream and remaining 25g butter.
•Season and stir until smooth.
•Remove the brisket and the rest of the dish, loosely covered with foil, for 10 minutes. •Return casserole to medium-high heat and cook onion sauce for another 5 minutes or until thickened.
•Shred the brisket into thick slices and divide among plates with the horseradish mash and carrots and top with the onion sauce to serve.

Beef and Plum Casserole with Steamed Broccoli

INGREDIENTS:

2 tablespoons olive oil
750g gravy beef, trimmed, cut into 3cm cubes
1 large brown onion, finely chopped
2 garlic cloves, crushed
2 medium carrots, peeled, halved, sliced
3 medium parsnips, peeled, chopped
2 tablespoons plain flour
2 dried bay leaves
4 sprigs fresh rosemary
1 tablespoon Worcestershire sauce
1/2 cup plum jam
2 1/2 cups Beef Stock
Steamed broccoli, to serve

INSTRUCTIONS:

•Warm oven to 350 F.
•Heat half of the oil in a large, heavy-based, flameproof casserole dish over medium-high heat.

•Brown the beef, in batches, for 5 to 6 minutes and then transfer it to a bowl.
•Heat remaining oil in dish and add onion, garlic, carrot and parsnip.
•Cook while stirring gradually for 5 minutes or until onion has softened.
•Return beef to dish and flour.
•Cook, stirring, for 1 minute and then add bay leaves and rosemary.
•Stir in Worcestershire sauce, plum jam and stock.
•Cover dish and bring to a boil.
•Transfer to oven and bake for 2 hours or until beef is tender.
•Remove and discard bay leaves.
•Serve with broccoli.

Moroccan Spice Beef and Pear Tagine

INGREDIENTS:

2/3 cup honey
1 large lemon, juiced
2 firm pears, cores removed, cut into thick wedges
1 tsp. ground cinnamon
1 tsp. ground allspice
2 tbsp. olive oil
2kg chuck steak, cut into 3cm cubes
2 brown onions, finely chopped
2 garlic cloves, crushed
3cm piece fresh ginger, peeled, grated
3 to 4 tbsp. Master foods Moroccan Spice Blend
20g butter

INSTRUCTIONS:

•Combine 1 1/2 cups cold water, honey, 1/4 cup lemon juice, pears, cinnamon and all spice in a saucepan over medium-high heat.
•Bring to a boil.
•Reduce heat to medium and let it simmer, uncovered, for 25 minutes or until pears are tender.
•Allow to cool and then drain, reserving the liquid.
•Set pears aside.
•Preheat oven to 350 F.
•Heat 1 tablespoon oil in a heavy-based saucepan over high heat.

•Brown the steak, in batches, for 3 minutes adding more oil as required.
•Transfer to a large plate.
•Reduce heat to medium and add onion to pan.
•Cook, stirring, for 5 minutes or until soft.
•Add garlic, ginger and spice to blend.
•Cook, stirring, for 1 minute.
•Return steak to pan with 1 1/3 cups reserved pear syrup.
•Bring to the boil.
•Transfer tagine to an ovenproof casserole dish and cover with a lid.
•Place in oven and cook for 1 1/2 hours.
•Meanwhile, heat butter in a non-stick frying pan over medium-low heat.
•Add pears and cook for 2 to 3 minutes each side or until golden.
•Remove tagine from oven and stir in pears.
•Return to oven and cook, uncovered, for 25 minutes or until steak is tender.
•Serve with pumpkin and chickpea salad and Moroccan bread.

Stock Beef, Potato and Mushroom Casserole

INGREDIENTS:

2 tbsp. olive oil
1 large onion, chopped
4 (500g) large Portobello mushrooms, sliced
1.3 kg gravy beef or boar blade roast, cut into chunks
10 small new potatoes, halved
2 cloves garlic, crushed
190g jar of sun-dried tomato or basil pesto
1 1/3 cups (330ml) Beef Stock
Salt & freshly ground pepper
Sour cream, to serve
Crusty bread, to serve

INSTRUCTIONS:

•Warm oven to 350 F
•Heat 1 tablespoon oil in a large heavy-based pan.
•Add onion and cook for 3-4 minutes or until golden.
•Add mushrooms and cook over high heat until browned.
•Take away the mushroom from the pan and set aside.

•Heat remaining oil and brown the meat in batches.
•Transfer to an ovenproof casserole dish.
•Add half the potatoes, mushrooms and onions.
•Spread over garlic.
•Top with remaining meat, potatoes and mushrooms.
•Add stock to pan and scrape base.
•Stir in pesto and let it simmer for 1 minute.
•Pour over and season the casserole.
•Cover and bake for 2 hours.
•Uncover, bake for 30 minutes more until tender.
•Serve topped with sour cream.

Beef and Carrots with Pasta Ragout

INGREDIENTS

1/4 cup plain flour
1kg gravy beef, cut into 5cm cubes
1/4 cup olive oil
2 large brown onions, cut into wedges
2 garlic cloves, crushed
1/2 cup tomato paste
1/2 cup red wine
1 cup Beef Stock
3 sprigs thyme
3 large carrots, peeled, roughly chopped
Cooked pappardelle pasta, to serve

INSTRUCTIONS

•Put flour in a snap-lock bag.
•Flavor with salt and pepper.
•Add beef and shake bag to lightly coat beef in flour and shaking off excess.
•Heat 1 tablespoon oil in a large frying pan over medium-high heat.
•Add half of the beef.
•Cook, stirring occasionally, for 3 to 5 minutes or until browned.
•Spoon into slow cooker and repeat the process with oil and the remaining beef.
•Reduce frying pan heat to medium.
•Add remaining oil and onion to pan.
•Cook, stirring often, for 2 minutes or until soft.

•Add garlic and tomato paste. Cook for 1 minute.
•Pour in wine and bring to a boil.
•Simmer, uncovered, for 5 minutes or until wine has reduced by half.
•Add stock beef, thyme and carrots and bring to a boil.
•Spoon sauce over beef and stir to combine.
•Cover and cook on high heat for up to 4 hours or in low heat for 6 hours.
•Season with salt and pepper.
•Spoon over pasta and serve.

Stuffed Beef Casserole

INGREDIENTS:

1 1/2 tablespoons olive oil
750g round steak, trimmed, cubed
1/4 cup seasoned flour
1 leek, trimmed, washed and sliced
1 clove garlic, crushed
1 tablespoon ground cumin
2 teaspoons ground ginger
2 cups salt-reduced beef stock
6 carrots (or 12 dutch carrots), cut into wedges
400g can diced tomatoes
1/2 cup stuffed green olives
1/4 cup preserved lemon, chopped
1/2 cup parsley, chopped
1/2 cup coriander leaves
Brown rice, to serve
Parsley, to serve

INSTRUCTIONS:

•Boil 1 tablespoon olive oil in a large deep frying pan over high heat.
•Powder the beef in flour.
•Cook and stirring it for 2-3 minutes or until lightly browned.
•Transfer to a plate.
•Heat remaining oil in same pan.
•Sauté leek and garlic for 1-2 minutes.
•Stir in spices and cook for 1-2 minutes.
•Return beef to pan with stock, carrots, tomatoes, olives, lemon and half of the herbs.

•Season to taste and let it simmer, uncovered for 35-40 minutes.
•Stir in remaining herbs and sprinkle with extra parsley.
•Serve with rice.

Tipsy Beer Beef Casserole

INGREDIENTS:

2 tbsp. olive oil
750g gravy beef, trimmed, cut into 3cm cubes
1 medium leek, trimmed, halved, washed, sliced
2 garlic cloves, crushed
4 middle bacon rashers, trimmed, chopped
200g cup mushrooms, sliced
2 tbsp. plain flour
2 large Desiree potatoes, peeled, chopped
2 dried bay leaves
4 sprigs fresh thyme
375ml bottle lager beer
1 1/2 cups Beef Stock
Sliced crusty bread, to serve

INSTRUCTIONS:

•Preheat oven to 350 F.
•Heat half the oil in a heavy-based, flameproof casserole dish over medium-high heat.
•Brown the beef, in batches, for 5 minutes and transfer to a bowl.
•Heat remaining oil in dish.
•Add leek, garlic, bacon and mushrooms.
•Cook, stirring, for 5 minutes or until onion has softened.
•Put back the beef to the dish.
•Add flour and cook for 1 minute.
•Add potato, bay leaves and thyme.
•Mix in beer and stock and cover the dish.
•Bring to a boil.
•Transfer to oven and bake for 2 hours or until beef is tender.
•Remove and discard bay leaves.
•Serve with bread.

Plain Chuck Steak Casserole

INGREDIENTS:

1 tbsp. vegetable oil
40g unsalted butter
1kg gravy beef or chuck steak, roughly chopped into 2.5cm chunks
2 onions, finely chopped
2 celery stalks, finely chopped
3 garlic cloves, finely chopped
2 large carrots, cut into 2cm cubes
2 tbsp. plain flour
1 tbsp. tomato paste
1 cup (250ml) dry red wine
2 cups (500ml) Beef Stock
400g can chopped tomatoes
2 tbsp. oregano leaves

INSTRUCTIONS:

•Heat half of the oil and half of the butter in a large wide-based casserole over high heat.
•Brown the beef in 3 batches for about 2 minutes.
•Transfer to a bowl.
•Heat the remaining oil and butter in same pan over low heat.
•Add the onion, celery, garlic and carrots.
•Cook, stirring for 3-5 minutes or until the onion is soft.
•Combine the flour and tomato paste and cook, stirring, for another minute.
•Increase the heat to high and return the beef and juices to the pan with the red wine.
•Cook, stirring, for 2 minutes or until wine is reduced by half.
•Reduce heat to medium-low, then add stock and tomatoes and let it simmer, uncovered, for 1 1/2-1 3/4 hours.
• Stirring occasionally, until the beef is tender and sauce is thick.
•Blending in the oregano leaves and serve.

Flavored Beef & Prune Tagine

INGREDIENTS:

2 tbsp. olive oil
500g Diced Beef
1 brown onion, finely chopped
1 garlic clove, crushed
3 tsp. ground cumin
2 tsp. ground coriander
1 tsp. ground turmeric
1/2 tsp. ground ginger
400g can diced tomatoes
1 cup (250ml) beef stock
3/4 cup (125g) seeded prunes, coarsely chopped
150g pack Baby Spinach Leaves
1 1/2 cups (300g) Couscous
1 tbsp. finely chopped flat-leaf parsley
Steamed baby carrots & broccoli, to serve

INSTRUCTIONS:

•Heat the half of the oil in a large saucepan over medium-high heat.
•Put half of the beef, and cook, turning over, for 3-4 minutes or until brown. Transfer to a plate.
•Repeat process with the remaining beef.
•Heat the remaining oil in the pan over medium heat.
•Add the onion and cook while stirring for about 5 minutes or until softened.
•Add the garlic, cumin, coriander, turmeric and ginger.
•Cook, stirring, for 1-2 minutes or until fragrant.
•Add the tomato and stock and bring to the boil.
•Return the beef to the pan and reduce heat to simmer for 15 minutes, covered.
•Add the prunes and let it simmer, uncovered, for 15-20 minutes or until beef is tender and sauce solidifies slightly.
•Add the spinach and cook while stirring for 2 minutes or until wilted.
•Meanwhile, place the couscous in a heatproof bowl and pour over 1 1/2 (375ml) cups boiling water.
•Cover and set aside for 5 minutes or until all the liquid is absorbed.
•Use a fork to separate grains.
•Add the parsley and toss to combine.

•Divide the couscous among serving bowls and top with the tagine to serve.
•Serve with baby carrots and broccoli.

Beef and Vegetable Casserole with Brandy

INGREDIENTS:

2 tbsp. plain flour
1.5kg beef casserole steak (such as chuck steak or gravy beef), cut into 4cm pieces
2 tbsp. olive oil
1 brown onion, halved, thinly sliced
3 carrots, peeled, cut into 2cm-thick slices
4 whole star anise
4cm-piece fresh ginger, peeled, thinly sliced
2 stems lemon grass, pale section only, halved
500ml (2 cups) Beef Stock
125ml (1/2 cup) brandy
90g (1/3 cup) tomato paste
300g green beans, topped
Fresh coriander leaves, to serve
Steamed Sun Rice White Medium Grain Rice, to serve

INSTRUCTIONS:

•Preheat oven to 350 F
•Season the flour with salt and pepper in a plate.
•Add the beef and toss to coat and shake off any excesses.
•Heat half of the oil in a 4L (16-cup) capacity flameproof, ovenproof casserole dish over medium heat.
•Add half of the beef and cook for 2-3 minutes on each side or until brown.
•Transfer to a plate and repeat process with the remaining oil and beef, reheating the dish between batches.
•Add onion and carrots to the pan and cook, stirring, for 5 minutes or until onion is soft. •Add the star anise, ginger and lemon grass, and stir to combine.
•Add the beef, stock, brandy and tomato paste to the dish.
•Cover and bake for 1 1/2 hours or until the beef is tender.
•In the meantime, cook the beans in a medium saucepan with boiling water for 3-4 minutes or until bright green and tender crisp.
•Drain the beans and add to the beef mixture and stir to combine.

•Top the beef mixture with coriander.
•Serve with steamed rice.

Potato with Cheese Dumplings

INGREDIENTS:

2 large (about 400g) Desiree potatoes, peeled
185ml (3/4 cup) milk
60g butter
225g (1 1/2 cups) self-rising flour
65g (3/4 cup) coarsely grated cheddar
40g (1/2 cup) finely grated parmesan
2 tbsp. chopped fresh continental parsley
Salt

INSTRUCTIONS:

•Preheat oven to 350 F.
•Heat half of the oil in a 2L (8-cup) capacity heatproof, ovenproof ceramic casserole dish over medium-high heat.
•Add half of the beef and cook, stirring, for 2 minutes or until brown and transfer to a bowl.
•Repeat the process with the remaining beef.
•Heat remaining oil over medium heat.
•Add onion, bacon and garlic, and cook, stirring, for 5 minutes or until bacon is crisp.
•Add beef, mushrooms, tomato, stock, tomato paste and vinegar.
•Spice with salt and pepper and bring to the boil.
•Cover and bake in oven for 1 1/2 hours.
•For the meantime, to make potato dumplings, place potatoes in a saucepan and cover with cold water.
•Bring to the boil over medium-high heat and cook, uncovered, for 10 minutes or until tender.
•Drain well and return to pan.
•Add milk and butter and use a potato masher to mash until smooth. Stir in flour, cheddar, parmesan and parsley.
•Taste and season with salt.
•Remove casserole from oven.
•Use a 60ml (1/4-cup) capacity measuring cup to shape potato mixture into 6 dumplings. •Assemble over casserole.
•Cook, uncovered, for a further 20 minutes.

•Remove from oven and set aside for 5 minutes to cool slightly before serving.

Parmesan Dumpling and Beef Casserole

INGREDIENTS:

1kg gravy beef, cut into 2cm chunks
1 tablespoon olive oil
1 onion, chopped
6 bacon rashes, chopped
500g button mushrooms, halved
4 whole garlic cloves, peeled
2 tbsp. plain flour
2 cups (500ml) Beef Stock
1 cup (250ml) red wine
2 fresh thyme sprigs
3 bay leaves
50g butter
2 cups (300g) self-raising flour
1/2 cup (45g) parmesan
3/4 cup (185ml) milk

INSTRUCTIONS:

•Brown the gravy beef and cut into 2cm chunks, in 1 tablespoon olive oil over medium heat. •Remove and transfer to a plate.
•Combine chopped onion, 6 bacon rashes, button mushrooms, and 4 peeled garlic cloves, and cook until soft.
•Stir in 2 tablespoons plain flour.
•Add 2 cups beef stock, 1 cup red wine, 2 fresh thyme sprigs and 3 bay leaves.
•Bring to a boil and then reduce heat to low.
•Add beef and simmer, covered for 1 1/2 hours.
•Spoon into a 2 liter ovenproof dish.
•Preheat oven to 400 F.
•Brush 50g butter into 2 cups self-rising flour.
•Stir in 1/2 cup parmesan and 3/4 cup milk.
•Bring all together and roll into 20 balls.
•Place on beef and bake for 20 minutes.

Beef Estofado Topped with Polenta

INGREDIENTS:

1 tbsp. olive oil
1kg beef chuck steak, cut into 4cm pieces
2 large brown onions, finely chopped
1 chorizo, coarsely chopped
4 large garlic cloves, finely chopped
2 carrots, peeled, coarsely chopped
3 tsp. Ground Paprika
1 tsp. ground oregano
1/2 tsp. ground cinnamon
4 (about 550g) tomatoes, coarsely chopped
250ml (1 cup) white wine
185ml (3/4 cup) Beef Stock
140g (2/3 cup) polenta
150g (1 cup) self-raising flour
2 eggs, lightly whisked
330ml (1 1/3 cups) buttermilk
100g manchego, cut into 1cm pieces
150g (1 cup) frozen broad beans, thawed, peeled
1-2 long fresh red chillies, thinly sliced

INSTRUCTIONS:

•Heat oil in a saucepan over medium-high heat.
•Cook beef, in 2 batches, for 2-3 minutes or until browned and transfer to a bowl.
•Reduce heat to medium and then stir the onion, chorizo and garlic for 3-5 minutes or until onion is golden.
•Stir in the carrot, paprika, oregano and cinnamon for 1 minute or until aromatic.
•Stir in the beef, tomato, wine and stock and season.
•Bring to a boil.
•Reduce heat to low and let it simmer, covered, for 11/2 hours.
•Uncover and simmer for another 1 hour or until the beef is tender.
•Spoon the mixture into a large baking dish. Cool completely.
•Preheat oven to 350 F
•Place polenta and flour in a bowl.
•Gradually stir in egg and buttermilk until combined.
•Stir in two-thirds of the manchego.

•Sprinkle broad beans over the beef and put spoonful of polenta mixture over the beef, leaving gaps.
•Sprinkle over the remaining manchego and top with the chili.
•Bake for 35-40 minutes or until golden.

Mashed Sweet Potato in Beef Goulash

INGREDIENTS:

2 tbsp. pure olive oil
175g outdoor bred short cut bacon, chopped
2 leeks, washed, sliced
2 cloves garlic, crushed
1.8kg chuck steak, cubed
1 red capsicum, chopped
2 tbsp. smoked paprika
2 gluten-free beef stock cubes
400g can chopped tomatoes
4 sprigs thyme
500g sweet potato, chopped
3 potatoes, chopped
20g butter
2 tablespoon parsley, chopped

INSTRUCTIONS:

•Heat 1 tablespoon oil in a large flameproof casserole pan over medium heat.
•Cook bacon for 2 minutes, or until brown.
•Add leek and cook for 5 minutes, or until soft.
•Add garlic and cook for 1 min, or until fragrant and then remove it from pan.
•Heat remaining oil in same pan on high-heat.
•Brown the beef in batches, stirring, for 2-3 minutes.
•Add leek mixture to pan with capsicum and paprika.
•Stir to combine.
•Mix together 2 cups boiling water and stock cubes.
•Stir until it dissolves.
•Add to beef mixture with tomato and thyme sprigs.
•Bring to boil.
•Reduce heat to low. And let it simmer, covered, for 2 hours, or until beef is very tender.

•Meanwhile, cook sweet potato and potato in a large pan of boiling, salted water for 15-20 minutes, or until soft.
•Drain and return it to the pan.
•Add butter and mash it until smooth.
•Season with the spices.
•Sprinkle parsley over goulash and serve with sweet potato mash.

Pot Roast Beef with Silver Beet and Chickpeas

INGREDIENTS

2 tbsp. olive oil
1.5kg beef silverside roast
1 large brown onion, cut into wedges
2 garlic cloves, crushed
3 tsps. Smoked paprika
1/4 cup plain flour
1 liter Beef Stock
400g can diced tomatoes
400g can chickpeas, drained, rinsed
1/2 bunch silver beet, trimmed, chopped
1/4 cup chopped fresh coriander leaves, to serve

INSTRUCTIONS

•Preheat oven to 325 F.
•Heat the oil in a large, flameproof, ovenproof dish over medium heat.
•Brown the beef for 3 to 5 minutes on each side.
•Transfer the browned beef to a plate.
•Heat remaining oil in a dish and add onion.
•Cook, stirring occasionally, for 4 minutes or until softened.
•Add garlic and paprika then cook while stirring for 30 seconds or until fragrant.
•Add flour and continue stirring for 1 minute.
•Gradually add stock beef, stirring until become smooth.
•Mix in the tomato and combine with the beef in the dish.
•Cover and bring to a boil.
•Transfer the dish to the oven.
•Bake for 1 hour and 30 minutes.
•Add chickpeas and continue to cook, uncovered, for 50 minutes or until beef is just cooked through and tender.

•Add silver beet.
•Cook for another 5 minutes or until silver beet has just wilted.
•Serve beef mixture with coriander.

Sweet Potato with Beef and Bacon Goulash

INGREDIENTS:

2 tbsp. pure olive oil
175g outdoor bred short cut bacon, chopped
2 leeks, washed, sliced
2 cloves garlic, crushed
1.8kg chuck steak, cubed
1 red capsicum, chopped
2 tablespoons smoked paprika
2 gluten-free beef stock cubes
400g can chopped tomatoes
4 sprigs thyme
500g sweet potato, chopped
3 potatoes, chopped
20g butter
2 tbsp. parsley, chopped

INSTRUCTIONS:

•Heat 1 tablespoon oil in a large flameproof casserole pan on medium heat.
•Cook bacon for 2 minutes, or until brown.
•Add leek and cook for another 5 minutes, or until soft.
•Add garlic and cook for 1 min, or until fragrant.
•Remove from pan and set aside.
•Heat remaining oil in same pan on high heat.
•Brown the beef in batches, stirring, for 2-3 minutes, or until browned all over.
•Return leek mixture to pan with capsicum and paprika.
•Stir to combine.
•Mix together 2 cups boiling water and stock cubes.
•Stir until it dissolved.
•Add to beef mixture with tomato and thyme sprigs.
•Bring to boil.

•Reduce heat to low and simmer, covered, for 2 hours, or until beef is very tender.
•Meanwhile, cook sweet potato and potato in a large pan of boiling, salted water for 15-20 minutes, or until soft.
•Drain and return to pan.
•Add butter and mash until smooth.
•Season to taste.
•Scatter parsley over goulash and serve with sweet potato mash.

Braised Duck Tagliatelle Pasta

INGREDIENTS:

4 duck Maryland's
1 large onion and 1 carrot, chopped
2 garlic cloves, crushed
1/4 cup (70g) tomato paste
1 tbsp. plain flour
2 cups (500ml) dry red wine
300ml Chicken
2 bay leaves and 2 tablespoons thyme leaves
Pared rind and juice of 1 orange
500g Tagliatelle
2 tablespoons chopped flat-leaf parsley
Watercress, fennel & orange salad and grated parmesan, to serve

INSTRUCTIONS:

•Preheat the oven to 325 F
•Place a large flameproof casserole over medium heat.
•Add duck, skin-side down, and cook for 6 minutes, then turn and cook for a further 4 minutes.
•Remove duck and drain fat, leaving 2 tablespoons in the pan.
•Add the onion, carrot and garlic and cook, stirring, for 2-3 minutes.
•Add the tomato paste and cook for a further minute.
•Strew the flour and stir to combine.
•Add the wine, stock, herbs, rind and juice.
•Bring to a boil and season to taste.
•Put back the duck to the pan, cover and cook in the oven for 2 hours.
•Remove the duck from the sauce and get the remaining fat from the surface.
•Put the casserole over medium heat.

•Simmer for 3-4 minutes until sauce has reduced slightly.
•When duck is cool enough to handle, discard skin and bones and shred meat.
•Return meat to casserole.
•To serve, cook pasta according to packet instructions, then drain.
•Put pasta in the pan, add the sauce and toss to combine.
•Divide pasta among plates and serve sprinkled with parsley and grated parmesan, with the watercress, fennel and orange salad.

Braised Beef Cheeks with Salsa Verde

INGREDIENTS:

750ml bottle red wine
2 tbsp. olive oil
6 beef cheeks, trimmed
2 tbsp. plain flour, seasoned, to dust
2 onions, chopped
4 garlic cloves, chopped
2L (8 cups) good-quality beef stock
2 bay leaves
Mashed potato, to serve
Salsa Verde
1/3 cup (80ml) extra virgin olive oil
2 cups flat-leaf parsley leaves
1 cup basil leaves
1/2 cup mint leaves
2 tbsp. each Dijon mustard, red wine vinegar and rinsed, salted capers
2 anchovy fillets (optional)

INSTRUCTIONS:

•Heat the oven to 325 F.
•Place the wine in a pan and simmer over medium heat for 10 minutes or until reduced by half and then set aside.
•Heat oil in a large flameproof casserole over medium-high heat.
•Dust beef in flour, shaking off excess.
•Brown the beef, in batches, for 2 minutes each side, adding more oil if necessary.
•Remove and set aside.
•Add the onion to the pan, reduce heat to medium and cook, stirring, for 5 minutes or until softened.
•Stir in garlic, then return beef to the pan.

•Add the remaining wine, stock and bay leaves, then season.
•Completely covered the meat with liquid and top up with water if necessary.
•Cover and cook in the oven for 2 1/2 hours or until the beef is meltingly tender.
•Meanwhile, to make the salsa Verde, place the ingredients in a blender and blend to form a smooth paste.
•Season to taste.
•Transfer beef to a plate, then cover with foil to keep warm.
•Place casserole over medium-high heat for 10 minutes or until the sauce thickens.
•Serve the beef with the sauce, mashed potato and salsa Verde.

Flamed Potato Salad with Casseroled Beef

INGREDIENTS:

500g gravy beef, cut into 3cm cubes
1 tablespoon olive oil
1 medium brown onion, cut into large dice
1/4 punnet fresh thyme sprigs
2 cloves garlic, crushed
1 tablespoon Italian red wine vinegar
1 cup beef stock
2 cups water
480g brushed potatoes, washed
1/2 small shallot, finely chopped
4 tablespoons extra virgin olive oil
40g loose rocket
1 medium carrot, peeled, shaved into ribbons with vegetable peeler
1/2 small red onion, thinly sliced

INSTRUCTIONS:

•Position an oven rack in the center of the oven and preheat the oven to 350 F
•Season the beef with salt and pepper.
•Heat a heavy medium casserole pan over medium-high heat.
•Add the oil, then the beef and cook, turning as needed, for about 10 minutes, or until the beef is brown on all sides.
•Add the onion, thyme, and garlic and cook, stirring to scrape up the brown bits on the base of the pan, for about 2 minutes, or until the onion is translucent.
•Reduce heat to medium, add the vinegar and then the stock, stirring to scrape up any remaining brown bits.
•Add the water to just cover the beef.
•Cover the pan and transfer it to the oven.
•Braise for about 2 hours, or until the beef is just tender.
•Remove the pan from the oven and place it over medium-low heat on the stove.
•Simmer gently, uncovered, for about 15 minutes, or until the sauce has reduced to about one-quarter of its original volume.
•Remove the thyme stems.
•Season to taste with salt and pepper.

•In the meantime, to make the potato salad, place potatoes in a medium saucepan and add enough water to cover.
•Add salt, and bring the water to the boil over medium-high heat.
•Reduce the heat to medium-low and simmer for about 5-7 minutes, or until a knife inserted into a potato slides in easily but still has some resistance in the center.
•Drain, then place the potatoes on a plate for 10 minutes, or until cool enough to handle.
•While potatoes are cooling, in a medium bowl, whisk the shallot and vinegar to blend. •Slowly add 3 tablespoons of the oil whilst whisking to blend.
•Season to taste with salt and pepper.
•Heat a chargrill pan over medium-low heat or an outdoor barbecue to medium.
•Quarter the potatoes, then place in a large bowl and toss to coat.

Braised Beef with Potatoes and Broccoli Florets

INGREDIENTS:

1 tbsp. olive oil
500g Beef Chuck Steak, cut into 4 equal pieces
1 medium brown onion, cut into medium dice
2 small carrots, peeled, cut into 2.5cm pieces
2 cloves garlic, crushed
2 tbsp. Red Wine Vinegar
1 cup Real Beef Stock
2 large sprigs fresh thyme
200g gold sweet potatoes, peeled and quartered
3 medium (450g) red washed potatoes, quartered
150g broccoli florets

INSTRUCTIONS:

•To braise the beef: Position the rack in the center of the oven and preheat the oven to 350 F
•Heat a large, heavy-based deep saucepan over medium-high heat.
•Add the oil and heat it for 1 minute.
•Season the beef with salt and pepper.
•Add the beef to the pan and cook until browned all over, about 2 minutes per side.
•Transfer the beef to a bowl and set aside.

•Add the onion and carrots to the pan and cook for 2 minutes, or until the vegetables have started to develop some color.
•Add the garlic and stir for 30 seconds, or until fragrant.
•Add the vinegar and cook, stirring to scrape up the brown bits on the bottom of the pan, for 1 min, or until the vinegar reduces by half.
•Return the beef and its juices to the pan.
•Add the stock and thyme, then add enough water to almost cover the meat (about 21/2 cups). Bring the liquid to a simmer, then cover the pan and transfer it to the oven.
•Braise the beef mixture for 2 hours, or until beef is tender.
•Using a slotted spoon, transfer the braised beef and vegetables to a large bowl and cover with foil to keep warm.
•Simmer the braising liquid over medium-high heat for about 5 minutes, or until reduced to 1 cup.
•Return the beef and vegetables to the braising liquid and season to taste with salt and pepper.
•Meanwhile, to roast the vegetables, position the rack in the center of the oven and preheat the oven to 350 F.
•In a large bowl, toss the sweet potato, potato and broccoli with the olive oil to coat.
•Season with salt and pepper.
•Transfer vegetables to a heavy, large baking tray, spacing them evenly apart.
•Roast vegetables without turning them, for 30 minutes, or until they are tender and beginning to brown.
•Stand for 2 minutes before serving.
Divide the roasted vegetables between 4 plates. Place a piece of beef alongside the vegetables on each plate. Divide the carrots and onions among the plates. Spoon the braising liquid over the beef and serve.

Spiced Chicken Braised with Witlof

INGREDIENTS:

1 tbsp. oil
4 (about 800g-1kg) chicken thigh cutlets
1 large leek, washed, trimmed, cut into 4 pieces
2 witlof, halved lengthways
2 garlic cloves, thinly sliced
1/2 cup (125ml) dry white wine
2 fresh bay leaves
2 tablespoons tarragon leaves
1 cup (250ml) Chicken
4 large silver beet leaves, washed, center stalk removed
Crusty bread, to serve

INSTRUCTIONS:

•Heat oven to 350 F.
•In a large flameproof casserole dish boil oil over medium-high heat.
•Add chicken and cook for 2-3 minutes each side or until well browned.
•Transfer chicken to a plate and season with salt and pepper.
•Pour off excess fat from pan, leaving about 1 tablespoon.
•Add leek and witlof to the pan and cook for 2 minutes each side or until light golden.
•Add the garlic and cook for 30 seconds.
•Add the wine, bay leaves and half the tarragon and cook for 2 minutes.
•Add the chicken stock and return chicken to pan.
•Sprinkle with remaining tarragon.
•Bring to the boil.
•Remove from heat and cover with a tight-fitting lid.
•Bake in preheated oven for 20 minutes or until chicken is just cooked through.
•Add the silver beet to the pan, tucking in under chicken.
•Bake for another 5-10 minutes or until chicken and silver beet is cooked through.
•Serve chicken and vegetables in a large shallow bowl with some of the stock poured over and with slices of crusty bread.

Flavored Chicken with Rosemary Gremolata Casserole

INGREDIENTS:

1 tbsp. extra-virgin olive oil
8 (130g each) chicken thigh cutlets, skin on
2 brown onions, halved, sliced
2 carrots, halved lengthways, thickly sliced
4 celery stalks, thickly sliced
8 middle bacon rashers, trimmed, chopped
4 garlic cloves, crushed
1/2 cup fresh sage leaves
1 cup dry white wine
1/2 cup plain flour
1 liter salt-reduced chicken stock
Mashed potato, to serve
Rosemary gremolata
2 tbsp. fresh rosemary leaves, roughly chopped
1 tsp. lemon zest
1 garlic clove, crushed

INSTRUCTIONS:

•Turn on oven to 350 F
•Heat oil in a large heavy-based, flameproof casserole dish over medium-high heat.
•Cook chicken, in batches, for 5 to 6 minutes or until golden.
•Transfer to a bowl.
•Add onion, carrot, celery and bacon.
•Cook, stirring, for 5 minutes or until onion has softened.
•Add garlic and sage then cook for 1 minute or until fragrant.
•Add wine and bring to a boil.
•Mix the flour and continue to cook for 1 minute.
•Slowly add stock while stirring constantly.
•Return chicken to dish.
•Cover and bring to a boil.
•Transfer to oven and bake for 1 hour.
•Remove the lid and bake, uncovered, for another hour or until chicken is tender.

•Make Rosemary gremolata by combining the rosemary, lemon zest and garlic in a bowl. •Serve casserole with mashed potato, sprinkled with Rosemary gremolata.

Chicken Casserole with Hunters Sauce

INGREDIENTS:

2 tbsp. plain flour
1 kilogram mixed chicken pieces
2 tbsp. olive oil
20 gram butter
1 bunch spring onions, trimmed, bulbs halved
200g button mushrooms, halved
2 garlic cloves, crushed
2 sprigs fresh thyme
1/2 cup dry white wine
2 tbsp. cognac (optional)
2 tbsp. tomato paste
2 cups chicken stock
Mashed potato and steamed broccoli, to serve

INSTRUCTIONS:

•Combine flour and chicken in a large bowl and then season it with salt and pepper.
•Toss to coat.
•Remove chicken and shaking off excess flour.
•Heat 1 tablespoon oil in a large, heavy-based flameproof casserole dish over medium-high heat.
•Cook chicken, in batches, turning, for 8 to 10 minutes or until golden.
•Transfer cooked chicken to a plate.
•Add butter and the remaining oil in a dish.
•Add the onion, mushrooms, garlic and thyme.
•Cook, stirring, for 4 to 5 minutes or until onion has softened and mushrooms are golden. •Add wine and cognac and simmer for 30 seconds.
•Add tomato paste.
•Cook, stirring, for 1 minute.
•Stir in chicken stock.
•Put back chicken to the pan and bring to boil.

•Reduce heat to low and let it simmer for 1 hour or until chicken is tender and sauce has reduced.
•Serve with mash and steamed broccoli.

Cannellini Bean with Chipolata Casserole

INGREDIENTS:

1 tablespoon olive oil
500g beef chipolata sausages
1 brown onion, finely chopped
3 carrots, peeled, finely chopped
3 celery sticks, ends trimmed, finely chopped
2 garlic cloves, crushed
1 x 800g can diced tomatoes
250ml (1 cup) salt-reduced chicken stock
2 x 400g cans cannellini beans, rinsed, drained
100g baby spinach leaves
2 tablespoons chopped fresh continental parsley
Crusty bread, to serve

INSTRUCTIONS:

•Preheat oven to 170 degree Celsius.
•Heat oil in a large flameproof casserole dish over medium heat.
•Add sausages and cook, turning occasionally, for 2-3 minutes or until lightly browned. •Transfer cooked sausages to a plate and set aside.
•Add the onion, carrot, celery and garlic to the dish.
•Cook, stirring often, for 6 minutes or until the onion starts to soften.
•Add the tomato and chicken stock.
•Increase heat to high and cover the dish and bring to a boil.
•Put the sausages again to the dish and cover.
•Bake in oven for 30 minutes.
•Stir in the beans.
•Stir in the spinach and parsley.
•Flavor with salt and pepper.
•Divide the casserole among serving dishes.
•Serve with bread.

Creamy Polenta Chicken Casserole

INGREDIENTS:

8 small free-range chicken legs
1/4 cup (40g) plain flour
2 tbsp. olive oil
200 gram bacon rashers, rind removed and cut into 2cm cubes
500 gram button mushrooms, halved
1 onion, chopped
2 garlic cloves, crushed
800 gram can diced tomatoes
140 gram container tomato paste
Salt and freshly ground pepper, to season
Sour cream and chopped continental parsley on creamy polenta, to serve

INSTRUCTIONS:

•Heave 8 small free-range chicken legs in 1/4 cup (40g) plain flour until coated.
• In a frying pan heat 2 tablespoons olive oil over high heat.
•Add chicken and cook, turning until golden. Place in a 3.5-litre crockpot.
•Add 200g bacon rashers, rind removed and cut into 2cm cubes, 500g button mushrooms, halved, 1 onion, chopped, and 2 garlic cloves, crushed, to the frying pan and cook for 5 minutes or until golden.
•Add to the crockpot with 800 gram diced tomatoes and 140 gram tomato paste.
•Cook, covered, on low heat for 4-6 hours or on high heat for 2-3 hours.
•Season well with salt and freshly ground pepper.
•Serve with a dollop of sour cream and spread with chopped continental parsley on creamy polenta.

Provençale Chicken Casserole

INGREDIENTS:

4 chicken breast fillets, trimmed
1/3 cup plain flour
50 gram butter, chopped
1 medium brown onion, finely chopped
1/2 cup dry sherry
400 gram can diced tomatoes
1/4 cup kalamata olives
2 tbsp. chopped fresh flat-leaf parsley leaves
Steamed potatoes and broccoli, to serve

INSTRUCTIONS:

•Preheat oven to 350 F.
•Place flour in a snap-lock bag. Season with salt and pepper. Add chicken breasts, 2 at a time, shaking to coat. Shake off excess. Place on a plate.
•Melt butter in a frying pan over medium-high heat. Add chicken. Cook for 2 to 3 minutes each side or until golden. Transfer to a 5cm-deep, 20cm x 30cm (base) baking dish.
•Reduce heat to medium-low. Add onion to pan. Cook, stirring occasionally, for 5 minutes or until softened. Increase heat to medium-high. Add sherry. Bring to the boil. •Boil for 1 minute. Add tomatoes. Cook, stirring occasionally, for 5 to 6 minutes or until boiling. Spoon tomato mixture over chicken. Cover.
•Bake for 30 minutes or until chicken is cooked through, adding olives for the last 5 minutes. Sprinkle with parsley. Serve with potatoes and broccoli.

Pineapple Topped with Crackers Casserole

INGREDIENTS

54 oz. pineapple chunks, drained
¼ cup granulated sugar
¼ cup all purpose flour
1 cup shredded sharp cheddar cheese
1 sleeve Ritz crackers
3 tbsps. Melted butter

INSTRUCTIONS:

•Heat oven to 350 degrees Fahrenheit.
•Combine pineapple, sugar, flour, and cheese in a large mixing bowl.
•In a greased 8 x 8 casserole dish pour the mixture.
•Crush crackers and sprinkle over the top of the pineapple mixture.
•Pour melted butter evenly over cracker layer.
•Bake the pineapple casserole for about 25 minutes or until golden brown and slightly bubbly.

Cheesy Pineapple Casserole

INGREDIENTS:

30 ounces pineapple chunks (drained)
1 cup white sugar
3/4 cup all-purpose flour
2 cups shredded sharp cheddar cheese
25 crackers (buttery round, crumbled)
1/2 cup melted butter

INSTRUCTIONS:

•Preheat oven to 350 degrees F (175 degrees C).
•Spread pineapple in the bottom of a 2 quart casserole dish.
•Combine white sugar, flour and cheese.
•Mix well.
•Sprinkle crackers over the top of pineapple and cheese mixture.
•Pour melted butter over the top and bake for 30 minutes.

Mashed Potatoes Casserole

INGREDIENTS:

4 1/2 cups cooked and mashed sweet potatoes
1/2 cup butter, melted
1/3 cup milk
1 cup white sugar
1/2 tsp. vanilla extract
2 eggs, beaten
1 cup light brown sugar
1/2 cup all-purpose flour
1/3 cup butter
1 cup chopped pecans

INSTRUCTIONS:

•Heat oven to 350 degrees Fahrenheit (175 degrees C).
•Oil a 9x13 inch baking dish with cooking spray.
•Mix together mashed sweet potatoes, 1/2 cup butter, milk, sugar, vanilla extract, and eggs in a large bowl.
•Arrange sweet potato mixture into the prepared baking dish.
•In a small bowl, mix together brown sugar and flour. Cut in 1/3 cup butter until mixture is crumbly, and then stir in pecans.
•Sprinkle pecan mixture over the sweet potatoes.
•Bake for 25 minutes in the preheated oven, or until golden brown.

Tilapia Casserole

INGREDIENTS

4 tsps. Extra-virgin olive oil, divided
1 medium onion, very thinly sliced
1/2 cup dry white wine
8 oz. cod or tilapia, cut into 2 pieces
1 tsp. chopped fresh thyme or 1/4 teaspoon dried
1/4 tsp. kosher salt
1/4 tsp. freshly ground pepper
3/4 cup finely chopped whole-wheat country bread, (about 1 slice)
1/4 tsp. paprika
1/4 tsp. garlic powder
1/2 cup finely shredded Gruyère or Swiss cheese

INSTRUCTIONS:

•Heat up oven to 400°F.
•Cook the oil in a medium ovenproof skillet over medium-high heat,.
•Add onion, stirring often for about 4 to 6 minutes or until just starting to soften.
•Pour wine to the skillet and then increase heat to high and then cook for 2 to 4 minutes or until the wine is slightly reduced.
•Put the fish on top of the onion and sprinkle with thyme, salt, and pepper.
•Cover tightly the pan with foil transfer to the oven and bake for 12 minutes.
•Toss the bread with the remaining 2 teaspoons oil, paprika and garlic powder in a small bowl. •Uncover the fish; top with the bread mixture and cheese. Bake, uncovered, until the fish is just cooked through, 8 to 10 minutes.

Cheesy Baked Fillet of Fish Casserole

INGREDIENTS:

1 cup sour cream
2 tbsps. butter
2 tbsps. lemon juice
1 -1 1/2 lb. of firm white fish fillet (halibut, or ling cod work well)
Salt
Pepper
1/2 medium onion, thinly sliced and separated into rings
1 -1 1/2 cup grated cheddar cheese

INSTRUCTIONS:

•Heat oven to 350 degrees.
•Melt butter and blend in the lemon juice and sour cream.
•Salt and pepper the fish to taste and place in a casserole dish.
•Spread the onion rings evenly on top.
•Pour the sour cream mixture over fish spread evenly and top with the cheese.
•Bake for 35 minutes or until fish flakes with a fork.

Tomato & Spinach Dinner Strata

INGREDIENTS:

4 tsps. Extra-virgin olive oil, divided
1 medium onion, chopped
8 oz. mushrooms, thinly sliced
1/2 tsp. freshly ground pepper, divided
1/4 tsp. salt
1 15-oz. container part-skim ricotta cheese
1 10-oz. package frozen chopped spinach, thawed and squeezed dry, or
1 1/2 pounds fresh spinach, cooked, squeezed dry and chopped
1/8 tsp. freshly grated nutmeg
2 cups prepared marinara sauce, divided
6 slices whole-grain sandwich bread, preferably day-old
1 cup shredded part-skim mozzarella cheese
3 large eggs
1 cup low-fat milk
1/4 cup freshly grated Parmesan cheese
2 tbsp. chopped fresh parsley

INSTRUCTIONS:

•Covering a 7-by-11-inch (or similar-size) baking dish with cooking spray.
•In a large nonstick skillet heat 2 teaspoons oil over medium heat.
•Sauté onion by stirring often for about 5 to 8 minutes or until softened but not browned. •Transfer the sautéed onion to a bowl.
•Add 2 teaspoons oil to the pan and then increase heat to medium-high.
•Add mushrooms and cook, stirring 4 to 5 minutes or until the moisture has evaporated. •Combine mushroom with the onions, add 1/4 teaspoon pepper and salt in a bowl.
•Combine ricotta, spinach, nutmeg and the remaining 1/4 teaspoon pepper in another bowl.
•Get 1 cup marinara sauce into the prepared baking dish.
•Break each slice of bread into 4 roughly equal pieces and then arrange half of the bread on the sauce.
•Spoon the ricotta mixture over the bread.
•Arrange the remaining bread over the ricotta.
•Scatter the mushroom mixture over the bread and top with mozzarella.

•Spoon the remaining marinara sauce over the top until the pan will be very full.
•Beat eggs and milk in a small bowl.
•Pour the mixture slowly over the casserole, poking the filling gently with the tip of a knife until the egg mixture is evenly distributed and the bread is soaked.
•Coat a piece of foil with cooking spray on one side and cover it to the casserole, sprayed-side down.
•Refrigerate for at least 2 hours or up to 1 day.
•Preheat oven to 375°F.
•Bake the strata for 40 minutes, uncovered.
•Sprinkle with Parmesan cheese and bake for another 10 minutes more or until puffed and golden brown.
•Let stand for 10 minutes and serve sprinkled with parsley.

Baked Tortellini

INGREDIENTS:

1 tbsp. extra-virgin olive oil
2 tbsp. all-purpose flour
2 1/2 cups low-fat milk, heated
1/2 cup grated fontina cheese, divided
1/2 tsp. ground nutmeg
Salt & freshly ground pepper, to taste
1 lb. fresh or frozen cheese tortellini, preferably low-fat
1/4 cup fine dry breadcrumbs
2 tbsp. freshly grated Parmesan cheese

INSTRUCTIONS:

•Heat oven to 350°F.
•Coat 6 individual gratin dishes or a 1 1/2-quart shallow baking dish with cooking spray.
•Cook pasta by following the package directions.
•Heat oil in a large saucepan over medium heat.
•Add flour and cook for 1 to 2 minutes, whisking constantly.
•Add hot milk and bring to a simmer, beating 3 to 4 minutes or until smooth and slightly thickened.
•Remove from heat and add 1/4 cup fontina cheese and nutmeg, stirring to melt the cheese. •Season with salt and pepper.

•In the meantime, cook tortellini until just tender for about 6 to 8 minutes or according to package directions.
•Drain and rinse well.
•Combine the tortellini with the cheese sauce and toss.
•Transfer to the prepared dishes or baking dish.
•Top with the remaining 1/4 cup fontina.
•Combine breadcrumbs and Parmesan and sprinkle evenly over the tortellini.
•Bake the tortellini for about 15 to 25 minutes or until golden and bubbly,.
•Serve immediately.

Cheesy Potato Casserole

INGREDIENTS:

Canola oil cooking spray
2 lbs. red potatoes, diced
1 cup low-fat milk
2 tbsp. cornstarch
8 oz. sharp Cheddar cheese, shredded
1 cup nonfat Greek yogurt
1 medium onion, chopped
1/2 tsp. plus a pinch of salt, divided
1/2 tsp. freshly ground pepper
2 cups crushed unsweetened corn flakes

INSTRUCTIONS:

•Heat oven to 350°F.
•Grease a 9-by-13-inch (or similar-size) baking dish with cooking spray.
•Place potatoes in a large pot then pour water to cover the potatoes and bring it to a boil.
•Immediately drain and rinse with cold water and return it to the pot.
•In the meantime beat the milk and cornstarch in a large saucepan.
•Let it simmer over medium-high heat, beating often for about 2 to 4 minutes or until bubbling and thickened enough to coat the back of a spoon.
•Remove the mix milk and cornstarch from the heat and combine with Cheddar cheese, yogurt, onion, 1/2 teaspoon salt and pepper.
•Pour the sauce over the potatoes and mix well.

•Spread evenly in the prepared pan.
•Sprinkle the casserole with corn flakes.
•Coat the corn flakes with cooking spray and use the short burst and then sprinkle with the remaining pinch of salt.
•Bake for about an hour until browned and bubbly at the edges.
•Let cool for 20 minutes before serving.

Shrimp Chili Cornbread Casserole

INGREDIENTS:

2 tsps. Canola oil
1 large onion, chopped
1 medium green bell pepper, chopped
4 cloves garlic, minced
3 medium zucchini, diced (about 5 cups)
1 1/2 tbsp. chili powder
1 1/2 tsp. ground cumin
1 tsp. ground cinnamon
1 tsp. salt
2 14-oz. cans no-salt-added diced tomatoes
1 1/2 lbs. raw shrimp, peeled and deveined
1/2 cup chopped fresh cilantro
1 cup yellow cornmeal
1 cup all-purpose flour
2 tsps. Baking powder
1/2 teaspoon salt
3/4 cup nonfat milk
1/4 cup canola oil
1 large egg
1 tbsp. honey

INSTRUCTIONS:

•To prepare the filling just heat 2 teaspoons oil in a Dutch oven over medium heat.
•Add onion and bell pepper and then cook, stirring often about 3 minutes, until softened,.
•Add garlic and cook, stirring, for 30 seconds.
•Stir in zucchini; cook, stirring often, for 3 minutes. Stir in chili powder, cumin, cinnamon and 1 teaspoon salt; cook for 20 seconds. Pour in tomatoes and their juice; bring to a simmer.
•Remove from the heat.

•Stir in shrimp and cilantro.
•Pour into a 9-by-13-inch baking pan.
•Preheat oven to 350°F.
•To prepare cornbread topping just whisk cornmeal, flour, baking powder and 1/2 teaspoon salt in a large bowl.
•Whip milk, 1/4 cup oil, egg and honey in a medium bowl until smooth.
•Add the wet ingredients to the dry ingredients and stir just until moistened.
•Drop by heaping tablespoons over the shrimp mixture.
•Bake the casserole, uncovered for 40 to 45 minutes or until the top is browned and the filling is bubbling.
•Let stand for 10 minutes before serving.

Zucchini Rice Casserole

INGREDIENTS

1 1/2 cups long-grain brown rice
3 cups reduced-sodium chicken broth
4 cups diced zucchini, and/or summer squash (about 1 pound)
2 red or green bell peppers, chopped
1 large onion, diced
3/4 tsp. salt
1 1/2 cups low-fat milk
3 tbsps. All-purpose flour
2 cups shredded pepper Jack cheese, divided
1 cup fresh or frozen (thawed) corn kernels
2 tsps. Extra-virgin olive oil
8 oz. turkey sausage, casings removed
4 oz. reduced-fat cream cheese, (Neufchâtel)
1/4 cup chopped pickled jalapeños

INSTRUCTIONS:

•Heat oven to 375°F.
•Pour rice into a 9-by-13-inch baking dish.
•Bring broth to a simmer in a small saucepan.
•Stir hot broth into the rice along with zucchini (and/or squash), bell peppers, onion and salt.
•Cover the pan with foil.
•Bake for 45 minutes.

•Remove foil and continue baking until the rice is tender and most of the liquid is absorbed, for around 35 to 45 minutes more.
•In the meantime, whisk milk and flour in a small saucepan.
•Cook over medium heat until bubbling and thickened for about 3 to 4 minutes.
•Reduce heat to low and then add 1 1/2 cups Jack cheese and corn and cook, stirring often until the cheese is melted.
•Set aside.
•Heat oil in a large skillet over medium heat and add sausage.
•Cook and break the sausage into small pieces with a spoon, until lightly browned and no longer pink for about 4 minutes.
•When the rice is done, stir in the sausage and cheese sauce.
•Sprinkle the remaining 1/2 cup Jack cheese on top and dollop cream cheese by the teaspoonful over the casserole.
•Top with jalapeños.
•Return the casserole to the oven and bake for about 10 minutes or until the cheese is melted.
•Let stand for about 10 minutes before serving.

Buffalo Chicken Casserole

INGREDIENTS:

12 oz. whole-wheat elbow noodles
2 tbsp. canola oil
3 medium carrots, sliced
3 medium stalks celery, sliced
1 large onion, chopped
1 tbsp. minced garlic
2 lbs. boneless, skinless chicken breast, trimmed and cut into 1-inch cubes
1/3 cup cornstarch
4 cups low-fat milk
1/8 tsp. salt
5 tbsps. Hot sauce
3/4 cup crumbled blue cheese (about 4 ounces)

INSTRUCTIONS:

•Preheat oven to 400°F.
•Bring a Dutch oven of water to a boil.
•Cook noodles until barely tender, about 2 minutes less than package directions.
•Drain, rinse and set aside.
•Heat oil in the pot over medium heat.
•Add carrots, celery, onion and garlic and cook until beginning to soften, about 5 minutes.
•Add chicken and cook until no longer pink on the outside, 5 to 7 minutes.
•Whisk cornstarch and milk in a medium bowl; add to the pot along with salt.
•Bring to a boil over medium-high heat, stirring often, until bubbling and thick enough to coat the back of a spoon, about 4 minutes.
•Remove from the heat and stir in hot sauce.
•Spread the noodles in a 9-by-13-inch (or similar 3-quart) baking dish.
•Top with the chicken mixture; sprinkle with blue cheese.
•Bake the casserole until it is bubbling, about 30 minutes.
•Let stand for 10 minutes before serving.

Brussels Sprout Gratin

INGREDIENTS:

2 1/2 pound Brussels sprouts, trimmed and halved (quartered if large; about 8 cups)
2-3 tbsp. extra-virgin olive oil, divided
1 medium onion, thinly sliced
3 tbsp. all-purpose flour
3/4 tsp. salt
1/4 tsp. white or black pepper
2 1/2 cups low-fat milk
1 1/2 cups fresh whole-wheat breadcrumbs or 1/2 cup shredded or crumbled cheese

INSTRUCTIONS:

•Position racks in upper and lower third of oven; preheat to 425°F.

•Toss Brussels sprouts in a large bowl with 1 tablespoon oil until well coated.

•Divide between 2 baking sheets and spread in an even layer.

•Roast, stirring once and rotating the pans top to bottom about halfway through, until tender and beginning to brown for about 20 to 25 minutes.

•Meanwhile, heat 1 tablespoon oil in a large saucepan over medium heat.

•Add onion and cook, stirring frequently, until very soft and golden brown, 5 to 8 minutes. •Add flour, salt and pepper; cook, stirring, for 1 minute more.

•Add milk and continue to stir, scraping up any browned bits.

•Cook, stirring, until the sauce bubbles and thickens enough to coat the back of a spoon, about 4 minutes. Remove from the heat.

•When the Brussels sprouts are done, remove from the oven. Preheat the broiler.

•Transfer half the Brussels sprouts to a 2-quart, broiler-safe baking dish.

•Spread half the sauce over the Brussels sprouts.

•Add the remaining Brussels sprouts and top with the remaining sauce.

•Combine breadcrumbs and the remaining 1 tablespoon oil in a small bowl (skip this step if you are topping with cheese).

•Sprinkle the breadcrumb mixture over the gratin.

•Place under the broiler and broil, watching closely, until the gratin is bubbling and beginning to brown on top, 1 to 5 minutes, depending on your broiler.
•Let stand for 10 minutes before serving.

Creamy Hamburger Noodle Casserole

INGREDIENTS:

2 bunches scallions, trimmed
8 oz. 90%-lean ground beef
1 1/2 tsp. canola oil
1/2 cup bulgur
2 cloves garlic, minced
2 8-oz. cans tomato sauce
1/2 cup water
1/4 tsp. salt, divided
Freshly ground pepper, to taste
6 oz. no-yolk whole-wheat egg noodles
1 cup low-fat cottage cheese
1 cup reduced-fat sour cream
1/4 cup shredded extra-sharp Cheddar cheese

INSTRUCTIONS:

•Preheat oven to 350°F.
•Coat a 2-quart baking dish with cooking spray.
•Put a large pot of water on to boil.
•Separate white and green parts of scallions; thinly slice and reserve separately.
•Cook beef in a large skillet over medium-high heat, breaking up clumps with a wooden spoon, until no longer pink, 3 to 5 minutes. Transfer to a plate lined with paper towels.
•Wipe out the pan, add oil and reduce heat to medium-low. Add bulgur, garlic and the reserved scallion whites.
•Cook, stirring, until the scallions soften, 5 to 7 minutes. Add tomato sauce, water and the beef; bring to a simmer. Cover and simmer gently until the bulgur is tender and the sauce is thickened, 15 to 20 minutes. Season with 1/8 teaspoon salt and pepper.
•Meanwhile, cook noodles until just tender, 6 to 8 minutes or according to package directions.
•Drain and rinse under cold water.

•Puree cottage cheese in a food processor until smooth. Transfer to a medium bowl; fold in sour cream and the reserved scallion greens. Season with the remaining 1/8 teaspoon salt and pepper.
•Spread half the noodles in the prepared pan. Top with half the cottage cheese mixture and half the meat sauce. Repeat with the remaining noodles, cottage cheese and sauce.
•Sprinkle Cheddar over the top.
•Bake the casserole until bubbly, 30 to 40 minutes. Let stand for 10 minutes before serving.

Quick Shrimp Enchilada Bake

INGREDIENTS:

1 pound peeled cooked shrimp, tails removed, diced
1 cup frozen corn, thawed
2 4-ounce cans chopped green chiles, (not drained)
2 cups canned green enchilada sauce, or green salsa, divided
12 corn tortillas
1 15-ounce can nonfat refried beans
1 cup reduced-fat shredded cheese, such as Mexican-style cheese blend, Monterey Jack or Cheddar
1/2 cup chopped fresh cilantro
1 lime, cut into wedges

INSTRUCTIONS:

•Preheat oven to 425°F. Coat a 9-by-13-inch glass baking dish with cooking spray.
•Combine shrimp, corn, chiles and 1/2 cup enchilada sauce (or salsa) in a microwave-safe medium bowl.
•Cover and microwave on High until heated through, about 2 1/2 minutes.
•Spread 1/4 cup enchilada sauce (or salsa) in the prepared baking dish. Top with a layer of 6 overlapping tortillas.
•Spread refried beans evenly over the tortillas.
•Top the beans with the shrimp mixture, followed by the remaining 6 tortillas.
•Pour the remaining sauce (or salsa) over the tortillas. Cover with foil.
•Bake the casserole until it begins to bubble on the sides, about 20 minutes. Remove the foil; sprinkle cheese on top.
•Continue baking until heated through and the cheese is melted, about 5 minutes more. Top with cilantro and serve with lime wedges.

Vegan Pies

INGREDIENTS:

1 lb. Yukon Gold or white potatoes, peeled and cut into 1-inch chunks
1/2 cup buttermilk
1 tbsp. butter
3/4 tsp. salt, divided
1/2 tsp. freshly ground pepper, divided
1 tbsp. extra-virgin olive oil
1 large onion, finely diced
1/2 cup finely diced carrot
1 tbsp. water
3/4 cup frozen corn kernels, thawed
1 tsp. chopped fresh thyme or 1/2 teaspoon dried
3 tbsp. all-purpose flour
1 14-oz. can vegetable broth
1 1/2 cups cooked or canned (rinsed) lentils

INSTRUCTIONS:

•Put potatoes in a large saucepan and cover with 2 inches of water.
•Bring to a simmer over medium-high heat.
•Reduce heat to medium, partially cover and cook until tender for about 10 to 15 minutes. •Drain and return the potatoes to the pot.
•Add buttermilk, butter and 1/4 teaspoon each salt and pepper.
•Mash with a potato masher until mostly smooth.
•While the potatoes are cooking, position rack in upper third of oven; preheat broiler.
•Coat four 10- to 12-ounce broiler-safe ramekins (or an 8-inch-square broiler-safe baking dish) with cooking spray.
•Place ramekins on a broiler-safe baking sheet.
•Heat oil in a large skillet over medium-high heat.
•Add onion, carrot and water.
•Cover and cook, stirring occasionally, until softened for 3 to 5 minutes.
•Stir in corn, thyme and the remaining 1/2 teaspoon salt and 1/4 teaspoon pepper; cook, stirring occasionally, for 2 minutes.
•Sprinkle with flour and stir to coat.
•Stir in broth and bring to a simmer; cook, stirring, for 1 minute.
•Stir in lentils and cook, stirring constantly, for 2 minutes.

•Divide the hot lentil mixture among the prepared ramekins (or spread in the baking dish). •Top with the mashed potatoes.
•Broil, rotating halfway through for about 6 to 10 minutes or until the potato is lightly browned in spots.

Relleno with Chilies Casseroles

INGREDIENTS:

2 4-oz. cans diced green chilies, drained and patted dry
3/4 cup frozen corn, thawed and patted dry
4 scallions, thinly sliced
1 cup shredded reduced-fat Cheddar cheese
1 1/2 cups nonfat milk
6 large egg whites
4 large eggs
1/4 tsp. salt

INSTRUCTIONS:

•Heat oven to 400°F.
•Coat eight 6-ounce or four 10-ounce heatproof ramekins with cooking spray and put on a baking sheet.
•Equally divide green chilies, corn and scallions among the ramekins.
•Top each with cheese.
•Beat milk, egg whites, eggs and salt in a medium bowl until combined.
•Divide the egg mixture evenly among the ramekins.
•Bake the mini casseroles until the tops begin to brown and the eggs are set for about 25 minutes for 6-ounce ramekins and about 35 minutes for 10-ounce ramekins.

Tuna with Mushroom Noodle Casserole

INGREDIENTS:

8 oz. whole-wheat egg noodles
1 tbsp. extra-virgin olive oil
1 medium onion, finely chopped
8 oz. mushrooms, sliced
1/2 tsp. salt
1/2 cup dry white wine
6 tbsps. All-purpose flour
3 cups nonfat milk
1/2 tsp. freshly ground pepper
12 oz. canned chunk light tuna drained
1 cup frozen peas, thawed
1 cup finely grated Parmesan cheese, divided
1/2 cup coarse dry whole-wheat breadcrumbs

INSTRUCTIONS:

•Boil a large pot of water and cook noodles according to package directions.
•Drain and rinse the noodles.
•Position rack in upper third of oven and preheat broiler.
•Meanwhile, heat oil in a large ovenproof skillet over medium-high heat.
•Add onion, mushrooms and salt and cook, stirring often, until the onion is softened but not browned for about 5 minutes.
•Add wine and cook until evaporated for about 4 to 5 minutes.
•Scatter flour over the vegetables and mix to coat.
•Add milk and pepper and bring to a simmer, stirring constantly.
•Stir in tuna, peas and 1/2 cup Parmesan until evenly combined.
•Stir in the noodles to fully cover the pan.
•Remove from the heat.
•Dash the casserole with breadcrumbs and the remaining 1/2 cup Parmesan.
•Broil for about 3 to 4 minutes or until bubbly and lightly browned on top.

Potatoes with Cheese Scalloped

INGREDIENTS:

2 lbs. Yukon Gold potatoes, cut into 1/4-inch-thick slices (about 8 cups)
2-3 tbsps. Extra-virgin olive oil, divided
1 medium onion, thinly sliced
3 tbsps. All-purpose flour
3/4 tsp. salt
1/4 tsp. white or black pepper
2 1/2 cups low-fat milk
1 1/2 cups fresh whole-wheat breadcrumbs or 1/2 cup shredded or crumbled cheese

INSTRUCTIONS:

•Position racks in upper and lower third of oven and then preheats to 425°F.
•Mix potatoes in a large bowl with 1 tablespoon oil until well coated.
•Place potatoes between 2 baking sheets, equally divided and evenly spread in a layer.
•Roast, stirring once and rotating the pans top to bottom about halfway through, until tender and beginning to brown for around 20 to 25 minutes.
•Meanwhile, heat 1 tablespoon oil in a large saucepan over medium heat.
•Add onion and cook for 5 to 8 minutes, stirring frequently, until very soft and golden brown.
•Add flour, salt and pepper; cook, stirring, for 1 minute more.
•Add milk and continue to stir, scraping up any browned bits.
•Cook and stirring for about 4 minutes or until the sauce bubbles and thickens enough to coat the back of a spoon.
•Remove from the heat.
•When the potatoes are done, remove from the oven. Preheat the broiler.
•Transfer half the potatoes to a 2-quart, broiler-safe baking dish.
•Spread half the sauce over the potatoes.
•Add the remaining potatoes and top with the remaining sauce.
•Combine breadcrumbs and the remaining 1 tablespoon oil in a small bowl (skip this step if you are topping with cheese).
•Sprinkle the breadcrumb mixture (or cheese) over the gratin.

•Place under the broiler and broil, watching closely, until the gratin is bubbling and beginning to brown on top for about 1 to 5 minutes or depending on your broiler.
•Let stand for 10 minutes before serving.

Meringue-Topped Sweet Potato Casserole

INGREDIENTS:

2 1/2 lbs. sweet potatoes (about 3 medium), peeled and cut into 2-inch chunks
2 large eggs
2 tbsps. Brown sugar
1/4 tsp. ground cinnamon
1 tablespoon canola oil
1 cup low-fat evaporated milk
1 tsp. vanilla extract
1/2 tsp. salt
1 8-ounce can crushed pineapple, un-drained
1/2 cup chopped pecans, toasted
4 tsps. Dried egg whites reconstituted according to package directions, or 2 large pasteurized egg whites, at room temperature
1/4 cup granulated sugar

INSTRUCTIONS:

•Boil the sweet potatoes in a large saucepan covered with water.
•Reduce heat to a simmer and cook until tender for about 10 to 15 minutes.
•Drain well and transfer to a food processor.
•Process until smooth.
•Preheat oven to 350°F.
•Coat an 8-inch-square (or similar 2-quart) broiler-safe baking dish with cooking spray.
•Beat whole eggs, brown sugar, cinnamon, oil, evaporated milk, vanilla and salt in a large bowl until smooth.
•Add the sweet potato; whisk until smooth.
•Stir in pineapple and its juice.
•Spread the mixture in the prepared baking dish.
•Sprinkle with pecans.
•Bake the casserole for 35 to 45 minutes or until heated through and the edges are bubbling. •Set aside while you make the topping.

•To prepare meringue topping: Position rack in top third of oven and preheat the broiler. •Beat egg whites in a medium bowl with an electric mixer at high speed until soft peaks form

•Beat in granulated sugar in a slow, steady stream.

•Continue beating until stiff peaks form.

•Spoon the meringue into a gallon-size sealable bag.

•Seal the bag, prang out as much air as possible.

•Cut a 1/2-inch hole in one corner.

•Pipe the meringue onto the casserole, making marshmallow-size dots. (Alternatively, use a pastry bag fitted with a 1/2-inch tip or spread the meringue over the casserole as if you were frosting a cake.)

•Broil for 30 to 90 seconds or until lightly browned while watching carefully to prevent burning.

Chicken and Potato with Lemon Casserole

INGREDIENTS:

2.5 cups condensed cream of mushroom OR cream of chicken soup
1/2 cup milk
1.5 lbs. Yukon gold potatoes, very thinly sliced (no thicker than 1/8")
2 cloves garlic, minced
1 small white onion, peeled and thinly sliced
1.5 lbs. boneless, skinless chicken breasts
Salt and freshly-ground black pepper
1 lemon, thinly sliced and halved (into half coins)
(Optional garnish: chopped fresh parsley or fresh thyme)

INSTRUCTIONS:

•Heat oven to 425 degrees Fahrenheit.
•Add condensed soup and milk to a saucepan and whisk to combine.
•Heat over medium-high heat until simmering while stirring frequently.
•When it reaches a simmer, remove from heat and set aside.
•Meanwhile, in a separate large mixing bowl, put potatoes, onion, garlic, and chicken.
•Pour in the condensed soup mixture, along with a generous pinch of salt and pepper, and gently toss to combine until the potato and chicken mixture is evenly coated.
•Transfer mixture to a 9 x 13 baking dish.
•Tuck lemon wedges into the mixture randomly.
•Then cover the top of the pan with aluminum foil.
•Bake for 1 hour or until the potatoes are tender.
•Carefully remove the foil, and change oven to the high "broil" setting.
•Broil the casserole for an extra 2-3 minutes to crisp up the top, watching very carefully so that it does not burn.
•Remove pan from oven and serve warm.

Shrimp with Quinoa and Cajun Casserole

INGREDIENTS:

¾ lb. large shrimp, peeled and deveined
4 medium tomatoes cut into chunks
1 jalapeno, seeded and chopped
½ cup chopped sweet onion
2 cloves of garlic, minced
1 tbsp. tomato paste
3 tbsp. olive oil
2½ tsp. Cajun seasoning
Salt and pepper to taste
2½ cups cooked quinoa
1 cup shredded fontina cheese
Fresh cilantro for garnish

INSTRUCTIONS:

•Mix the shrimp and Cajun seasoning together, set aside.
•Mix the tomatoes with olive oil and Cajun seasoning, set aside.
•Heat olive oil over medium heat in a cast iron skillet (or any oven-safe skillet.)
•Cook the shrimp until opaque for about 2-3 minutes per side.
•Remove from the pan and set aside.
•Add the remaining olive oil to the pan along with the onion, jalapeno and garlic.
•Cook until the onion and jalapeno are tender while stirring often.
•Mix in the quinoa, tomato paste, Cajun seasoning and tomato chunks.
•Top with the shrimp and then sprinkle with the fontina cheese.
•Put in the oven and bake at 350°F for 15 minutes.
•During the last 2 minutes, turn on the broiler to high and broil until the cheese is slightly brown and bubbly.
•Garnish with fresh cilantro.

Hot Mussels with Tomatoes and Fennel

INGREDIENTS:

1 tbsp. olive oil
1 red onion, thinly sliced
2 baby fennels, halved, thinly sliced
2 garlic cloves, thinly sliced
300ml white wine
400g can chickpeas, rinsed, and drained
400g can chop tomatoes
1 tbsp. tomato paste
1 tsp. smoked paprika (pimento), plus extra to serve
1kg pot-ready mussels
2 tbsps. coriander leaves
Pinch of dried chili flakes

INSTRUCTIONS:

•In a large saucepan heat oil over medium-high heat.
•Add onion, fennel and garlic, then cook, stirring, for 5 minutes or until softened.
•Add the white wine and bring to the boil.
•Stir in the chickpeas, tomatoes, tomato paste and paprika, then simmer for 5 minutes or until slightly reduced.
•Add the mussels, cover the pan, increase the heat to high and cook for 2 minutes.
•Give the pan a big shake and look inside.
•If some mussels have not yet opened, cover and simmer for a further 1 minute.
•Discard any mussels that are closed.
•Divide mussels and sauce among shallow bowls and sprinkle with coriander, chili, extra paprika and some black pepper.

Zesty Meatball Casserole

INGREDIENTS:

500g pork mince
1 egg
1/2 cup fresh breadcrumbs
1/2 tsp. smoked paprika
Olive oil cooking spray
1 medium brown onion, finely chopped
1 medium red capsicum, chopped
2 garlic cloves, crushed
1 long red chili, finely chopped
2 tsps. Ground cumin
400g can chop tomatoes
100g baby spinach
Couscous, to serve

INSTRUCTIONS:

•Combine pork mince, egg, breadcrumbs and paprika in a bowl.
•Roll into 16 balls.
•Spray a saucepan with oil.
•Heat over medium-high heat.
•Cook meatballs, in batches, for 4 to 5 minutes or until browned.
•Transfer to a plate.
•Add onion to pan.
•Cook, stirring, for 3 to 4 minutes or until softened.
•Add capsicum, garlic and chili.
•Cook, stirring, for 2 to 3 minutes or until capsicum has softened.
•Add cumin and cook, stirring, for 1 minute or until fragrant.
•Add tomato and 3/4 cup cold water.
•Return meatballs to pan and put in the freezer.
•Bring to the boil.
•Reduce heat to low.
•Simmer, uncovered, for 15 to 20 minutes or until meatballs are cooked through.
•Stir in spinach.
•Cook, covered, for 2 to 3 minutes or until spinach wilts.
•Serve with couscous.

Spiced Beef, Sausage & Bean Casserole

INGREDIENTS:

2 tbsps. Olive oil
800g beef or pork chipolata sausages
4 onions, thinly sliced
1 cup (250ml) Beef Stock
2 cups arrabbiata (or other spicy) tomato pasta sauce
440ml can Guinness or other stout bee
4 tbsps. (1/3 cup) brown sugar
2 bay leaves
800g canned borlotti beans, rinsed, drained
Chopped parsley and potatoes, to serve

INSTRUCTIONS:

•Preheat the oven to 350 F
•Heat the oil in a large flameproof casserole over medium-high heat.
•Cook sausages for 5-6 minutes until browned all over.
•Set aside.
•Drain some of the oil from the pan if necessary, then add onion and cook over medium-low heat for 5-6 minutes until soft.
•Add stock, sauce, beer, sugar and bay leaves, and then bring to the boil.
•Reduce heat to medium-low and return sausages to pan with beans.
•Transfer to the oven for 40 minutes until thick.
•Stir in chopped parsley and serve with baked potatoes if desired.

Spiced Chorizo and Tater Casserole

INGREDIENTS:

2 tbsps. Olive oil
500g chorizo sausages, chopped into 3cm pieces
150g rindless bacon, roughly chopped
2 cloves garlic, chopped
1 teaspoon paprika
400g can dice tomatoes
2 cups chicken stock
3 cups frozen mixed vegetables
1/2 cup parsley, chopped
1 onion, halved, thinly sliced

INSTRUCTIONS:

•Heat oil in a large, heavy-based saucepan on high heat.
•Cook sausage pieces for 1-2 minutes each side until brown.
•Drain on kitchen paper.
•Cook bacon and onion in same pan for 5 minutes on medium heat until onion is soft.
•Add garlic and paprika and cook for 1 minute.
•Add tomato and stock and bring to the boil.
•Return sausages to pan and simmer on low for 10 minutes.
•Add vegetables and simmer uncovered for 10 minutes.
•Stir through parsley.
•Serve with steamed rice.

Steak and Pineapple Casserole

INGREDIENTS:

1/2 cup plain flour, seasoned
1kg chuck steak cut into 3cm cubes
1 large onion, thinly sliced
440g can pineapple pieces in natural juice
420g can tomato soup
2 tablespoons Worcestershire sauce
3 to 4 Desiree potatoes, washed and thinly sliced
Steamed green beans, to serve

INSTRUCTIONS:

•Heat oven to 200°C.
•Put seasoned flour into a large plastic bag.
•Toss steak in flour, shake off excess.
•Put into a large casserole dish.
•Arrange onion over meat.
•Drain pineapple, reserving juice, then layer over onion.
•Mix reserved juice, soup and Worcestershire sauce.
•Pour over casserole.
•Layer potatoes over casserole.
•Cover dish, then bake for 50 minutes.
•Remove lid and cook for a further 25 minutes or until potatoes are golden.
•Serve with steamed green beans.

Italian Beef Consommé Casserole

INGREDIENTS:

2 tablespoons olive oil
1kg beef rump steak, trimmed, diced
1 large brown onion, chopped
2 garlic cloves, crushed
3 medium carrots, peeled, chopped
1 tablespoon plain flour
1 tablespoon tomato paste
400g can dice Italian tomatoes
2 cups beef consommé
1 medium red capsicum, chopped
3/4 cup frozen peas
80g baby spinach
1/2 cup fresh basil leaves, torn
Cooked pasta or crusty bread, to serve

INSTRUCTIONS:

•Simmer 1 tablespoon oil in a heavy-based saucepan over medium-high heat.
•Browned the beef, in batches, for about 5 minutes.
•Transfer to a bowl.
•Heat remaining oil in pan.
•Add onion and garlic.
•Cook and stirring, for 3 minutes or until softened.
•Add carrot and then cook while stirring for 5 minutes or until carrot starts to brown.
•Return beef and juices to pan.
•Add flour and tomato paste and then cook, stirring, for 1 minute.
•Add tomato and consommé.
•Cover and bring it to a boil.
•Reduce heat to low and then let it simmer for 1 hour.
•Stir in capsicum and simmer, covered, for 1 hour or until beef is tender.
•Add peas, spinach and basil.
•Season with salt and pepper.
•Cook for 2 to 3 minutes or until peas are heated through.
•Serve with pasta or bread.

Chicken Fusilli Pasta Cacciatore

INGREDIENTS:

1 tbsp. olive oil
1.5kg mixed chicken pieces, trimmed
1 brown onion, roughly chopped
1 red capsicum, chopped
200g cup mushrooms, sliced
575g jar Napoletana pasta sauce
1/2 cup pitted kalamata olives, halved
1/2 cup small fresh basil leaves
Cooked fusilli (spiral) pasta, to serve

INSTRUCTIONS:

•In a large non-stick saucepan heat oil over medium-high heat.
•Cook chicken in batches, turning, for 5 minutes or until browned.
•Transfer to a plate.
•Add onion, capsicum and mushroom to pan.
•Cook, stirring, for 3 minutes or until softened.
•Return chicken to pan and then add the sauce.
•Cover and bring it to a boil.
•Reduce heat to low and let it simmer for 25 to 30 minutes or until chicken is cooked through.
•Stir in olives.
•Season with salt and pepper.
•Top with basil.
•Serve with pasta.

Pesto Dumplings, Prosciutto & Lamb Casserole

INGREDIENTS:

40g (1/4 cup) plain flour
1.5kg mini lamb round roasts, cut into 3cm pieces
3 tbsps. Olive oil
8 slices prosciutto, coarsely chopped
1 large brown onion, halved, thinly sliced
1 x 800g can diced tomatoes
250ml (1 cup) Chicken
4 dried bay leaves
1 x 500g pack frozen broad beans, thawed, peeled
Pesto dumplings
190g (1 1/4 cups) self-raising flour
70g chilled butter, chopped
60ml (1/4 cup) milk
1 tbsp. basil pesto

INSTRUCTIONS:

•Heat oven to 350 F.
•Place flour on a plate and season with salt and pepper.
•Add lamb and toss to coat and shake off excess.
•Heat 1 tablespoon oil in a 4L (16-cup) capacity flameproof casserole dish over medium heat.
•Add half the lamb and cook for 2-3 minutes each side or until brown and then transfer to a plate.
•Repeat with 1 tablespoon of oil and the remaining lamb, reheating dish between batches.
•Heat the remaining oil in dish and then add the prosciutto and onion.
•Cook, stirring, for 2-3 minutes or until onion is soft.
•Return the lamb to the dish.
•Add the tomato, stock and bay leaves.
•Cover and bake in oven for 1 1/2 hours or until the lamb is tender.
•Meanwhile, to make pesto dumplings, place flour in a bowl.
•Use your fingertips to rub the butter into the flour until it resembles fine breadcrumbs. •Pour in milk.
•Use a round-bladed knife in a cutting motion to mix until evenly incorporated.
•Add pesto and mix to create a swirled effect.
•Divide dough into 12 equal portions.

•Roll each portion into a ball.
•Increase oven temperature to 220°C.
•Add the broad beans to the lamb mixture and combine.
•Top with the dumplings.
•Bake, uncovered, for 10-15 minutes or until the dumplings are golden.
•Serve.

Balsamic Beef with Tomato Casserole

INGREDIENTS

2 tbsp. olive oil
800g beef chuck steak, trimmed, cut into 3cm pieces
3 medium carrots, peeled, chopped
2 tbsps. Balsamic vinegar
420g can Heinz Big Red condensed salt-reduced tomato soup
2 cups Beef Stock
1 cup dried puy lentils

INSTRUCTION

•In a large heavy-based casserole dish heat oil over medium-high heat.
•Brown the beef, in batches, for 5 to 6 minutes.
•Transfer to a bowl.
•Return beef to pan.
•Add carrots and vinegar.
•Cook while stirring for 2 minutes or until vinegar is reduced slightly.
•Stir in soup and stock.
•Cover and bring it to a boil.
•Reduce heat to low and let it simmer for 2 hours or until beef is tender.
•Meanwhile, cook lentils according to packet directions.
•Drain and add lentils to beef mixture.
•Season with salt and pepper.
•Stir to combine.
•Serve.

Tomato, Mustard and Coriander Lamb

INGREDIENTS:

1 tbsp. Alfa One rice bran oil
2kg leg of lamb
2 large brown onions, halved, thinly sliced
2 garlic cloves, crushed
2 tsps. Ground coriander
2 cinnamon sticks
1/4 tsp. ground cloves
2 tsps. Mustard seeds
2cm piece fresh ginger, peeled, finely chopped
1/4 tsp. ground turmeric
1 tsp. hot chili powder
410g can tomato puree
1 cup chicken stock
Chopped fresh coriander, steamed rice and lime halves, to serve

INSTRUCTIONS:

•In a large heavy-based flameproof casserole dish heat oil over medium-high heat.
•Brown the lamb for 5 minutes each side and then transfer it to a plate.
•Reduce heat to medium.
•Cook onion, stirring, for 5 minutes or until softened.
•Add garlic, coriander, cinnamon, cloves, mustard seeds, ginger, turmeric and chilli.
•Cook, stirring, for 1 minute or until fragrant.
•Return lamb to dish and then add puree, stock and 1 cup cold water.
•Season with salt and pepper.
•Cover and bring it to a boil.
•Reduce heat to low and let it simmer for 2 hours and 30 minutes to 3 hours or until lamb is tender, turning halfway during cooking.
•Shred the lamb using forks.
•Serve with coriander, rice and lime halves.

Tomato and Olive Lamb Casserole

INGREDIENTS:

2 tbsps. plain flour
8 (1kg) lamb neck chops
1 tbsp. olive oil
1 medium brown onion, halved, thinly sliced
1 large carrot, peeled, chopped
2 celery stalks, chopped
2 garlic cloves, crushed
1 cup chicken stock
2 x 400g cans dice tomatoes
2 tbsps. Fresh oregano leaves
1/2 cup pitted kalamata olives
Crusty bread, to serve

INSTRUCTIONS:

•Put flour on a large plate.
•Toss lamb in flour and shaking off excess.
•Transfer to a plate.
•Heat half the oil in large heavy-based saucepan over medium-high heat.
•Brown the lamb in batches for 3 minutes on each side.
•Transfer to a plate and set aside.
•Sauté onion, carrot and celery in a heated pan with oil.
•Cook, stirring, for 5 minutes or until vegetables are just tender.
•Add garlic and cook, stirring, for 1 minute or until fragrant.
•Stir in stock and tomatoes.
•Return lamb to pan and then cover.
•Bring to a boil and then reduce heat to low.
•Simmer for 30 minutes and then remove the lid.
•Simmer for another 30 minutes more or until lamb is cooked through.
•Stir in oregano and olives.
•Season with pepper.
•Serve with bread.

Beef Braised in Wine

INGREDIENTS:

1 onion, chopped
1 carrot, chopped
1 celery, chopped
2 tsps. Quarter spices (a mix of pepper, cloves, nutmeg and ginger)
2 garlic cloves, bruised
2 bay leaves
1/4 cup (60ml) brandy
1.5L (6 cups) dry red wine
1kg lean braising beef, such as chuck steak, cut into 3cm cubes
1/4 cup (60ml) olive oil
60g unsalted butter
1 1/2 tbsps. Tomato paste
2 tbsps. Plain flour
400ml Beef Stock
12 eschalots
2 tsps. sugar
250g thickly sliced pancetta or speck, cut into strips
150g button mushrooms
Aligot to serve

INSTRUCTIONS:

•Put the chopped onion, carrot, celery, spice, garlic, bay leaves, brandy, wine and beef in a bowl.
•Cover and marinate in the fridge for at least 4 hours, preferably overnight.
•Heat the oven to 170°C.
•Drain the beef mixture, reserving marinade.
•Bring the marinade to a boil in a pan over medium-high heat for 5-6 minutes.
•Heat half each of the oil and butter in a large flameproof casserole over medium-high heat. •Brown the beef in batches, then set aside.
•Add reserved vegetables and cook, stirring, for 2-3 minutes and then pour tomato paste and stir for 1 minute, then stir in the flour.
•Return the meat to the pan with marinade and stock.
•Bring to a boil, then cover and cook in the oven for 1 1/2 hours.
•Meanwhile, mix eschalots, sugar and enough water to cover in a saucepan and bring to boil over medium-high heat.

•Reduce heat to medium and simmer for 8-10 minutes until onions are tender.
•Set aside until needed.
•Heat remaining butter and oil in a fry pan over medium heat.
•Cook pancetta or speck, stirring, for 2-3 minutes until it starts to crisp, then remove with a slotted spoon and set aside.
•Add mushrooms to the pan, and then cook for 2-3 minutes until softened. Set aside with pancetta.
•Skim any fat from the surface of the beef pan.
•Strain, returning the liquid to the pan and setting beef and vegetables aside in a bowl. •Return pan to medium-high heat for 3-4 minutes to reduce and thicken sauce and then add beef with eschalots, pancetta and mushrooms.
•Simmer for another 5 minutes to heat through. Serve with aligot, and a salad if desired.

Tuna with Tomato Casserole

INGREDIENTS:

2 tbsps. Olive oil
1 leek (white part only), thinly sliced
1 carrot, finely chopped
1 celery stalk, finely chopped
400g can chop tomatoes
2 x 400g cans cannellini beans, rinsed
200ml chicken or vegetable stock
1 tbsp. Dijon mustard
2 x 200g yellow fin tuna fillets
1 cup (50g) panko breadcrumbs
1 garlic clove, crushed
1 tbsp. finely chopped flat-leaf parsley

INSTRUCTIONS:

•Heat 1 tablespoon oil in a pan over medium-low heat.
•Cook leek, carrot and celery for 10 minutes, stirring, until softened.
•Add tomato, beans and stock and simmer over medium heat for 20 minutes until slightly reduced, then add in mustard.
•Heat the oven to 200° C.
•Grease a 4 individual baking dishes or ramekins.
•Heat a lightly oiled pan over high heat.

•Blister tuna for 1 minute each side.
•Cut into bite-sized pieces.
•Layer beans, then tuna, then more beans in the dishes.
•Mix panko, garlic, parsley and 1 tablespoon oil, and then scatter on top.
•Bake for 20 minutes until golden and bubbling.
•Serve with a salad.

Tuna Casserole with Béchamel Sauce

INGREDIENTS:

200g large pasta shells
1 tbsp. olive oil
1 onion, chopped
2 tsps. Crushed garlic
425g can tuna chunks in spring water, drained
1/2 cup semi-dried tomatoes, from the deli, chopped
1/2 cup pitted kalamata olives, from the deli, halved
300ml cooking cream
1/4 cup shredded parmesan
2 tbsps. Chopped flat-leaf parsley, to serve

INSTRUCTIONS:

•Cook pasta following package directions and then drain well with water.
•Meanwhile, heat oil in a frying pan over medium-high heat.
•Sauté onion for 1-2 minutes or until softened.
•Put garlic and cook for another 30 seconds.
•Add tuna, tomatoes, olives and cream.
•Stir for 2-3 minutes to combine and heat through.
•Preheat grill on high.
•Spoon pasta mixture into four 1 1/2-cup ovenproof dishes and sprinkle with parmesan. •Cook under grill for 4-5 minutes or until golden and bubbly.
•Sprinkle with parsley.

Spicy Lamb with Pumpkin Couscous

INGREDIENTS:

60ml (1/4 cup) olive oil
6 lamb shanks, French trimmed
2 red onions, halved, thinly sliced
3 garlic cloves, crushed
2 cinnamon sticks
3 tsps. Ground cumin
2 tsps. Ground coriander
2 tsps. Ground paprika
Large pinch of saffron threads
1L (4 cups) Beef Stock Salt Reduced
2 x 400g cans cherry tomatoes
2 tbsps. Brown sugar
1/2 cup chopped fresh coriander
1/2 cup chopped fresh mint
800g Butternut pumpkin, peeled, cut into 3cm pieces
380g (2 cups) couscous

INSTRUCTIONS:

•Heat oven to 350 F.
•Heat 1 tablespoon oil in a flameproof casserole dish over medium-high heat.
•Brown the lamb in 2 batches, turning, for 5 minutes.
•Transfer to a large bowl.
•Heat the remaining oil in the dish over medium heat.
•Cook the onion for 5 minutes or until soft.
•Stir in the garlic, cinnamon, cumin, ground coriander, paprika and saffron for 1 minute or until aromatic.
•Stir in the stock, tomato, sugar, half the fresh coriander and half the mint.
•Bring to a boil and season.
•Add lamb and then cover.
•Bake for 1 hour and 30 minutes.
•Add pumpkin and then cover.
•Bake for 30 minutes or until pumpkin is soft.
•Transfer lamb and 2 cups of sauce to a heatproof bowl.
•Cover to keep warm and then add couscous to the pumpkin mixture.
•Stir until just combined and cover.

•Set aside for 5 minutes or until liquid has absorbed.
•Divide among bowls.
•Top with the lamb and sauce, and the remaining coriander and mint.

Pancetta and Rosemary Rabbit

INGREDIENTS:

1.6kg whole rabbit, jointed
2 tbsps. Plain flour, seasoned
1/4 cup (60ml) olive oil
1 tsp. fennel seeds
2 onions, finely chopped
6 slices flat pancetta, chopped
4 garlic cloves, chopped
1 cup (250ml) white wine
1/3 cup (80ml) balsamic vinegar
400g can chop tomatoes
400g can cherry tomatoes
2 rosemary sprigs, leaves chopped
2 tbsps. Chopped flat-leaf parsley
Cooked soft polenta, to serve

INSTRUCTIONS:

•Preheat the oven to 350 F
•Dust rabbit in flour, shaking off excess.
•Heat 2 tablespoons oil in a fry pan over medium heat and cook rabbit, in batches, for 2 minutes each side or until golden.
•Place in a baking dish.
•Heat remaining 1 tablespoon oil and cook fennel, onion, pancetta and garlic, stirring, for 3-4 minutes until soft and golden.
•Add wine and half the vinegar, and simmer for 3-4 minutes until reduced by half.
•Add tomatoes and rosemary, season and bring to the boil.
•Pour over rabbit, cover and cook for 1 1/4 hours or until rabbit is tender.
•Stir in remaining 2 tablespoons vinegar and scatter with parsley.
•Serve with polenta.

Braised Beef Cheek Casserole

INGREDIENTS:

6 beef cheeks trimmed
2 tbsps. Plain flour, seasoned
2 tbsps. Olive oil
1 large onion and 1 carrot, chopped
2 garlic cloves, crushed
1 cup (250ml) dry red wine
2 cups (500ml) Beef Stock
1 vanilla bean, split
1/4 firmly packed cup (50g) brown sugar
2 each of thyme sprigs and bay leaves
Mashed potato and vegetables, to serve

INSTRUCTIONS:

•Preheat oven to 350 F.
•Pat beef dry with paper towel, then toss in seasoned flour.
•Heat oil in a large flameproof casserole.
•Cook beef, in batches, over medium heat for 2 minute each side or until sealed.
•Stir onion, carrot and garlic in same pan for 1 minute.
•Add wine, stock, vanilla, sugar and herbs.
•Bring to the boil.
•Return beef to pan.
•Place a circle of baking paper on the surface and cover with a lid.
•Cook in oven for 2 hours.
•Remove beef, and then reduce sauce over high heat for 2-3 minutes until reduced slightly. •Season, then return beef to pan.
•Serve with mash and vegetables.

Carol's Chicken Stew Casserole

INGREDIENTS:

2 tbsp. olive oil
1 small chicken cut into serving pieces
2 crushed garlic cloves
1 diced large onion
1 can diced tomatoes
2 bay leaves
1 tsp. salt
1 tbsp. black pepper
1 1/2 cups water
2 large cubed potatoes
1 green cubed capsicum

INSTRUCTIONS:

•Heat the oil in a large saucepan and brown the chicken lightly.
•Then remove and set aside.
•Add garlic and stir-fry until golden.
•Then stir-fry the onions until translucent.
•Return the chicken and add the tomatoes, bay leaves, water, salt & pepper.
•Simmer for 20 minutes over low heat.
•Add the potatoes and simmer for 15 minutes or until nearly cooked.
•Add the capsicum and simmer for 5 minutes.
•Serve hot with plain steamed rice.

Chicken & Pineapple Adobo- Filipino Style

INGREDIENTS:

2-3lbs. chicken thighs or breasts
1 cup drained pineapples, cut into bite sized chunks
4-6 cloves of garlic, chopped
1/2 large onion, diced
1/2 cup white/ apple cider vinegar
1/3 cup dark soy sauce
1 tbsp. fish sauce
1/2 cup water
2-3 bay leaves
Salt and pepper to taste

INSTRUCTIONS:

•Take a big pot and marinate the chicken with garlic, onion, apple cider vinegar, soy sauce, fish sauce, water, bay leaves and pepper.
•Put in the fridge overnight.
•Turn it around a couple of times in between.
•Bring the whole mixture to a boil and then reduce the heat to medium-low.
•Let it simmer for around 30-40 minutes or until the chicken is fully cooked.
•Add pineapples and salt then stir.
•Serve hot with rice.

Beef Pares ala Pinoy Style

INGREDIENTS:

1 kilo sliced in cubes Beef (preferably with fat)
4pcs star anise,
1/4 cup brown sugar
1/8 cup white sugar
1tbsp.salt
1 beef cube
1/8 cup soy sauce
2 tbsp. Cornstarch or flour
1 whole garlic crushed
chopped onion spring (for garnishing)
3 tbsp. oil

INSTRUCTIONS:

•Simmer sliced beef in soy sauce, white sugar, brown sugar, star anise, beef cube and salt for 2 hours in medium heat or pressure cooked it for 1 hour.
•Lower the heat and continue simmering until beef is tender.
•In 1/2 cup of water, add cornstarch and stir until cornstarch or flour is properly dissolved. •Pour cornstarch mixture to the boiling beef pares.
•You can add more flour depending on the consistency of the sauce.
•In a separate pan, fry the crushed garlic in slow heat until the garlic is brown and crispy.
•Serve Beef Pares with rice and garnish it with garlic and spring onions on top.

Goat Stew with Vegie

INGREDIENTS:

1 lb. bone-in goat meat, cut into large chunks
1/4 cup vinegar
1/4 cup soy sauce
4 cloves garlic, crushed
1 tbsp. vegetable oil
1 onion, chopped
1 red bell pepper, cut into 1-inch squares
1 cup tomato sauce
2 cups beef stock
1 potato, peeled and cut into large chunks
2 carrots, peeled and cut into large chunks
1/2 cup green peas
1/2 tsp. salt
1/4 tsp. pepper
1 pinch cayenne pepper

INSTRUCTIONS:

•Mix goat meat with vinegar, soy sauce, and garlic in a large bowl.
•Cover and refrigerate from 1 to 8 hours.
•For best flavor, marinate at least 6 hours.
•Remove meat from marinade and pat dry with paper towels.
•Set aside marinade and garlic cloves.
•Heat vegetable oil in a large pot over medium-high heat.
•Brown the goat meat, working in batches if necessary for 10 to 15 minutes.
•Set goat meat aside.
•Cook and stir onion, red bell pepper, and garlic cloves from the marinade over medium heat until onion is translucent for about 5 minutes.
•Pour in tomato sauce and bring mixture to a simmer.
•Cook for about 5 minutes.
•Return goat meat to the sauce and pour in the marinade and beef stock.
•Bring to a boil; reduce heat to low, and let it simmer covered until goat meat is partially tender for about 30 to 40 minutes.
•Mixing in potato, carrots, and peas.
•Season with salt, black pepper, and cayenne pepper.

•Simmer until goat meat is very tender and potato and carrots are cooked through for about 20 to 30 more minutes.
•Adjust seasonings before serving.

Potato Casserole With Hamburger

INGREDIENTS:

1 lb. ground beef
1 can beef broth
1 small can cream of potato soup
1 20 oz. pkg. shredded hash browns
1 C. shredded mozzarella cheese

INSTRUCTIONS:

•Heat oven to 450°
•Brown the beef in skillet and then drain.
•Add broth and soup.
•Spread hash browns in greased 9"x13" baking dish.
•Top with beef and broth mixture.
•Bake covered for 20 minutes.
•Uncover and cook for another 10 minutes.
•Sprinkle with cheese before serving.

Fusilli Hamburger Casserole

INGREDIENTS:

1 lb. ground chuck or sirloin
3 cups cooked Fusilli, or bow-tie pasta
1 onion, chopped
1 bell pepper, chopped
3 celery stalks, chopped
1 28 oz. can diced tomatoes
7 oz. can tomato sauce or 1 cup V-8
3 cups shredded cheddar cheese, divided
1 tsp. oregano
1 tsp. basil
Louisiana hot sauce
Salt and pepper

INSTRUCTIONS:

•Lightly brown the meat and drain.
•Add veggies and continue cooking until wilted and meat is cooked through.
• Add tomatoes and sauce or V-8.
•Add oregano and basil.
•Remove from heat and stir in 2 cups cheese and add pasta.
•Adjust seasonings and add three or four dashes of Louisiana hot sauce.
•Place in casserole and bake with additional cheese sprinkled on top.
•Let the cheese melt and casserole is bubbly before serving.

Hot Taco with Tortilla Casserole

INGREDIENTS:

1 lb. ground beef
1 can (15 oz.) chili beans
1 can (8 oz.) tomato sauce
2 tbsps. Taco sauce
4 tsps. Chili powder
1/2 tsp. garlic powder or salt
1 tomato, chopped
2 cups tortilla chips
1 cup sour cream
1/2 cup sliced green onions with tops
1 cup cheddar cheese, shredded

INSTRUCTIONS:

•Brown the beef and drain.
•Stir in beans, tomato sauce, taco sauce, chili powder and garlic powder.
•Heat to boiling.
•Put chips in 12x8x2-inch baking dish, ungreased.
•Top with beef mixture.
•Spread with sour cream.
•Sprinkle with onions, tomatoes and cheese.
•Bake, uncovered, at 350° F for 20-30 minutes or until hot.
•Arrange additional tortilla chips around edge of casserole.
•Serve with shredded lettuce, chili peppers and taco sauce, if desired.

Crockpot Beef Bouillon with Mushroom Casserole

INGREDIENTS:

1 cup uncooked wild rice, rinsed and drained
1 cup chopped celery
1 cup chopped carrots
2 cans (4 oz. each) mushroom stems and pieces, drained
1 large onion, chopped
1 garlic clove, minced
1/2 cup slivered almonds
3 beef bouillon cubes
2-1/2 tsps. Seasoned salt
2 lbs. boneless round steak, cut into 1-inch cubes
3 cups water

INSTRUCTIONS:

•Put wild rice, celery, carrots, mushroom stems, onion, garlic clove, almonds, beef bouillon cubes, salt, steak, and water in a crockpot in the order listed (do not stir).
•Cover and cook on low heat for 6-8 hours or until rice is tender.
•Stir before serving.

Cheesy Chicken Dorito Casserole

INGREDIENTS:

1 regular bag of cheese Doritos (crushed in the bag)
4 chicken breast or 4-5 chicken filets (can also use a whole chicken).
1 bell pepper (diced)
1 cup of green onions (diced)
1 yellow onion (diced)
seasoning
parsley
3 chicken bouillon cubes
1 can of cream of mushroom soup
1 can of cream of chicken soup
1 can of rotel tomatoes
1 can of enchilada sauce (regular size can) can use mild or hot
1-2 cans of ranch style beans
1-2 bags of Mexican shredded cheese or shredded cheese of your choice
Jalapenos (optional)

INSTRUCTIONS:

•Cook chicken with all the vegetables, seasonings, parsley and bouillon cubes until done.
•Save broth.
•In a different boiler, mix the soups, beans, rotel tomatoes and enchilada sauce.
•Remove vegetables from broth and place in this mixture also.
•Heat and make sure all ingredients are mixed well.
•If mixture is too thick add small of amounts of broth.
•Put crushed Dorito chips in the bottom of a deep casserole dish, greased the dish with pam.
•Cut chicken into bite size pieces and place on top of Doritos.
•If using ground hamburger chuck, spread evenly over chips.
•Cover Doritos and chicken with mixture.
•Top with shredded cheese and jalapenos. (optional)
•Bake at 375 degrees Fahrenheit for 30 minutes or until cheese has melted and the side are bubbly.

Chicken Mushroom Roll Casserole

INGREDIENTS:

6 tbsp. melted butter, divided
4 cups cubed sourdough rolls
1/3 cup grated Parmesan cheese
2 tbsp. chopped fresh parsley
2 medium-size sweet onions, sliced
1 (8-oz.) package sliced fresh mushrooms
1 cup white wine
1 (10 3/4-oz.) can cream of mushroom soup
1/2 cup drained and chopped jarred roasted red bell peppers
2 1/2 cups shredded cooked chicken

INSTRUCTIONS:

•Mix melted butter with cube sourdough rolls, grated parmesan cheese and chopped fresh parsley, and then set aside.
•In a large skillet, sauté the onion with the remaining butter over medium to high heat for about 15 minutes or until it become golden brown.
•Add mushroom and cook in 5 minutes.
•Pour wine, mushroom soup, roasted bell peppers and shredded chicken while stirring constantly until it become bubbly and cooked.
•Spoon the mixture into the 9 inch square baking dish, slightly greased and top it with bread mixture, evenly.
•Bake the casserole at around 400°F for about 15 minutes or until golden brown.

Vegetable Casserole with Ham

INGREDIENTS

1/4 cup butter
1/4 cup all-purpose flour
3 1/2 cups milk
1/2 tsp. dried thyme
1 tsp. chicken bouillon granules
2 cups diced cooked ham
1 (10-oz.) package frozen sweet peas and mushrooms
1 cup frozen crinkle-cut carrots
1 (14.1-oz.) package refrigerated piecrusts

INSTRUCTIONS

•Heat oven to 450°F.
•Melt butter in a large saucepan over medium heat.
•Slowly whisk in flour, and cook, whisking constantly for about 1 minute.
•Add milk, dried thyme, and chicken bouillon granules, stir constantly until cook or in about 6 to 8 minutes when become thick and bubbly.
•Add ham, frozen crinkle –cut carrots, and refrigerated pie crust, let it cook for about 4 to 5 •minutes or until the mixture is thoroughly heated.
•Spoon it into a lightly greased 11 x 7 – inch baking dish.
•Unroll each piecrust on a lightly floured surface.
•Cut the piecrust into 1 ¼ - inch – wide strips and arrange it in a lattice design over the ham mixture.
•Then bake the casserole in a 450° F for about 40 minutes or until crust is brown and the filling is bubbly.

Beef Burger Casserole

INGREDIENTS:

1 lb. ground beef
1/4 C. chopped onion
1- 8 oz. can tomato sauce
1/4 C. ketchup
1/2 tsp. salt
1- 8 oz. pkg. American cheese slices
1- 8 oz. pkg. crescent rolls

INSTRUCTIONS:

•Preheat oven to 400°F.
•Brown the beef and onions in skillet and then drain well.
•Stir in tomato sauce, ketchup and salt.
•Layer the beef mixture and cheese in a 2 qt. casserole dish, alternately.
•Put crescent rolls around edge.
•Bake for 20-25 minutes or until rolls are golden brown.

Mushroom Burrito Casserole

INGREDIENTS:

1 lb. ground beef
1/2 chopped onion
1 pack of taco seasoning
Flour tortillas
1 can refry beans
3 cups shredded cheddar cheese
1 can cream of mushroom soup
8 oz. sour cream

INSTRUCTIONS:

•Brown the beef and drain.
•Add taco seasoning, prepare following the package directions.
•Add refried beans.
•Mix soup with sour cream.
•Spread this mixture over bottom of casserole dish.
•Put meat in the tortillas, wrap up and place seam down in dish.
•Put the remaining sour cream and soup over top of burritos.
•Sprinkle cheese on top and bake in 350°F oven for 30 minutes.
•Garnish with green onions and tomatoes.
•Serve picate sauce and Dorito chips on side.

Beef and Corn Noodle Casserole

INGREDIENTS:

Easy Country Ground Beef and Corn Casserole
1 1/2 pounds of lean ground beef
1 cup of chopped onion
1 - 12 ounce can of whole kernel corn, drained
1 can of cream of chicken soup
1 can of cream of mushroom soup
1 cup of sour cream
1 small can tomato sauce
1/4 cup of chopped pimiento
3/4 teaspoon of salt
1/4 teaspoon of black pepper
3 cups of noodles, cooked and drained
3 tablespoons of butter, melted
1 cup of soft breadcrumbs

INSTRUCTIONS:

•Brown the ground beef and then add the onion and cook until tender.
•Add the corn, soup, tomato sauce, sour cream, pimiento, salt, and pepper.
•Mix well and then stir in the cooked noodles.
•Taste and add more seasoning if needed.
•Pour into a 2-1/2 quart casserole dish and add the melted butter to the breadcrumbs and sprinkle over the top of the casserole.
•Bake at 350 degrees for 30 minutes or until hot & bubbly.

Taco Pie with Cheese

INGREDIENTS:

1 lb. rigatoni
1 lb. ground beef
1 package taco seasoning
4 oz. cream cheese
1 1/2 cups salsa
1 cup cheddar cheese
1 1/2 cups Monterrey jack cheese

INSTRUCTIONS:

•Boil the pasta until not quite al dente and drain well when done.
•Meanwhile, brown the ground beef and drain.
•Add the taco seasoning following the packet directions.
•Cook for a few minutes over low heat and then add the cream cheese.
•Allow the cream cheese to fully melt into the meat mixture.
•Remove from heat and stir in 1 cup of salsa.
•Spray the spring form pan with Pam and position the rigatoni noodles up in the pan.
•Scatter the meat mixture on top of the noodles and use a chopstick, skewer or straw to poke the meat down into the holes of the noodles.
•Then pour the remaining half cup of salsa over the top.
•Sprinkle the top with the remaining 2 cups of cheese.
•Bake at 350 degrees Fahrenheit for about 20 minutes.
•Remove from oven and let stand for 10 minutes before removing the sides of the pan and cutting

Turkey with Spinach Casserole

INGREDIENTS:

3 tbsp. butter, divided
2 large sweet onions, diced
1/2 cup all-purpose flour
1 tsp. salt
1 tsp. pepper
4 (12-oz.) turkey tenderloins cut into 1 1/2-inch cubes
2 tbsp. vegetable oil
1 1/2 cups chicken broth
1 cup milk
1 (10-oz.) package fresh spinach, torn

INSTRUCTIONS:

•Thaw butter in a large skillet over medium-high heat.
•Add onions and sauté for 15 minutes or become caramelized.
•Put onions in a bowl, and set aside.
•Combine all-purpose flour, salt, and pepper, and then dredge turkey tenderloins in flour mixture.
•Melt remaining 2 tablespoons butter with oil in skillet over medium-high heat.
•Brown the turkey tenderloins on all sides.
•Gradually stir in chicken broth and milk.
•Bring to a boil, and cook, stirring constantly, 1 minute or until thickened.
•Stir in onions and add spinach, stirring just until wilted.
•Pour turkey mixture into a lightly greased 13- x 9-inch baking dish.
•Bake, covered, at 350°F for 30 minutes.
•Remove from oven, and arrange desired amount of Cranberry-Pecan Crusts over pie before serving.

Original Vermicelli Chicken Casserole

INGREDIENTS:

1 1/2 (8-oz.) vermicelli
1/2 cup butter
1/2 cup all-purpose flour
4 cups milk
1/2 cup dry white wine
2 tbsps. Chicken bouillon granules
1 tsp. seasoned pepper
2 cups freshly grated Parmesan cheese
4 cups diced cooked chicken
1 (6-oz.) jar sliced mushrooms, drained
3/4 cup slivered almonds

INSTRUCTIONS:

•Heat oven to 350°Fahrenheit..
•Prepare pasta according to package directions.
•In the meantime, melt butter in a Dutch oven over low heat and then whisk in flour until smooth.
•Cook for 1 minute while whisking constantly.
•Gradually whisk in milk and wine; cook over medium heat, whisking constantly for about 8 to 10 minutes or until mixture is thickened and bubbly.
•Whisk in bouillon granules, seasoned pepper, and 1 cup Parmesan cheese.
•Remove from heat; stir in diced cooked chicken, sliced mushrooms, and hot cooked pasta.
•Spoon mixture into a lightly greased 13- x 9-inch baking dish and then sprinkle with slivered almonds and remaining 1 cup Parmesan cheese.
•Bake at 350°F for 35 minutes or until bubbly.

Spiced Tomato and Egg Casserole

INGREDIENTS:

1 ½ pounds fingerling potatoes
Kosher salt
¼ cup vegetable oil
1 yellow onion, diced
1 pepper, seeded if desired, finely chopped
2 jalapeño peppers, seeded if desired, finely chopped
2 tbsps. Finely chopped peeled ginger
3 garlic cloves, finely chopped
1 tsp. ground cumin
1 tsp. ground garam masala
½ tsp. ground coriander
1 28-oz. cans whole peeled tomatoes
¼ cup chopped fresh mint, more for garnish
2 tbsps. Chopped cilantro or basil, more for garnish
6 eggs
Black pepper

INSTRUCTIONS:

•Boil a large pot with salted water.
•Place potatoes in the large pot and bring it to a boil until potatoes are cooked and become tender.
•Remove and drain the potatoes.
•Slice it into 1/2-inch-thick rounds.
•Heat oil in a large skillet over medium-high heat and then add the onion followed by peppers, ginger, garlic, cumin, garam masala and coriander.
•Cook it for about 10 minutes.
•Stir in tomatoes and 1/2 teaspoon salt and simmer it over medium-low heat for around 15 minutes.
•Break tomatoes with a fork and mix in mint, cilantro or basil.
•Taste and adjust seasonings.
•Heat oven to 375°F.
•Place potatoes in a 9-inch-square baking dish and file it in a single layer.
•Pour the hot tomato sauce over potatoes.
•Set the pan to oven and bake for about 20 minutes.
•Make six wells in the tomato mixture.

•Crack the eggs and put it into the wells.
•Season with salt and pepper.
•Bake until egg whites are set but yolks are still runny, this will take for about 8 to 13 minutes, depending on how much the potatoes and sauce cooled before baking.
•Serve garnished with herbs.

Egg Noodles Casserole

INGREDIENTS:

1 lb. Ground beef
2 cloves Garlic, crushed
2 tsp. Salt
2 tsp. Sugar
2 -8oz Cans Tomato Sauce
1 C. Sour Cream
1-8 oz. Pkg. Cream Cheese, softened
6 Green Onions, chopped finely
1-8 oz. Pkg. Egg Noodles, cooked and drained
1 C. Cheddar cheese, grated

INSTRUCTIONS:

•Preheat oven to 350°F.
•Brown beef with garlic.
•Add salt, sugar and tomato sauce and simmer.
•Combine Sour Cream, Cream Cheese, and Onion.
•Spray 2-3 qt. casserole with cooking spray.
•Put 1/2 of the noodles and 1/2 of the tomato sauce mixture in bottom.
•Layer with Sour Cream mixture.
•Top with remaining noodles and tomato sauce mixture.
•Bake for 35 minutes.

Cottage Cheese Beef Casserole

INGREDIENTS

2 lbs. lean ground beef
1 large white onion
12 oz. can tomato paste
16 oz. container cottage cheese
16 oz. container sour cream
2 packages shredded cheddar cheese
1 lb. noodles

INSTRUCTIONS:

•Heat oven to 375.
•Brown the beef and onion.
•Cook noodles and then add sour cream and cottage cheese.
•Mix meat and tomato paste in a separate bowl.
•Layer noodles and meat then put cheddar cheese on top.
•Cover casserole and bake for about 45 minutes.

Full House Casserole

INGREDIENTS:

1 box elbow macaroni (shells, or rotini)
Olive Oil
Kosher Salt
Butter
1.5 - 2 lbs. 93% lean ground beef
1 medium white onion, chopped
1 T. chopped garlic
2 tsps. Worcestershire Sauce
Italian Seasoning
Seasoned Salt
Garlic Pepper
1 tub fresh mushrooms, sliced (or one large jar, drained)
1 Large can diced tomatoes
1 can cream of mushroom soup
1 package shredded cheese, halved

INSTRUCTIONS:

•Bring large pot of water to boil.
•Add olive oil, butter, macaroni, and an armful of kosher salt

•Cook according to package directions.
•In the time being, heat oven to 350 degree Fahrenheit.
•Brown meat, onion, mushrooms with Worcestershire, Italian seasoning, seasoned salt, and garlic pepper in large skillet.
•Once cook, transfers to large mixing bowl and then add cooked pasta, tomatoes, soup, and half the cheese.
•Stir together well to combine.
•Spread in casserole dish.
•Cover with remaining cheese.
•Bake about 25 minutes or until cheese is melted and become bubbly.
•Serve with salad and garlic bread.

Beefy Chile Relleno Casserole

INGREDIENTS:

1 27 oz. can whole green chilies
1 lb. Monterey Jack or Pepper Jack cheese, grated/shredded
1 lb. cheddar cheese, grated/shredded
1-1/2 to 2 lbs. ground beef, browned
2 garlic cloves, minced or finely chopped
1 tomato, seeded and diced
3 eggs, beaten
3 Tbsp. flour
1 small can evaporated milk
1 15 oz. can tomato sauce or you can use salsa sauce

INSTRUCTIONS:

•Wash chilies, slice open, remove seeds, and pat dry.
•In a 9" x 13" pan, layer half of the chilies, half of the cooked ground beef, garlic mixture with tomatoes, and then half the cheese.
•Repeat layers and save some 1/2 cup cheese for topping.
•Combine the eggs with the flour and milk and beat until it blended well.
•Pour the egg mixture over the chilies, meat, and cheese.
•Bake at 350°F for 35 minutes.
•Spread tomato sauce evenly over the top, sprinkle with the reserved cheese and bake for another 15 minutes.
•Cut into squares and then serve.

Casserole Stuffed Pizza

INGREDIENTS:

1 lb. lean ground beef, browned and drained
1 small onion, chopped
1/3 green pepper, chopped
1 clove garlic, minced
1 (4-oz.) can mushrooms, drained
½ cup chopped pepperoni
½ cup sliced black olives
1 (6-oz.) can tomato paste
2 cups cooked noodles
2 cups water
1 tsp. salt
1/8 tsp. pepper
1/8 tsp. basil
1/8 tsp. oregano
¼ cup grated Parmesan cheese
Mozzarella cheese, for topping

INSTRUCTIONS:

•Heat the oven to 350 degrees Fahrenheit.
•Mix all ingredients together in a large bowl, excluding the mozzarella.
•Pour the mixture into a casserole dish and then bake for 30 to 40 minutes.
•When done, sprinkle with mozzarella cheese and let it melt.

Spicy Corn Pie Casserole

INGREDIENTS:

Crust
1 1/4 cups albers yellow cornmeal
1/2 tsp. salt
1 1/2 cups Carnation Evaporated Milk
1 cup water
Filling
1 lb. ground beef
1 clove garlic, finely chopped
1 cup chopped onion
1/4 cup chopped green bell peppers
1 cup cream-style corn
1/2 cup sliced black olives, drained
4 oz. can dice green chilies
1 cup tomato sauce
1 tbsp. chili powder
1 tsp. salt
1/4 tsp. black pepper
1/3 cup shredded cheddar cheese

INSTRUCTIONS:

•For crust, combine the cornmeal, salt, evaporated milk and water in a small saucepan.
•Cook over medium heat, stirring frequently for 5 to 7 minutes or until thickened.
•Remove 1/2 cup, cover with plastic wrap.
•Spread the remaining cornmeal mixture on bottom and sides of greased 8-inch square baking dish.
•Cool for 2 to 3 minutes if necessary.
•Bake in preheated 425-degree oven for 10 minutes.
•Remove from heat.
•For filling, brown the beef, garlic, onion and bell pepper in large skillet and then drain.
•Add corn, olives, chilies, tomato sauce, chili powder, salt and pepper.
•Mix well.
•Spoon into cornmeal crust.
•Drop rounded teaspoons of remaining cornmeal mixture on top of meat, sprinkle with cheese.
•Return to oven and bake for 15 minutes.

Cheesy Beef and Spinach Casserole

INGREDIENTS:

1-1/2 lb. ground beef
1 medium onion chopped
3 garlic cloves chopped
2 cans drained (4 oz.) mushrooms
1 tsp. salt
1 tsp. oregano
1/2 tsp. pepper
1 tsp. garlic powder
1 tsp. smoked paprika
1/2 cup chopped (drained well) roasted peppers or 1 red or green pepper chopped
3 packages (10 oz.) frozen spinach, thawed & squeezed well
1 can of condensed cream of mushroom or celery soup
1-1/4 cup sour cream
8 oz. shredded mozzarella cheese
1/2 cup Parmesan cheese
1 bag of wide egg noodles
4 tbsp. butter
Paprika, parsley

INSTRUCTIONS:

•Brown the beef and drain well.
•Add olive oil to meat and then add chopped onions, garlic, mushrooms, peppers and cook till tender (do not overcook).
•Add seasonings and stir.
•Add soup, spinach, sour cream and blend well.
•Add mozzarella cheese and Parmesan.
•Transfer the mixture to a 9 x 11 inch greased baking pan.
•Bake uncovered for 30 minutes at 350 degrees Fahrenheit until hot and bubbly.
•In the meantime, cook noodles in salted water and drain well done.
•Add butter, parsley and paprika to the hot pan.
•Stir in noodles.
•Mix all and cook.
•Serve over buttered noodles.

Mushroom Casserole

INGREDIENTS:

1/2 cup butter
1/2 cup celery, chopped
16 oz. fresh mushrooms, sliced
1 cup beef stock or broth
2 tbsps. Cornstarch
1/2 tsp. dried marjoram
2 tbsps. Fresh parsley, minced
1/2 cup saltine cracker crumbs
2 tbsps. Parmesan cheese, grated
1 tbsp. butter, melted

INSTRUCTIONS:

•Melt 1/2 cup butter in large skillet and then add celery and mushrooms.
•Sauté until softened.
•In small bowl, whisk together stock, cornstarch and marjoram.
•Add to the skillet and cook over medium heat until sauce is thickened.
•Remove from heat and stir in parsley.
•Spoon into a greased 1 quart casserole.
•Stir together cracker crumbs, cheese and butter.
•Sprinkle over top.
•Bake at 350 degrees Fahrenheit for 20 minutes.
•Serve with broiled or grilled beef.

Manwich Beef Casserole

INGREDIENTS:

1 lb. Ground beef, browned in skillet
1 small can baked beans
2 tsp. Instant minced onion
2 tbsp. Brown sugar
3/4 c. Manwich
1 c. Shredded sharp cheese
1 (10 count) can flaky biscuits, cut in half

INSTRUCTIONS:

•Brown beef and then add beans, Manwich, onions, and brown sugar.
•Add biscuits (on top, cut side down) and sprinkle with cheese.
•Bake at 350 degrees Fahrenheit for 20 minutes.

Pineapple with Plum and Cabbage Casserole

INGREDIENTS:

1 large cabbage
1 lb. Ground Beef
2 cups cooked rice
1 clove garlic, minced
1 egg
1/4 cup breadcrumbs
1/4 cup ketchup
1 tsp. salt
1/4 tsp. pepper
6 tbsp. chopped fresh parsley, divided
1 tsp. vegetable oil
1 onion, chopped
1 clove garlic, finely chopped
1/4 cup brown sugar
2 tbsp. lemon juice
1 28-oz cans plum tomatoes, with juices
1/2 cup cranberry juice or pineapple juice
Salt and pepper to taste

INSTRUCTIONS:

•Freeze whole cabbage for 2 days.
•Defrost, remove core and separate the leaves.

•Combine beef, cooked rice, minced garlic, egg, breadcrumbs, ketchup, salt, pepper and parsley in large bowl.
•Heat oil in large non-stick saucepan on medium heat.
•Cook onion and garlic for a couple of minutes until fragrant but not brown.
•Add sugar, lemon juice, tomatoes and cranberry juice and then bring to boil.
•Add parsley and cook for another 15 minutes, breaking up tomatoes with spoon.
•If too thick, add about 1/2 cup water or juice.
•Season with salt and pepper.
•Line bottom of 11 x 7-inch baking dish with one-third of the cabbage leaves.
•Spread with half of the meat mixture and one-third of the sauce.
•Repeat with cabbage, meat and sauce.
•Top with remaining cabbage and sauce.
•Bake in 350°F oven for 45 minutes.
•Sprinkle with remaining parsley and allow resting for 10 minutes before cutting into squares.

Shell Macaroni in Crock Pot Casserole

INGREDIENTS:

1 lb. lean ground beef
1 small onion, chopped
1 tsp. salt
1/4 tsp. garlic powder
1 tsp. Worcestershire sauce
1/4 cup flour
1-1/4 cup hot water
2 tsp. beef bouillon
2 tbsp. red wine
6 oz. shell macaroni
1 can (2 oz.) sliced mushrooms, drained
1 cup dairy sour cream

INSTRUCTIONS:

•Brown the ground beef and onion in a large skillet.
•Drain meat and place in slow-cooker.
•Stir in salt, garlic powder, Worcestershire sauce, and flour.
•Add water bouillon, and wine and then mix well.

•Cover and cook on low heat for 2 to 3 hours.
•In the meantime, cook macaroni according to package directions.
•Add cooked macaroni, mushrooms, and sour cream to slow-cooker and then stir to mix ingredients.
•Cover and cook on high for 10 to 15 minutes.

Cheesy Pizza Casserole

INGREDIENTS:

1 lb. ground beef or ground turkey
1 pkg. Velveeta Shells & Cheese Dinner
2 cans pizza sauce
1 pkg. shredded mozzarella cheese

INSTRUCTIONS:

•Brown meat and drain thoroughly.
•Stir in pizza sauce.
•Cook Shells & Cheese Dinner as directed.
•Drain and put in bottom of casserole dish.
•Top with meat mixture and mozzarella cheese.
•Bake at 350 degrees for 20 minutes.

Beef with Blue Cheese Stovetop Casserole

INGREDIENTS:

Vegetable oil spray
1.5 lbs. lean ground beef
2 Tbsp. Worcestershire sauce
1 Tbsp. chopped garlic
Seasoned Salt
Garlic Pepper
3 medium onions, chopped
1 1/4 cups red potatoes, diced
8 oz. button mushrooms, sliced
1 cup beef broth (or water)
1 tsp. dried oregano, crumbled
1/2 cup crumbled blue cheese
1/4 to 1/2 cup snipped fresh parsley

INSTRUCTIONS:

•Heat a Dutch oven over medium-high heat.
•Lightly spray the heated Dutch oven with vegetable oil spray.
•Cook the beef with the onion, garlic, seasoned salt, garlic pepper and Worcestershire or until no longer pink in the center, stirring occasionally to turn and break up the beef.
•Drain well and then set aside.
•Wipe the Dutch oven with a paper towel.
•Lightly spray with vegetable oil spray.
•Stir in the potatoes, mushrooms, broth, and oregano.
•Increase the heat to high.
•Bring to a boil.
•Reduce the heat and simmer, covered, for 10 minutes, or until the potatoes are tender.
•Remove from the heat.
•Stir in the beef and the remaining ingredients.
•Let stand for 2 minutes to absorb flavors.

Chicken Breast and Dried Beef Casserole

INGREDIENTS:

8 boneless, skinless chicken breast halves
8 strips bacon
1 cup sour cream
1 can (10 3/4 ounces) condensed cream of mushroom soup
1 jar dried beef, chopped

INSTRUCTIONS:

•Roll each chicken breast half and wrap a strip of bacon around.
•Arrange the dried beef lining in a large casserole dish.
•Place the 8 chicken breast rolls above the beef.
•Combine sour cream and soup and then pour into the chicken.
•Bake slowly, at 300°F for 2 hours, or until chicken is cooked and bacon is crispy.

Beef with Okra Casserole

INGREDIENTS:

1 1/2 lb. Okra
1 tsp. Salt
6 Tbsps. Vegetable oil
3 Tbsps. Yogurt, plain
1 ea. Onion - chopped fine
3 Tbsps. Sour cream
6 ea. Tomatoes - peeled, chopped
1/2 t Pepper, white
1 lb. Beef
1 ea. Tomato - thinly sliced
1 cup Stock
1 ea. Lemon - thinly sliced
2 ea. Garlic cloves - crushed

INSTRUCTIONS:

•Cut the okra stalks.
•Heat 3 tablespoons oil in a large saucepan.
•Add okra and then sauté for 6 minutes.
•Drain sautéed okra on paper towels.
•Discard oil and then wipe pan with paper towels.
•Heat 2 more tablespoons oil in saucepan.

•Add onion and tomatoes and then sauté until heated through.
•Add beef and cook, stirring occasionally until browned.
•Add stock and then bring to a boil.
•Add garlic and salt.
•Simmer until most of liquid has evaporated.
•Preheat oven to 350 degrees Fahrenheit.
•Brush a large baking pan with oil.
•Stir yogurt, sour cream and white pepper into beef mixture.
•Spoon half of the beef mixture and pour into the bottom of oiled pan.
•Cover with okra, then with remaining beef mixture.
•Sprinkle with remaining oil.
•Bake for about 50-60 minutes.
•Garnish with tomato and lemon slices.

Egg Grits Casserole

INGREDIENTS:

1/12 cups grits
6 cups water (salted)
1 and 1/2 cups shredded cheddar, plus a little to sprinkle on the top
1 stick butter
garlic (1 and 1/2 tsp. minced fresh or 1/2 tsp. granulated) optional
3 eggs
1 and 1/4 cup milk

INSTRUCTIONS:

•Coat a 9 x 13 dish casserole dish with Pam
•Heat oven to 350 degrees Fahrenheit.
•Cook grits in boiling salted water in about 12-15 minutes or until done.
•Add butter and cheese while stirring until melted.
•Lightly beat eggs and milk together, and then add to grits.
•Pour into prepared pan, sprinkling with extra cheese.
•Bake in prepared oven for about 45-60 minutes.

Egg with Cottage Cheese Casserole

INGREDIENTS:

5 beaten eggs
1 cup small curd cottage cheese
1/4 cup melted and cooled butter
1 (4 Oz) can diced chopped green chilies
1/4 cup all purpose flour
1/2 tsp. baking powder
2 cups grated/shredded Colby jack cheese

INSTRUCTIONS:

•Combine eggs, cheese, butter, chilies, flour and baking powder together and then add 2 cups grated/shredded Colby jack cheese.
•Pour above mixture into olive oil.
•Grease a nine inch square baking dish.
•Sprinkle top of mixture with cayenne pepper, black pepper, onion powder, garlic powder and parsley flakes.
•Bake in 350 degrees Fahrenheit oven until lightly browned on top and the center is puffed.

Blackberry Jam French Toast

INGREDIENTS:

1 cup blackberry jam
1 (12-oz.) French bread loaf, cut into 1 1/2-inch cubes
1 (8-oz.) package 1/3-less-fat cream cheese, cut into 1-inch cubes
4 large eggs
2 cups half-and-half
1 tsp. ground cinnamon
1 tsp. vanilla extract
1/2 cup firmly packed brown sugar
Toppings: maple syrup, whipped cream

INSTRUCTIONS:

•Cook jam in a small saucepan over medium heat for 1 to 2 minutes or until melted and smooth, stirring once.
•Place half of bread cubes in the bottom of a lightly greased 13- x 9-inch baking dish.
•Top with cream cheese cubes, and drizzle with melted jam.

•Top with remaining bread cubes.
•Whisk together eggs, half-and-half, cinnamon and vanilla.
•Pour over bread mixture.
•Sprinkle with brown sugar.
•Cover tightly, and chill 8 to 24 hours.
•Preheat oven to 325°F.
•Bake, covered, 20 minutes.
•Uncover and bake for 10 to 15 minutes or until bread is golden brown and mixture is set. •Serve with desired toppings.

Brie Casserole

INGREDIENTS:

1 large sweet onion, halved and thinly sliced
1 large red bell pepper, diced
1 large Yukon gold potato, peeled and diced
2 tbsps. Olive oil
1 (8-oz.) Brie round
1 (12-oz.) package sourdough bread loaf, cubed
1 cup (4 oz.) shredded Parmesan cheese
8 large eggs
3 cups milk
2 tbsps. Dijon mustard
1 tsp. Seasoned salt
1 tsp. n pepper

INSTRUCTIONS:

•Sauté onion, bell pepper and potato in hot oil for 10 to 12 minutes or just until vegetables are tender and onion slices begin to turn golden.
•Trim and discard rind from Brie.
•Cut cheese into 1/2-inch cubes.
• Layer a lightly greased 13- x 9-inch baking dish with half each of bread cubes, onion mixture, Brie cubes, and Parmesan cheese.
•Whisk together eggs, milk, mustard, and salt.
•Pour half of egg mixture evenly over cheeses.
•Repeat layers once.
•Cover and chill at least 8 hours or up to 24 hours.
•Bake at 350° for 45 to 50 minutes or until lightly browned on top and set in center.

Herb & Cheese Frittatas

INGREDIENTS:

12 large eggs
1 cup half-and-half
1/2 tsp. Salt
1/4 tsp. freshly ground pepper
2 tbsps. Chopped fresh chives
1 tbsp. chopped fresh parsley
1 tsp. chopped fresh oregano
1 pt. grape tomatoes, halved
1 1/2 cups (6 oz.) shredded Italian three-cheese blend

INSTRUCTIONS:

•Heat oven to 450°F.
•Process first 4 ingredients in a blender until blended.
•Stir together chives and next 2 ingredients in a small bowl.
•Place 8 lightly greased 4-inch (6-oz.) ramekins on 2 baking sheets; layer tomatoes, 1 cup cheese, and chive mixture in ramekins.
•Pour egg mixture over top, and sprinkle with remaining 1/2 cup cheese.
•Bake at 450° for 7 minutes, placing 1 baking sheet on middle oven rack and other on lower oven rack.
•Switch baking sheets, and bake 7 to 8 more minutes or until set.
•Remove top baking sheet from oven; transfer bottom sheet to middle rack, and bake 1 to 2 more minutes or until lightly browned.
•Tomato-Herb Frittata: Prepare recipe as directed, substituting a lightly greased 13- x 9-inch baking dish for ramekins and increasing bake time to 18 to 20 minutes or until set.

Hot Beef with Mushroom Casserole

INGREDIENTS:

2 lbs. ground beef
1 small finely chopped yellow onion
1 can corn
1/4 c. taco seasoning
1 can cream of mushroom soup
1 can cream of tomato soup
1 can refry beans
2 8oz. cans hot red sauce
34 cups shredded cheese
34 flour tortillas cut into strips chili powder and cumin, to taste

INSTRUCTIONS:

• Heat oven to 350°F.
•Brown the ground beef with onions and drain the excess fat.
•Place the beef in a large over medium heat oven and add taco seasoning by mixing it well.
•Stir in corn and refried beans and then mix it well.
•Add and mix well the cream of mushroom, tomato soup, and both cans of enchilada sauce
•Stir in chili powder and cumin to taste.
•Lightly grease a 9 x 13-inch baking dish, and place a single layer of tortilla strips down.
•Place half of the meat mixture over the top of the first layer.
•Add enough cheese to lightly cover the layer and add another layer of tortilla strips
•Add the remaining meat mixture and another small amount of cheese.
•Add another layer of tortilla strips that is enough to completely cover the mixture.
• Top the last layer of tortillas with enough cheese to completely cover the tortillas.
•Cover dish with foil.
•Bake at 350°F for about 30 minutes.
•Let stand about 5 minutes to cool and enjoy.

Mushroom Soup with Tuna Casserole

INGREDIENTS:

1 can tuna
1 can cream of mushroom soup
1 1/2 cups of grated cheese
1/2 cup frozen peas
1 cup milk
3 cups of macaroni, parboiled

INSTRUCTIONS:

•Mix the tuna with one cup grated cheese.
•Combine the cream of mushroom soup.
•Stir together, then add salt and pepper to taste.
•Blend tuna mushroom soup and milk with parboiled noodles and then add frozen peas.
•Bake at 300°F for about an hour.
•Ten minutes before removing from oven, sprinkle with cheese and continue to bake until cheese melts and becomes bubbly.

Tuna or Chicken Noodle Casserole

INGREDIENTS:

6 oz. egg noodles
2 tbsps. Butter
1 (10 3/4 ounce) can condensed cream of mushroom soup, undiluted
1/2-1 tsp. garlic powder (or to taste, I use 1 teaspoon)
3 -4 tbsps. Grated parmesan cheese (optional)
3/4 cup milk (or can use half-and-half cream)
1/2 cup sour cream (can increase to 3/4 cup)
1/4-1/2 tsp. Seasoning salt (or to taste, or use white salt)
1/2 tsp. fresh ground black pepper (or to taste)
1 small onion, finely chopped (can use 2 green onions)
1/4 cup pimiento, chopped
1 small green bell pepper, finely chopped
1 large celery rib, diced
1 (6 1/2 ounce) can tuna, drained and flaked
12 -15 butter flavored crackers, broken in pieces

INSTRUCTIONS:

•Heat oven to 375 degrees Fahrenheit.
•Grease a 2-quart casserole dish.
•Cook the egg noodles in boiling salted water; drain then toss with 2 tablespoons butter.
•Mix the undiluted mushroom soup, garlic powder, Parmesan cheese (if using) milk or half and half, sour cream, salt, pepper, chopped onion, pimiento, bell pepper and celery in a large saucepan.
•Cook over low heat, stirring frequently for 15 minutes.
•Add in the tuna or chicken and mix to combine.
•Combine the mixture with the cooked egg noodles.
•Transfer to prepare greased baking dish.
•Sprinkle top with the broken Ritz crackers.
•Bake for about 25 minutes.

Quinoa Enchilada Casserole

INGREDIENTS:

1 cup quinoa 1 (10ounce) can Old El Paso™ mild enchilada sauce
1 (4.5oz.) can Old El Paso™ chopped green chiles, drained
1/2 cup corn kernels, frozen, canned or roasted
1/2 cup canned black beans, drained and rinsed
2 tbsp. chopped fresh cilantro leaves
1/2 tsp. cumin
1/2 tsp. chili powder Kosher salt and freshly ground black pepper, to taste
3/4 cup shredded cheddar cheese, divided
3/4 cup shredded mozzarella cheese, divided
1 avocado, halved, seeded, peeled and diced
1 Roma tomato, diced

INSTRUCTIONS:

•Cook quinoa according to package directions.
• Set aside.
• Heat oven to 375 degrees F.
• Coat an 8x8 or 2 quart baking dish with nonstick spray.
• In a large bowl, combine quinoa, enchilada sauce, green chilies, corn, black beans, cilantro, and cumin and chili powder.
•Season with salt and pepper, to taste.
• Stir in 1/2 cup cheddar cheese and 1/2 cup mozzarella cheese.
• Spread quinoa mixture into the prepared baking dish.
• Top with remaining cheeses.
• Put into the oven and bake until bubbly and cheeses have melted for about 15 minutes.
• Serve immediately, garnished with avocado and tomato, if desired.

Sausage Brunch Casserole

INGREDIENTS:

1 1/2 pounds ground pork sausage
1 (8 ounce) package refrigerated
crescent roll dough
2 cups mozzarella cheese
4 eggs, beaten
3/4 cup milk
salt and pepper to taste

INSTRUCTIONS:

•Put sausage in a large, deep skillet.
•Sous-chef over medium high heat until evenly brown.
•Drain, crumble and set aside.
•Preheat oven to 425 degrees Fahrenheit or 220 degrees Celsius.
•Lightly grease a 9x13 inch baking pan.
•Lay crescent rolls flat in the bottom of the pan.
•Combine cooked sausage, cheese, eggs, milk, salt and pepper.
•Pour over crescent rolls.
•Bake in preheated oven for 15 minutes or until bubbly and rolls are baked.

Full Brunch Crockpot Casserole

INGREDIENTS:

2 boxes Betty Crocker Seasoned Skillets hash brown potatoes
1 ½ lb. bulk spicy pork sausage
2 medium red bell peppers, chopped (2 cups)
8 medium green onions, chopped (1/2 cup)
1 cup shredded Cheddar cheese (4 oz.)
1 cup shredded pepper Jack cheese (4 oz.)
2 cups milk
½ tsp. Salt
½ tsp. Pepper
6 eggs
Chopped fresh cilantro, if desired

INSTRUCTIONS:

•Spray 3-quart casserole dish with cooking spray.

•Boil potatoes with 10 cups of water in 4-quart bowl.
•Let stand for 3 minutes.
•Drain well and return potatoes to bowl.
•In 12-inch skillet, cook sausage over medium heat for 5 minutes.
•Add bell peppers and then cook for 4 minutes, stirring frequently, until sausage is no longer pink and peppers are tender.
•Drain.
•Add sausage mixture to potatoes in a bowl.
•Stir in onions and 1/2 cup of each of the cheeses.
•Spread in baking dish.
•In medium bowl, beat milk, salt, pepper and eggs until blended.
•Pour over sausage-potato mixture; sprinkle with remaining 1/2 cup of each cheese.
•Cover; refrigerate 8 hours or overnight.
•Heat oven to 375°F.
• Uncover baking dish.
•Bake for 50 minutes or until light golden brown and cheese is melted.
•Let stand for 10 minutes before serving.
• Sprinkle with cilantro.

Shrimp Zucchini Casserole

INGREDIENTS:

2 tsp. canola oil
1 large onion, chopped
1 medium green bell pepper, chopped
4 cloves garlic, minced
3 medium zucchini, diced (about 5 cups)
1 1/2 tbsp. chili powder
1 1/2 tsp. ground cumin
1 tsp. ground cinnamon
1 tsp. salt
2 14-oz. cans no-salt-added diced tomatoes
1 1/2 lbs. raw shrimp, (41-50 per pound) peeled and deveined
1/2 cup chopped fresh cilantro
1 cup yellow cornmeal
1 cup all-purpose flour
2 tsp. baking powder
1/2 tsp. salt
3/4 cup nonfat milk
1/4 cup canola oil
1 large egg
1 tbsp. honey

INSTRUCTIONS:

•To prepare the filling just heat oil in a Dutch oven over medium heat.
•Cook onion and bell pepper, stirring often for about 3 minutes or until softened.
•Add garlic and cook, stirring, for 30 seconds.
•Stir in zucchini; cook, stirring often, for 3 minutes.
•Stir in chili powder, cumin, cinnamon and 1 teaspoon salt; cook for 20 seconds.
•Pour in tomatoes and their juice and then bring to a simmer.
•Remove from the heat.
•Add the shrimp and cilantro.
•Pour into a 9-by-13-inch baking pan.
•Heat oven to 350°F.
•To prepare cornbread topping just whisk cornmeal, flour, baking powder and 1/2 teaspoon salt in a large bowl.
•Beat milk, 1/4 cup oil, egg and honey in a medium bowl until smooth.

•Add the wet ingredients to the dry ingredients and stir just until moistened.
•Drop by heaping tablespoons over the shrimp mixture.
•Bake the casserole, uncovered, until the top is browned and the filling is bubbling for around 40 to 45 minutes.
•Let stand for 10 minutes before serving.

Beef Nuggets Casserole

INGREDIENTS

1/4 cup extra-virgin olive oil
1 medium yellow onion, finely chopped (about 2 cups)
1 lb. 80-percent lean ground beef
Kosher salt and freshly ground black pepper
2 cups frozen cut green beans, thawed (8 oz.)
1 3/4 cups frozen corn kernels, thawed (8 oz.)
2 10-oz. cans cream of mushroom soup
1 lb. frozen shredded potato nuggets

INSTRUCTIONS

•Heat the oven to 350 degrees Fahrenheit.
•Boil oil and sauté onions for about 15 minutes or until soft and begin to brown.
•Add the beef to the onions and cook until the meat is brown, stirring and scraping the bottom of the skillet to release the yummy brown bits, about 10 minutes.
•Season with salt and pepper.
•Transfer the beef and onion mixture from the skillet into a 9-by-13-inch baking dish.
•Sprinkle the green beans and corn evenly on top.
•Spread the cream of mushroom soup over top.
•Add frozen potato nuggets on top.
•Uncovered and bake for 1 hour or until the potato nuggets should be golden brown.

Muffin Mix Corn Casserole

INGREDIENTS:

1 cans whole kernel yellow corn, un-drained
1 can cream style yellow corn
1 (8 oz.) sour cream
2 eggs, beaten
1 box Jiffy corn muffin mix
1 stick butter, melted

INSTRUCTIONS:

•Mix all together the ingredients.
•Pour into large, lightly greased casserole dish.
•Bake at 350°F for 55 to 60 minutes.
•Serve.

Feta Cheese in Eggplant Casserole

INGREDIENTS:

1/2 small eggplant
3/4 tsp. salt, divided
1 tsp. pepper, divided
1 cup Italian breadcrumbs
1/2 cup grated Parmesan cheese, divided
1/2 cup egg substitute
Vegetable cooking spray
1 medium onion, chopped
2 garlic cloves, minced
1 (28-oz.) can crushed tomatoes
1 tsp. sugar
1 tsp. dried basil
1/2 tsp. dried oregano
1 (16-ounce) container 1% low-fat cottage cheese
1/2 cup crumbled feta cheese

INTRODUCTIONS:

•Cut eggplant crosswise into 1/8-inch-thick slices.
•Sprinkle evenly with 1/2 teaspoon salt and 1/2 teaspoon pepper.
•Combine breadcrumbs and 3 tablespoons Parmesan cheese.
•Dip eggplant into egg substitute.
•Dredge in breadcrumb mixture.

•Coat eggplant evenly on both sides with cooking spray.
•Arrange slices on a rack coated with cooking spray and then put rack inside a roasting pan.
•Bake at 375°F for 16 minutes, turning over after 8 minutes.
•Sauté onion and garlic in a large saucepan coated with cooking spray over medium-high heat for 5 minutes or until onion is tender.
•Add tomatoes, remaining 1/4 teaspoon salt, remaining 1/2 teaspoon pepper, sugar, basil, and oregano; bring to a boil.
•Reduce heat, and simmer, stirring often for 10 minutes or until thickened.
•Spoon 1 cup tomato mixture into an 8-inch square baking dish coated with vegetable cooking spray and then arrange one-third of eggplant slices in a single layer over tomato mixture.
•Stir together cottage cheese and feta cheese and then spoon 1/3 cup cheese mixture over eggplant.
•Spoon 1 cup tomato mixture over cheese mixture.
•Repeat layers twice, ending with tomato mixture.
•Sprinkle with remaining Parmesan cheese.
•Bake at 350° for 35 to 40 minutes or until bubbly and golden brown.
•Part-skim ricotta cheese may be substituted for cottage cheese, if desired.

Squash with Crushed Crackers Casserole

INGREDIENTS:

6 cups sliced yellow squash
1 to 2 tbsps. Vegetable oil
1 large onion, sliced
4 tbsps. Butter
1/2 cup sour cream
1 tsp. Paula Dean's House Seasoning (salt, pepper, garlic powder)
1 cup grated Cheddar cheese
1 cup crushed butter crackers

INSTRUCTIONS:

•Pan-fry squash in vegetable oil until broken down in about 15-20 minutes and then drain. •Sauté onions in butter for 5 minutes.
•Mix squash and onions together and add remaining ingredients, except cracker crumbs. •Pour into casserole dish.
•Top with cracker crumbs.
•Bake at 350 degrees Fahrenheit for 25-30 minutes.

Crumbled Summer Squash Casserole

INGREDIENTS:

2 lbs. sliced yellow summer squash
1/2 tsp. sugar
1 tsp. salt
4 oz. butter
1- 1/2 cups shredded mild Cheddar cheese or Monterey Jack
1 cup butter crackers, crumbled
1/2 cup evaporated milk
2 eggs, beaten
Black pepper to taste

INSTRUCTIONS:

•Boil sliced squash in water with salt and sugar until just tender.
•Drain well and add butter, 1 cup of the cheese, 3/4 cup cracker crumbs, milk, eggs, and pepper.
•Mix well and pour into a buttered 2-quart casserole or baking dish.

•Scattering the reserved cheese and cracker crumbs over the top.
•Bake this summer squash casserole for 30 to 45 minutes at 325 degrees.

Buttered Squash Au Gratin

INGREDIENTS:

1/4 cup butter or margarine
4 cups thinly sliced summer squash
1 sliced onion
1 tsp. salt
Dash of pepper
1/4 cup water
1/2 cup grated cheese

INSTRUCTIONS:

•Melt butter in saucepan.
•Add squash, onion, salt, pepper, water.
•Cook, covered 10 to 15 minutes or until squash is tender.
•Sprinkle with cheese.

Hash Brown Potato Casserole

INGREDIENTS:

5 c. frozen hash brown potatoes
2 c. ham, diced (asks for ½" slices at the deli and cut into cubes)
½ c. green onion, diced
1 c. shredded cheddar or Colby jack cheese, divided
¼ tsp. garlic powder
½ tsp. kosher salt
Freshly ground black pepper to taste
4 eggs
12 oz. evaporated milk

INSTRUCTIONS:

•Heat oven to 375 degrees F.
•Spray 9 x 13" baking dish with cooking spray.
•Stir together potatoes, ham, ½ c. cheese, and green onions in a medium bowl.
•Spread mixture evenly in prepared baking dish.
•In a small bowl, whisk together eggs, evaporated milk, garlic powder, salt, and pepper.
•Pour evenly over potato mixture.
•Cover with foil, and bake for 40 minutes.
•Remove cover, and sprinkle remaining ½ c. cheese over casserole.
•Bake uncovered for an additional of 15 minutes or until hot and bubbly and knife inserted in center comes out clean.

Ritz Pineapple Chunks Casserole

INGREDIENTS:

54 oz. pineapple chunks, drained
¼ cup granulated sugar
¼ cup all-purpose flour
1 cup shredded sharp cheddar cheese
1 sleeve Ritz crackers
3 tbsps. Melted butter

INSTRUCTIONS:

•Heat the oven to 350 degrees Fahrenheit.
• combine pineapple, sugar, flour, and cheese in a large mixing bowl.
•Pour mixture into a greased 8 x 8 casserole dish.
•Crush crackers and sprinkle over the top of the pineapple mixture.
•Pour melted butter evenly over cracker layer.
•Bake casserole for 25 minutes or until golden brown and slightly bubbly.

Pineapple Cheddar Casserole

INGREDIENTS:

30 oz. pineapple chunks
1 cup white sugar
3/4 cup all-purpose flour
2 cups shredded sharp cheddar cheese
25 crackers (buttery round, crumbled)
1/2 cup melted butter

INSTRUCTIONS:

•Heat oven to 350 degrees Fahrenheit.
•Spread pineapple in the bottom of a 2 quart casserole dish.
•In a small bowl, stir together the sugar, flour and cheese.
•Add to casserole dish.
•Sprinkle crackers over the top of pineapple and cheese mixture.
•Pour melted butter over the top and bake for 30 minutes.

Pot Roast Beef with Silver Beet and Chickpeas

INGREDIENTS

2 tbsp. olive oil
1.5kg beef silverside roast
1 large brown onion, cut into wedges
2 garlic cloves, crushed
3 tsps. Smoked paprika
1/4 cup plain flour
1 liter Campbell's Real Stock Beef
400g can diced tomatoes
400g can chickpeas, drained, rinsed
1/2 bunch silver beet, trimmed, chopped
1/4 cup chopped fresh coriander leaves, to serve

INSTRUCTIONS

•Preheat oven to 325 F
•Heat the oil in a large, flameproof, ovenproof dish over medium heat.
•Brown the beef for 3 to 5 minutes on each side.
•Transfer the browned beef to a plate.
•Heat remaining oil in a dish and add onion.
•Cook, stirring occasionally, for 4 minutes or until softened.
•Add garlic and paprika then cook while stirring for 30 seconds or until fragrant.
•Add flour and continue stirring for 1 minute.
•Gradually add stock beef, stirring until become smooth.
•Mix in the tomato and combine with the beef in the dish.
•Cover and bring to a boil.
•Transfer the dish to the oven.
•Bake for 1 hour and 30 minutes.
•Add chickpeas and continue to cook, uncovered, for 50 minutes or until beef is just cooked through and tender.
•Add silver beet.
•Cook for another 5 minutes or until silver beet has just wilted.
•Serve beef mixture with coriander.

Bacon and Steak Goulash

INGREDIENTS:

2 tbsp. olive oil
175g short cut bacon, chopped
2 leeks, washed, sliced
2 cloves garlic, crushed
1.8kg chuck steak, cubed
1 red capsicum, chopped
2 tbsp. smoked paprika
2 gluten-free beef stock cubes
400g can chop tomatoes
4 sprigs thyme
500g sweet potato, chopped
3 potatoes, chopped
20g butter
2 tbsp. parsley, chopped

INSTRUCTIONS:

•Heat oil in a large casserole pan on medium heat.
•Cook bacon for 2 minutes, or until brown.
•Add leek and cook for another 5 minutes, or until soft.
•Add garlic and cook for 1 min, or until fragrant.
•Remove from pan and set aside.
•Heat remaining oil in same pan on high heat.
•Brown the beef in batches, stirring, for 2-3 minutes, or until browned all over.
•Return leek mixture to pan with capsicum and paprika.
•Stir to combine.
•Mix together 2 cups boiling water and stock cubes.
•Stir until it dissolved.
•Add to beef mixture with tomato and thyme sprigs.
•Bring to boil.
•Reduce heat to low and simmer, covered, for 2 hours, or until beef is very tender.
•Meanwhile, cook sweet potato and potato in a large pan of boiling, salted water for 15-20 minutes, or until soft.
•Drain and return to pan.
•Add butter and mash until smooth.
•Season to taste.

•Scatter parsley over goulash and serve with sweet potato mash.

Duck Pasta Casserole

INGREDIENTS:

4 duck
1 large onion and 1 carrot, chopped
2 garlic cloves, crushed
1/4 cup tomato paste
1 tbsp. plain flour
2 cups dry red wine
300ml Campbell's Real Stock Chicken
2 bay leaves and 2 tablespoons thyme leaves
Pared rind and juice of 1 orange
500g Tagliatelle
2 tablespoons chopped flat-leaf parsley
Watercress, fennel & orange salad (see related recipe) and grated parmesan, to serve

INSTRUCTIONS:

•Heat the oven to 325 F
•Place a large flameproof casserole over medium heat.
•Add duck, skin-side down, and cook for 6 minutes, then turn and cook for a further 4 minutes.
•Remove duck and drain fat, leaving 2 tablespoons in the pan.
•Add the onion, carrot and garlic and cook, stirring, for 2-3 minutes.
•Add the tomato paste and cook for a further minute.
•Strew the flour and stir to combine.
•Add the wine, stock, herbs, rind and juice.
•Bring to a boil and season to taste.
•Put back the duck to the pan, cover and cook in the oven for 2 hours.
•Remove the duck from the sauce and get the remaining fat from the surface.
•Put the casserole over medium heat.
•Simmer for 3-4 minutes until sauce has reduced slightly.
•When duck is cool enough to handle, discard skin and bones and shred meat.
•Return meat to casserole.

•To serve, cook pasta according to packet instructions, then drain.
•Put pasta in the pan, add the sauce and toss to combine.
•Divide pasta among plates and serve sprinkled with parsley and grated parmesan, with the watercress, fennel and orange salad.

Chicken Breast Cheesy Egg Noodle Casserole

INGREDIENTS:

2 skinless boneless chicken breasts cut into cubes
1/2 can reduced fat cream of chicken soup
1 tbsp. olive oil
1/4 lb. Velveeta cheese, cut into cubes
1/2 a bag egg noodles
1 can corn
1 tbsp. seasoned salt
1/2 tbsp. parsley flakes
1 tsp. pepper

INSTRUCTIONS:

•Boil egg noodles in water till chewy.
•Brown the chicken and salt in olive oil and then drain oil.
•Combine cream of chicken soup and egg noodles with chicken and heat until roasting.
•Reduce heat, and add Velveeta cheese, corn, and pepper.
•Cook until all of Velveeta is melted.
•Remove from heat and sprinkle with parsley flakes.

Egg Spinach & Cheese Casserole

INGREDIENTS:

10 oz. fresh spinach, whole (or 12 ounces of frozen chopped spinach)
1/4 cup onion, chopped
4 egg whites, well beaten
2 tbsps. Low-fat Parmesan cheese, grated
1 cup 1% milk
1/2 tsp. salt
1/3 cup celery, chopped
1/2 tsp. nutmeg, ground

INSTRUCTIONS:

•Wash fresh spinach and discard the stems.
•Let the leaves become wilted by covering the saucepan over low heat.
•Drain in a colander or sieve, press out liquid and chop spinach.
•Mix remaining ingredients together, and then fold in spinach.
•Pour mixture into a well-greased 9 inch pie plate.
•Bake at 375 degrees F for 45 minutes or until a knife inserted in the middle comes out clean.
•Cut into 6 wedges and serve warm.

Almond Tuna and Egg Noodle Casserole

INGREDIENTS:

2 cans reduced fat cream of celery soup
1/3 cup dry sherry
2/3 cup skim milk
2 tbsp. parsley flakes
10 oz. frozen mix vegetables
2 cans light tuna in water, drained
10 oz. whole grain egg noodles, cooked
2 tbsp. margarine
1/2 cup toasted almonds

INSTRUCTIONS:

•Combine soup, sherry, milk, and parsley flakes in a lightly greased slow cooker.
•Stir until well-blended and texture is consistent.

•Stir in vegetables and drained tuna.
•Fold in whole grain noodles until evenly distributed.
•Top with almonds and butter substitute.
•Cover and cook on low heat for 7 to 9 hours or high heat for about 2 to 3 hour until noodles are tender but not overdone.

Mexican Casserole

INGREDIENTS:

1 1/2 lb. 97% lean ground beef
3/4 cup onion, chopped finely
1/3 cup whole wheat cracker crumbs
2 egg whites, slightly beaten
3 tbsps. Skim milk
1 tbsps. Chili powder
3/4 tsp. salt
3 cups mashed potatoes
1 11-oz. whole kernel corn with red and green peppers, drained and rinsed
1/4 cup green onions, thinly sliced
1/2 cup reduced fat Mexican-style cheese blend

INSTRUCTIONS:

•Preheat oven to 375 degrees F.
•Combine ground beef, onions, cracker crumbs, egg whites, milk, chili powder and salt in a large bowl.
•Mix lightly but thoroughly and gently press into bottom of 9-inch square baking pan.
•Bake meatloaf for 20 to 25 minutes or until no longer pink and juices run clear.
•Carefully pour off drippings.
•Meanwhile, combine all remaining ingredients except the cheese in a medium bowl.
•Spread over meatloaf to edges of pan and then sprinkle the top with cheese.
•Broil 3 to 4 inches from heat for 3 to 5 minutes or until top is lightly browned
•Cut into 6 rectangular servings.

Corn, Bean Chicken Casserole

INGREDIENTS:

8 chicken drumsticks, skin removed and all excess fat removed
8 oz. low fat smoked sausage, sliced
32 oz. fat free barbecued baked beans
15 oz. frozen whole kernel corn, thawed
15 oz. can black beans, well rinsed and drained
1 3/4 cup frozen baby lima beans, thawed
1 1/2 cup onions, chopped
1 cup your favorite tomato sauce
1 1/2 cup baked corn tortilla chips, crushed

INSTRUCTIONS:

•Preheat oven to 375 degrees F.
•Have a shallow 3-quart baking dish ready.
•In the baking dish, mix together the chicken, sausage, baked beans, corn, black beans, lima beans, onions and tomato sauce.
•Cover and bake for 1 hour.
•Uncover and sprinkle with chips.
•Bake uncovered for 15 minutes longer, or until the chicken is cooked through.

Apple Chicken Drumstick Casserole

INGREDIENTS:

8 chicken drumsticks
1 onion
2 apples
1 package mushroom soup mix
1 tsp. dried thyme
2 tsp. whole grain mustard
1 1/2 cup water
1 cup plain yogurt
8 brown button mushrooms
Salt and pepper

INSTRUCTIONS:

•Remove chicken skin.
•Peel and finely slice onion.
•Peel, core and dice apples.
•Place chicken, onion and apple in a casserole dish with the mushroom soup mix, thyme, mustard and water.
•Put a tight fitting lid on top.
•Bake at 350 degrees F for 1 hour or until chicken is tender. Stir in yogurt.
•Clean mushrooms and cut in half.
•Mix through chicken in casserole and bake for another 15 minutes.
•Season with salt and pepper.

Casserole with Beef, Turkey and Mustard

INGREDIENTS:

1/2 lb. extra lean ground beef
½ lb. turkey bacon, diced
1 small onion, diced
1 can kidney beans, drained and rinsed well
1 can navy beans, drained and rinsed well
1 can butter beans, drained and rinsed well
1/3 cup SPLENDA brown sugar substitute
1/4 cup reduced sugar ketchup
1/2 tsp. dry mustard
2 tbsp. maple syrup

INSTRUCTIONS:

•Brown the ground beef, turkey bacon and onion in a skillet over medium-high heat.
•Drain any excess grease.
•Add the beef mixture with the hamburger mix the kidney beans, navy beans, butter beans, brown sugar substitute, ketchup, dry mustard and maple syrup in large baking dish.
•Make sure everything is thoroughly combined.
•Bake at 350 degrees F for 1 hour, or until everything is thoroughly heated through.

Easy and Simple Burger Casserole

INGREDIENTS:

1 lb. extra lean ground beef
1 can low fat cream of mushroom soup
3/4 cup skim milk
1/2 cup onion, chopped
1 pinch salt
1 pinch black pepper
3 cups raw potatoes, sliced
1/2 lb. reduced fat Cheddar cheese, grated
1/4 cup margarine

INSTRUCTIONS:

•Brown the ground beef and drain off fat and then set aside.
•Preheat oven to 350 degrees F.
•Combine low fat cream of mushroom soup, skim milk, onion, salt and pepper in a separate bowl.
•In large casserole dish, layer potatoes, soup mixture and hamburger.
•Repeat layers again, ending with hamburger and dot with margarine.
•Cover and bake for 1 1/4 to 1 1/2 hours.
•Sprinkle with grated low fat Cheddar cheese and bake just until cheese is melted.

Casserole with Sausages and Beans

INGREDIENTS:

1 tbsp. olive oil
500g beef sausages
1 brown onion, finely chopped
3 carrots, peeled, finely chopped
3 celery sticks, ends trimmed, finely chopped
2 garlic cloves, crushed
1 x 800g can diced tomatoes
250ml salt-reduced chicken stock
2 x 400g cans cannellini beans, rinsed, drained
100g baby spinach leaves
2 tbsps. Chopped fresh continental parsley
Crusty bread, to serve

INSTRUCTIONS:

•Heat oven to 170 degree Celsius.
•Simmer oil in a large flameproof casserole dish over medium heat.
•Add sausages and cook, turning occasionally, for 2-3 minutes or until lightly browned. •Transfer cooked sausages to a plate and set aside.
•Add the onion, carrot, celery and garlic to the dish.
•Cook, stirring often, for 6 minutes or until the onion starts to soften.
•Add the tomato and chicken stock.
•Increase heat to high and cover the dish and bring to a boil.
•Put the sausages again to the dish and cover.
•Bake in oven for 30 minutes.
•Stir in the beans.
•Stir in the spinach and parsley.
•Flavor with salt and pepper.
•Divide the casserole among serving dishes.
•Serve with bread.

Cheesy Mushroom and Black Bean Tortilla Casserole

INGREDIENTS:

2 tsps. Extra-virgin olive oil
3/4 lb. cremini or button mushrooms, trimmed and quartered
1 garlic clove, minced
1/4 tsp. cayenne pepper
Coarse salt and ground pepper
1 1/2 cups reserved cooked black beans from Spicy Black Bean Soup,
1 can (15.5 ounces) black beans, rinsed and drained
8 corn tortillas, warmed and halved
2 cups salsa
1 1/4 cups shredded Monterey Jack cheese (4 ounces)

INSTRUCTIONS:

•Heat oven to 400 degrees Celsius.
•In a large skillet, heat oil over medium-high.
•Add mushrooms and cook, stirring often, until browned for 7 minutes.
•Add garlic and cayenne and then season with salt and pepper.
•Add black beans and stir to combine.
•Cook until beans are warmed through, 2 minutes.
•Remove from heat.
•Arrange 5 tortilla halves in a 2-quart baking dish.
•Top with half the bean mixture and 1/2 cup salsa, and then sprinkle with one-third the cheese.
•Repeat with another layer of tortilla halves, bean mixture, salsa, and cheese.
•Top with remaining tortilla halves, salsa, and cheese.
•Cover with foil and bake until center is hot and cheese melts, 10 minutes.
•Uncover and bake until cheese is bubbling for 5 minutes.

Pasta in a Pan Casserole

INGREDIENTS:

12 oz. linguine
12 oz. cherry or grape tomatoes, halved or quartered if large
1 onion, thinly sliced (about 2 cups)
4 cloves garlic, thinly sliced
1/2 tsp. Red-pepper flakes
2 sprigs basil, plus torn leaves for garnish
2 tbsps. Extra-virgin olive oil, plus more for serving
Coarse salt and freshly ground pepper
4 1/2 cups water
Freshly grated Parmesan cheese, for serving

INSTRUCTIONS:

•Combine pasta, tomatoes, onion, garlic, red-pepper flakes, basil, oil, 2 teaspoons salt, 1/4 teaspoon pepper, and water in a large straight-sided skillet.
•Bring to a boil over high heat.
•Boil mixture, stirring and turning pasta frequently with tongs, until pasta is al dente and water has nearly evaporated for about 9 minutes.
•Season to taste with salt and pepper, divide among 4 bowls, and garnish with basil.
•Serve with oil and Parmesan.

Spiced Peanut Chicken Casserole

INGREDIENTS:

1/4 cup smooth peanut butter
1/4 cup water
1/4 tsp. toasted sesame oil
2 tbsps. Soy sauce
2 tsps. Sambal oelek
2 tsps. Rice vinegar
4 skinless chicken thighs
1 bunch Broccolini

INSTRUCTIONS:

•Preheat broiler.
•Mix together peanut butter, water, sesame oil, soy sauce, sambal oelek, and rice vinegar. •Toss chicken thighs and Broccolini in sauce, and place on a rimmed baking sheet.
•Broil 10 inches from heat until chicken is cooked through, about 10 minutes.

Andouille Okra Chicken Casserole

INGREDIENTS:

3 tbsps. Vegetable oil
1/3 cup all-purpose flour
2 red bell peppers (ribs and seeds removed), chopped
1 medium onion, chopped
4 garlic cloves, chopped
1 tsp. dried oregano
Coarse salt and ground pepper
1 package (10 ounces) frozen, cut okra
8 oz. smoked (precooked) Andouille sausage, halved lengthwise and sliced 1 inch thick
1 rotisserie chicken (about 2 1/2 lbs.), skin and bones removed, meat shredded
Store-bought or homemade cornbread, for serving (optional)

INSTRUCTIONS:

•In a 5-quart Dutch oven or heavy-bottomed pot, heat oil over medium.
•Add flour, and cook, whisking constantly, until pale golden for 5 to 7 minutes.

•Stir in bell peppers, onion, garlic, and oregano.
•Season with salt and pepper.
•Cook, stirring occasionally, until vegetables are crisp-tender, 10 to 12 minutes.
•Add 4 cups water; stir in okra and sausage.
•Bring to a boil.
•Stir in shredded chicken, and warm through, 1 to 2 minutes.
•Season with salt and pepper; if desired, serve with cornbread.

Cheesy Beef Cabbage Casserole

INGREDIENTS:

1 lb. lean ground beef
1 onion, diced
3 cloves garlic, minced
¼ tsp. ground thyme
1 tsp. dried oregano
¾ tsp. kosher salt
Black pepper
¼ tsp. caraway seeds, optional
1 c. brown rice, uncooked
14 oz. petite diced tomatoes, un-drained
8 oz. tomato sauce
2 cup beef broth
12 oz. bag shredded cabbage
1 cup mozzarella cheese
¼ cup grated parmesan cheese

INSTRUCTIONS:

•In a Dutch oven or large skillet over medium-high heat, sauté beef and onions.
•Mixing in oregano, thyme, salt, pepper, and caraway seeds while cooking.
•When meat is cooked through and onions are tender, add garlic and rice, and sauté 3 minutes longer.
•Stirring in beef broth, tomatoes, and tomato sauce.
•Bring to a boil, and then reduce heat to simmer and cover.
•Cook at least one hour, or up to 2 hours.
•Add the cabbage, and replace lid.
•Simmer over very low heat about 10 minutes longer.

•Turn broiler to high.
•Remove lid and turn off heat.
•Sprinkle cheeses over the top of the cabbage mixture, and place the pot under broiler for 3-5 minutes or until cheese is bubbly and starting to brown.

Parmesan Spinach Casserole

INGREDIENTS:

10 oz. fresh spinach, whole
1/4 cup onion, chopped
4 egg whites, well beaten
2 tbsp. low-fat Parmesan cheese, grated
1 cup 1% milk
1/2 tsp. salt
1/3 cup celery, chopped
1/2 tsp. nutmeg, ground

INSTRUCTIONS:

•Wash fresh spinach and remove the stems.
•Steamed in a covered saucepan over low heat until the leaves are wilted.
•Drain in a colander or sieve, press out liquid and chop spinach.
•Mix the onion, egg whites, cheese, milk, salt, celery and nutmeg by stirring it gradually.
•Folding in the spinach and then pour mixture into a well-greased 9 inch pie plate.
•Bake at 375 degrees Fahrenheit for 45 minutes.
•Cut into 6 wedges and serve warm.

Beef Broccolini Casserole

INGREDIENTS:

2 tbsps. Olive oil
750g gravy beef, trimmed, cut into 3cm cubes
1 large brown onion, finely chopped
2 garlic cloves, crushed
2 medium carrots, peeled, halved, sliced
3 medium parsnips, peeled, chopped
2 tbsps. Plain flour
2 dried bay leaves
4 sprigs fresh rosemary
1 tbsp. Worcestershire sauce
1/2 cup plums jam
2 1/2 cups Campbell's Real Stock Beef
Steamed broccolini, to serve

INSTRUCTIONS:

•Preheat oven to 350 F
•Heat half the oil in a large, heavy-based, flameproof casserole dish over medium-high heat. •Cook beef, in batches, for 5 to 6 minutes or until browned.
•Transfer to a bowl.
•Heat remaining oil in dish.
•Add onion, garlic, carrot and parsnip.
•Cook, stirring, for 5 minutes or until onion has softened.
•Return beef to dish. Add flour.
•Cook, stirring, for 1 minute.
•Add bay leaves and rosemary.
•Stir in Worcestershire sauce, plum jam and stock.
•Cover dish and bring to a boil.
•Transfer to oven and then bake for 2 hours or until beef is tender.
•Remove and discard bay leaves.
•Serve with broccolini.

Pear Beef Tagine Casserole

INSTRUCTIONS:

2/3 cup honey
1 large lemon, juiced
2 firm pears, cores removed, cut into thick wedges
1 tsp. ground cinnamon
1 tsp. ground allspice
2 tbsps. Olive oil
2kg chuck steak, cut into 3cm cubes
2 brown onions, finely chopped
2 garlic cloves, crushed
3cm piece fresh ginger, peeled, grated
3 to 4 tbsps. Master foods Moroccan Spice Blend
20g butter

INGREDIENTS:

•Place 1 1/2 cups cold water, honey, 1/4 cup lemon juice, pears, cinnamon and allspice in a saucepan over medium-high heat.
•Bring to the boil and then reduce heat to medium.
•Simmer, uncovered, for 25 minutes or until pears are tender.
•Allow to cool and then drain, reserving liquid.
•Set pears aside.
•Preheat oven to 180°C.
•Heat 1 tablespoon oil in a heavy-based saucepan over high heat.
•Cook steak, in batches, for 3 minutes or until browned, adding more oil as required. •Transfer to a large plate.
•Reduce heat to medium.
•Add onion to pan.
•Cook, stirring, for 5 minutes or until soft.
•Add garlic, ginger and spice blend.
•Cook, stirring, for 1 minute.
•Return steak to pan with 1 1/3 cups reserved pear syrup.
•Bring to the boil.
•Transfer tagine to an ovenproof casserole dish.
•Cover with a lid. Place in oven and cook for 1 1/2 hours.
•Meanwhile, heat butter in a non-stick frying pan over medium-low heat.
•Add pears and then cook for 2 to 3 minutes each side or until golden.

•Remove tagine from oven and stir in pears.
•Return to oven and cook, uncovered, for 25 minutes or until steak is tender.
•Serve with pumpkin and chickpea salad and Moroccan bread.

Beef Stock, Mushroom and Potato Casserole

INSTRUCTIONS:

2 tbsps. Olive oil
1 large onion, chopped
4 large portabello mushrooms, sliced
1.3 kg gravy beef or bolar blade roast, cut into chunks
10 small new potatoes, halved
2 cloves garlic, crushed
1 jar of sun-dried tomato or basil pesto
1 1/3 cup beef stock
Salt & freshly ground pepper
Sour cream, to serve
Crusty bread, to serve

INGREDIENTS:

•Preheat oven to 350 F
•Heat 1 tablespoon oil in a large heavy-based pan.
•Add onion and cook 3-4 minutes until golden.
•Add mushrooms and cook over high heat until browned.
•Remove from the pan and set aside.
•Heat remaining oil and brown the meat in batches.
•Transfer to an ovenproof casserole dish.
•Add half the potatoes, mushrooms and onions.
•Scatter over garlic.
•Top with remaining meat, potatoes and mushrooms.
•Add stock to pan and scrape base.
•Stir in pesto.
•Simmer for 1 minute.
•Pour over casserole.
•Season and then cover and bake for 2 hours.
•Uncover, bake for 30 minutes more until tender.
•Serve topped with sour cream.

Pork Tenderloin with Plums Casserole

INGREDIENTS:

1 lb. pork tenderloin, pounded thin
Coarse salt
Extra-virgin olive oil
Unsalted butter
4 plums cut into wedges
1 red onion, thinly sliced
1/4 cup red-wine vinegar

INSTRUCTIONS:

•Slice pork tenderloin, and season with salt.
•Brown pork in olive oil and butter over medium-high heat, and remove.
•Sauté plums and red onion over medium heat.
•Add vinegar, and stir until bubbling. Return pork to pan, and toss.

Salmon Fillet and Red Cabbage with Potatoes

INGREDIENTS:

4 cups shredded red cabbage (from half a small head)
10 halved new potatoes
Extra-virgin olive oil
Coarse salt and freshly ground pepper
1 lb. skinless salmon fillet
2 tbsps. Grainy mustard
2 tbsps. Horseradish
Zest of 1 lemon plus lemon juice

INSTRUCTIONS:

•Preheat oven to 400 degrees.
•Toss cabbage and potatoes with olive oil; season with salt and pepper.
•Roast for 25 minutes.
•Smear salmon with a mixture of mustard, horseradish and lemon zest.
•Nestle in pan, and roast 15 minutes.
•Squeeze lemon juice over all.

Brown Lentil Curry

INGREDIENTS:

1 tbsp. olive oil
1 medium onion, finely chopped
2 tbsps. Curry powder
1 lb. sweet potatoes, peeled and cut into 1-inch chunks
1 head cauliflower (2 1/2 lbs.), stemmed and separated into florets
1 cup brown lentils, picked over, well rinsed, and drained
2 cans (14.5 oz. each) diced tomatoes with juice
Coarse salt
Plain low-fat yogurt, for serving (optional)

INSTRUCTIONS:

•In a nonstick Dutch oven (5-quart pot with a tight-fitting lid), heat oil over medium heat. •Add onion, and cook, stirring frequently, until softened for about 7 minutes.
•Add curry powder and then cook, stirring constantly for 1 minute.
•Stir in sweet potatoes, cauliflower, lentils, tomatoes and their juice, and 1 1/2 cups water. •Season with salt.
•Bring mixture to a boil.
•Reduce heat to a simmer and cover, and cook until lentils and sweet potatoes are tender in about 30 minutes.
•Serve immediately with yogurt, if desired.

Hot Chicken Coconut Casserole

INGREDIENTS:

1 tbsp. olive oil
4 whole chicken legs (about 3 pounds total)
Coarse salt and ground pepper
1 can (14.5 oz.) light coconut milk
1 1/2 cups canned reduced-sodium chicken broth
1 to 2 tsps. Thai red curry paste
1 cup jasmine rice
2 red bell peppers (ribs and seeds removed), cut into 1-inch pieces
8 oz. green beans (stem ends removed), cut into 1-inch lengths
1/2 lemon, cut into wedges, for serving

INSTRUCTIONS:

•In a 5-quart Dutch oven or heavy pot, heat oil over medium-high.
•Season chicken with salt and pepper.
•Working in two batches, cook chicken until browned for 6 to 8 minutes and then transfer to a plate.
•To pot, add coconut milk, broth, 1/2 cup water, and curry paste; bring to a boil, and stir in rice.
•Add chicken (with any juices), arranging pieces in a single layer.
•Cover, and reduce heat to medium-low.
•Cook, without stirring, until rice is almost tender for 15 minutes.
•Scatter bell peppers and green beans on top of chicken mixture and cover, and then cook until vegetables are crisp-tender for 8 to 10 minutes.
•Serve with lemon wedges on the side.

Colby Egg Casserole

INGREDIENTS:

5 eggs, beaten
1 cup small curd cottage cheese
¼ cup butter, melted and cooled
1 (4 oz.) can green chilies, diced
¼ cup all-purpose flour
½ tsp. baking powder
2 cups Colby jack cheese, grated or shredded

INSTRUCTIONS:

•Mix the eggs, cottage cheese, butter, green chilies and all-purpose flour.
•Add 2 cups grated Colby jack cheese while mixing gradually.
•Pour the mixture into a 9 inch square baking dish olive with cooking spray.
•Sprinkle top of mixture with cayenne pepper, black pepper, onion powder, garlic powder and parsley flakes.
•Bake at 350 degrees Fahrenheit or until lightly browned on top and the center is puffed and firm.

Southwest Breakfast Casserole

Ingredients:

6 slices white bread, crust removed
1 lb. pork sausage
4 cups Colby or 4 cups Monterey jack cheese
6 eggs
2 (4 oz.) cans diced green chilies
1 tsp. salt
1 tsp. dry mustard
2 cups half-and-half
butter or margarine, softened

Directions:

Lightly butter both side of bread slices and place in 9x13-inch baking dish.
In a skillet, over medium-high heat, brown beef sausage; drain well and pat with paper towels.
Spread sausage over bread slices.
Spread cheese over sausage. Follow with a layer of chopped green chilies.
In medium bowl, whisk eggs lightly. Add salt, dry mustard and half-and-half.
Stir thoroughly. Pour over casserole.
Cover with foil and refrigerate overnight.
To bake, preheat oven to 350°F and bake casserole 45 minutes, or until lightly browned. Allow to cool 15 minutes to set.

Parmesan Cheese Potato Casserole

INGREDIENTS:

1 large sweet onion, halved and thinly sliced
1 large red bell pepper, diced
1 large Yukon gold potato, peeled and diced
2 tbsp. Olive oil
1 (8 oz.) Brie round
1 (12 oz.) package sourdough bread loaf, cubed
1 cup (4 oz.) shredded Parmesan cheese
8 large eggs
3 cups milk
2 tbsp. Dijon mustard
1 tsp. seasoned salt
1 tsp. pepper

INSTRUCTIONS:

•Stir-fry sweet onion, bell pepper and potato in hot oil for about 10 to 12 minutes or just until vegetables are tender and onion begin to turn golden.
•Sleek and discard rind from Brie.
•Cut cheese into 1/2-inch cubes.
•Layer a lightly greased 13- x 9-inch baking dish with half of each of the bread cubes, onion mixture, Brie cubes, and Parmesan cheese.
•Whisk together eggs, milk, mustard, salt and pepper.
•Pour half of egg mixture evenly over cheeses.
•Repeat layers once.
•Cover and chill at least for 8 hours or up to 24 hours.
•Bake at 350°F for 45 to 50 minutes or until lightly browned on top and set in center.

Beef Macaroni with Mushroom Casserole

INGREDIENTS:

1 lb. lean ground beef
1 small onion, chopped
1 tsp. salt
1/4 tsp. garlic powder
1 tsp. Worcestershire sauce
1/4 cup flour
1-1/4 cup hot water
2 tsp. beef bouillon
2 tbsp. red wine
6 oz. Macaroni
1 can (2 oz.) sliced mushrooms, drained
1 cup dairy sour cream

INSTRUCTIONS:

•Brown the beef and onion in a large skillet.
•Drain meat and place in slow-cooker.
•Mix in salt, garlic powder, Worcestershire sauce, and flour.
•Add water bouillon, and wine and then mix well.
•Cover and cook on low heat for 2 to 3 hours.
•Meanwhile, cook macaroni according to package directions.
•Add cooked macaroni, mushrooms, and sour cream to slow-cooker and then stir to mix ingredients.
•Cover and cook on high for 10 to 15 minutes.

Turkey Velveeta Pizza Casserole

INGREDIENTS:

1 lb. ground turkey
1 pkg. Velveeta Shells and Cheese Dinner
2 cans pizza sauce
1 pkg. shredded mozzarella cheese

INSTRUCTIONS:

•Brown the meat and drain thoroughly.
•Add the pizza sauce.
•Cook Shells & Cheese Dinner according to package directions..
•Drain and put in bottom of casserole dish.
•Top with meat mixture and mozzarella cheese.
•Bake at 350 degrees Fahrenheit for 20 minutes.

Beef with Blue Cheese Stovetop Casserole

INGREDIENTS:

Vegetable oil spray
1.5 lbs. lean ground beef
2 tbsp. Worcestershire sauce
1 tbsp. chopped garlic
Seasoned Salt
Garlic Pepper
3 medium onions, chopped
1 1/4 cups red potatoes, diced
8 oz. button mushrooms, sliced
1 cup beef broth
1 tsp. dried oregano, crumbled
1/2 cup crumbled blue cheese
1/4 to 1/2 cup snipped fresh parsley

INSTRUCTIONS:

•Preheat a Dutch oven over medium-high heat.
•Spray the heated Dutch oven with vegetable oil spray.
•Cook the beef with the onion, garlic, seasoned salt, garlic pepper and Worcestershire or until no longer pink in the center, stirring occasionally to turn and break up the beef.
•Drain well and then set aside.

•Wipe the Dutch oven with a paper towel.
•Lightly spray with vegetable oil spray.
•Stir in the potatoes, mushrooms, broth, and oregano.
•Increase the heat to high.
•Bring to a boil.
•Reduce the heat and simmer, covered, for 10 minutes, or until the potatoes are tender.
•Remove from the heat.
•Stir in the beef and the remaining ingredients.
•Let stand for 2 minutes to absorb flavors.

Sour Cream Chicken Casserole

INGREDIENTS:

8 chicken breast, halves and skinless
8 bacon, strips
1 cup sour cream
1 can (10 3/4 ounces) condensed cream of mushroom soup
1 jar dried beef, chopped

INSTRUCTIONS:

•Roll each chicken breast half and wrap a strip of bacon around.
•Arrange the dried beef lining in a large casserole dish.
•Place the 8 chicken breast rolls above the beef.
•Combine sour cream and soup and then pour into the chicken.
•Bake slowly, at 300°F for 2 hours, or until chicken is cooked and bacon is crispy.

Shrimp and Sausages with Tomato Casserole

INGREDIENTS:

1 tbsp. canola oil
6 oz. Andouille sausage, halved lengthwise and sliced into 1/4-inch-thick pieces
1 medium onion, diced
1 green bell pepper, ribs and seeds removed, diced
3 celery stalks, diced
2 garlic cloves, minced
Coarse salt and ground pepper
2 tsps. Paprika
8 plum tomatoes, seeded and chopped
1 cup long-grain white rice
1 lb. medium shrimp (about 30), peeled, deveined, and tails removed
1/2 cup thinly sliced scallions, for garnish

INSTRUCTIONS:

•Heat oil in a large skillet over medium-high heat.
•Add sausage and cook, turning occasionally, until browned on all sides for 4 to 6 minutes.
•Add onion, bell pepper, celery, and garlic; season with salt and pepper.
•Cook, stirring occasionally, until onion begins to soft for 5 to 6 minutes.
•Stir in paprika and cook until fragrant for about 1 minute.
•Add tomatoes, rice, and 3 cups water to skillet; cover, and simmer over medium heat until rice is cooked and has absorbed all water, about 15 minutes.
•Add shrimp to skillet and cook then cover, until shrimp are opaque throughout in about 3 to 4 minutes.
•Remove from heat and then season with salt and pepper, as desired.
•Serve hot, garnished with scallions.

Squash Baked Risotto with Butternut

INGREDIENTS:

2 tbsps. Extra-virgin olive oil
2 shallots, diced small
2 garlic cloves, minced
1 tsp. fresh thyme leaves
1 1/2 cups Arborio rice
Coarse salt and ground pepper
1/2 cup dry white wine
1 medium butternut squash (2 lb.), peeled and diced medium (4 cups)
4 cups low-sodium vegetable broth
1 bunch black (Tuscan) or curly kale, tough stems removed, cut crosswise into 1/2-inch-thick strips
Grated Parmesan, for serving

INSTRUCTIONS:

•Preheat oven to 400 degrees F.
•In a medium Dutch oven or heavy ovenproof pot with a tight-fitting lid, heat oil over medium-high.
•Add shallots and cook, stirring occasionally for about 3 minutes or until soft.
•Add garlic and thyme and cook until fragrant, about 1 minute.
•Add rice and cook, stirring frequently, until opaque for about 3 minutes.
•Season with salt and pepper.
•Add wine and cook, stirring, until completely absorbed, about 2 minutes.
•Add squash and broth; bring mixture to a boil. Stir in kale.
•Cover, transfer to oven, and bake until rice is tender and most of liquid is absorbed, about 20 minutes.
• To serve, sprinkle with Parmesan.

Mussels & Wine Casserole

INGREDIENTS:

3 tbsp. extra-virgin olive oil
1 large shallot, minced
2 garlic cloves, thinly sliced
1/4 tsp. crushed red-pepper flakes
2 cups dry white wine
3 cups canned crushed tomatoes with juice
4 oz. dried, hot chorizo, cut on the diagonal into 1/4-inch slices
1 tsp. coarse salt teaspoon coarse salt
Freshly ground pepper
2 lbs. mussels, scrubbed and debearded
1/3 cup coarsely chopped fresh flat-leaf parsley

INSTRUCTIONS:

•Heat oil in a large, heavy stockpot over medium heat.
•Add shallot and cook, stirring occasionally, until soft for about 3 minutes.
•Add garlic and red-pepper flakes and cook, stirring occasionally for 3 minutes.
•Add wine bring to a boil.
•Add tomatoes and chorizo.
•Reduce heat, and simmer, stirring occasionally, 15 minutes.
•Season with salt and pepper.
•Add mussels.
•Cover, and continue to cook, shaking pot occasionally.

Irish Stout Beef Casserole

INGREDIENTS:

4 lbs. beef chuck, cut into 1 1/2-inch cubes
1/4 cup all-purpose flour
2 cans (6 ounces each) tomato paste
2 1/2lbs. new potatoes, scrubbed
2 medium onions cut into 1-inch pieces
2 cans (14 1/2 ounces each) reduced-sodium beef broth
1 can (14.9 ounces) Irish stout beer
10 garlic cloves, sliced
Coarse salt and ground pepper
2 boxes (10 ounces each) frozen baby peas, thawed

INSTRUCTIONS:

•Preheat oven to 350 degrees Fahrenheit.
•In a 5-quart Dutch oven or heavy pot, toss beef with flour and stir in tomato paste.
•Add potatoes, onions, broth, beer, and garlic; season with salt and pepper.
•Cover, and bring to a boil over medium heat, stirring occasionally.
•Transfer pot to oven, and cook, covered, until meat is fork-tender for 2 1/2 to 3 hours.
• Stir in peas.
•Season with salt and pepper.

Chili Beef Burger Casserole

INGREDIENTS:

2 lbs. ground beef
1 tbsp. onion, minced
2 cans (10 3/4-ounce) tomato soup
1 tsp. chili powder
4 cups corn chips
8 oz. package shredded Cheddar cheese

INSTRUCTIONS:

•Preheat oven to 350° F.
•Brown the ground beef and onion together in a large skillet over medium heat and drain.

•Stir in soup and chili powder.
•Spread it in an ungreased 13"x9" baking pan and top it with corn chips.
•Bake, uncovered, at 350°F for about 20 to 25 minutes.
•Remove from oven and then sprinkle it with cheese.
•Bake for an additional 5 minutes until cheese melts.

Beef Elbow Casserole

INGREDIENTS:

1 lb. lean ground beef
7 oz. uncooked small elbow macaroni
1 can (14.5 oz.) cut tomatoes, drained
1 can (10.75 oz.) Italian tomato soup
1 small onion, chopped or 1 tbsp. dried instant onions
1 clove garlic, minced or 1/8 teaspoon dried minced garlic
1 can (4.5 oz.) sliced mushrooms, drained
1 tsps. Salt
1/2 tsp. chili powder
1 teaspoon Italian seasonings
1/4 teaspoon pepper

INSTRUCTIONS:

•Preheat the oven to 350° F.
•Brown the ground beef and drain.
•Cook macaroni according to package directions.
•Mix beef, macaroni and the remaining ingredients in a 2 quart casserole.
•Cover the casserole.
•Bake at 350° F for 30 minutes.

Spicy Chicken and Green Peas Casserole

INGREDIENTS:

2 tbsps. Olive oil
1 whole cut-up chicken (2 1/2 to 3 pounds), skins removed, breasts halved crosswise
Coarse salt and ground pepper
1 medium onion, chopped
4 cloves garlic, smashed
1 cup long-grain brown rice
4 plum tomatoes, diced
1 jar (12 oz.) roasted red peppers, drained and sliced into 1/2-inch strips
1 package (10 oz.) frozen green peas, thawed
Lemon wedges, for serving (optional)

INSTRUCTIONS:

•Heat oil in a large straight-sided skillet over medium heat.
•Season chicken with 1 teaspoon salt and 1/4 teaspoon pepper.
•Cook, turning, until golden on all sides for about 10 minutes and then transfer to a plate.
•Add onion, garlic, 1 teaspoon salt, and 1/4 teaspoon pepper to skillet.
•Cook, stirring frequently, until onion is softened, 3 to 5 minutes.
•Stir in rice, tomatoes, peppers, and 1 1/4 cups water; nestle chicken pieces in rice mixture. •Bring to a boil and reduce heat.
•Cover, and simmer over medium-low heat until rice is tender in about 55 to 60 minutes.
•If any liquid remains in skillet, remove lid and simmer until evaporated.
•Sprinkle peas over contents of skillet; cover, and remove from heat.
•Set aside until peas are heated through, about 10 minutes.
•Serve with lemon wedges, if desired.

Mouthwatering Monte Cristo Casserole

Ingredients:
1 cup nonfat milk
6 eggs or 1 1/2 cups egg substitute
2 (12 1/2 oz.) packages frozen French toast slices, thawed
8 oz. deli ham, diced
8 s deli turkey, diced
4 oz. Swiss cheese, grated
1/4 cup fresh parsley, snipped
1 Tbsp. powdered sugar
2 cups fresh strawberries, sliced
1/2 cup strawberry ice cream topping

Instructions:
Preheat oven to 375 degrees F.
Add milk to microwaveable container and heat until hot.
Beat eggs in small bowl and add hot milk to eggs, mix well.
Slice French toast into 3/4 inch cubes and put into in a large bowl.
Pour egg mixture over bread cubes, mix and set aside.
Add together ham, turkey, cheese and parsley in a bowl.
Grease a 13x9x2 inch baking pan with cooking spray.
Layer half the French toast cubes with half the meat mixture in bottom of pan.
Repeat.
Let stand for at least 10 minutes (It can be held overnight.)
Bake 30-35 minutes until golden brown and set in center.
Cool 10 minutes.

Quick & Easy Breakfast Casserole

Ingredients:
1 (12 oz.) cans crescent rolls
1 pound sausage, cooked and drained
1 pound fresh mushrooms, sliced
3/4 pound Monterey jack cheese, grated
6 eggs, beaten
1 (10 1/2 oz.) cans cream of onion soup

Instructions:
Arrange crescent rolls evenly in a 13x9-inch dish
Cover with sausage, mushrooms and half the cheese.
Whisk eggs with soup and spread over casserole.
Add remaining cheese on top.
Put in refrigerator overnight.
Bake at 350° for 1 hour.

Belly Filling Breakfast Casserole

Ingredients:
4 whole wheat English muffins, split
1 Tbsp. olive oil
2 medium tomatoes, chopped
1 pound mushroom, sliced
salt and pepper, to taste
8 eggs
1/2 cup low-fat milk
1/2 tsp. garlic powder
1/2 tsp. onion powder
2 tsp. dried basil
1 cup gruyere cheese, grated

Instructions:
Place English muffin halves in the bottom of a greased 9- x 13-inch baking dish
Add tomatoes, mushrooms, salt and pepper to a large skillet over medium heat and cook, mixing occasionally, until tender and liquid is thickened, around 10 minutes.

Scoop tomato mixture over the top of the English muffins, spreading it evenly; set aside to let cool.
In a bowl, beat together eggs, milk, garlic powder, onion powder, salt and pepper.
Spread evenly over tomato mixture, then sprinkle with basil.
Cover and refrigerate overnight.
When ready to cook, preheat oven to 350°F
Sprinkle casserole with cheese and bake, uncovered, until puffed, cooked through and cheese is golden brown, 45 to 50 minutes.
Serve immediately.

Conclusion

Thank you again for downloading this book!

I hope this book was able to help you discover some amazing Casserole Recipes. The next step is to get cooking!!!

Thank you and good luck!

Check Out My Other Favorite Books

Below you'll find some of my other favorite books that are popular on Amazon and Kindle as well. Simply search for these titles on the Amazon website to find them.

Ketogenic Diet: 365 Days of Keto, Low-Carb Recipes for Rapid Weight Loss

Dash Diet: 365 Days of Dash Diet Recipes For Weight Loss

Pressure Cooker: 365 Days of Pressure Cooker Recipes

Cooking for Two: 365 Days of Fast, Easy, Delicious Recipes for Busy Couples

Mason Jar Salads: 101 Quick and Easy Mason Jar Recipes for Meals on the Go

FREE Gift

FREE Gift -Holiday Casserole Recipes

As a "Thank You" for purchasing this book, I want to give you a gift absolutely 100% Free

Click Here to Download Holiday Casserole Recipes

Or go to http://freebookbonus.com/casseroles/

53382501R00194

Made in the USA
Middletown, DE
27 November 2017